THE MODERN INTERIOR

The Modern Interior

Penny Sparke

REAKTION BOOKS

For Molly, Nancy and Celia

Published by Reaktion Books Ltd
33 Great Sutton Street
London EC1V 0DX

www.reaktionbooks.co.uk

First published 2008

Printed and bound in Great Britain
by MPG Books Ltd, Bodmin, Cornwall

British Library Cataloguing in Publication Data
Sparke, Penny
    The modern interior
    1. Interior decoration – History
    I. Title
    747'.09
    ISBN-13: 978 1 86189 372 7

Contents

Introduction

An estate agent's photograph of an interior space in Montevetro – a Richard Rogers-designed, riverside apartment building in Battersea – published in a south-west London magazine in July 2007, portrayed an all-white living room furnished with hard-edged white sofas, a Le Corbusier chaise longue upholstered in white leather, low 'Japanese-style' white coffee tables and a huge plasma screen television. Described as 'contemporary and stylish', this room, and others like it, would undoubtedly fulfil most people's expectations of a 'modern interior'. Countless images of a similar nature reveal themselves to us through the glossy home-oriented magazines, furniture retailers' catalogues and television advertisements that form part of our daily lives. Indeed our sense of the early twenty-first-century modern interior is, arguably, largely formed by its presence in the mass media, where it is frequently represented as a highly desirable, uncluttered backcloth to an increasingly complex existence.

For those with a more historical frame of reference, however, the term 'the modern interior', may evoke an open-plan space from the 1920s featuring chromed tubular steel, black leather chairs and large expanses of glass. Whichever image comes to mind – contemporary or historical – it is likely that the epithet 'modern' is understood stylistically and that the interior in question is located in a domestic setting. This book adopts a different starting point, however. *The Modern Interior* sets out to demonstrate that 'the modern interior', which was formed and developed between the middle years of the nineteenth and twentieth centuries, went beyond style and encompassed many more inside spaces than those contained within the home. The modern interior addressed in this study is defined by its relationship with the everyday experiences of modernity during those years, which were as profound in the office, the factory, the

A shopping mall in Calgary, Alberta, 2005.

department store and the café – as well as in the modern hospital and church – as they were in the home. In addition, the visual languages through which it was expressed could range from Louis Quinze to Streamlined Moderne. The modern interior addressed in this study can be understood, therefore, in a very general sense, as the inside location of people's experiences of, and negotiations with, modern life.

One of the best documented of these negotiations was initiated by a group of progressive architects and designers who were committed to the idea that modern inside spaces not only mirrored modern experiences but that, more importantly, they also played a role in constructing them. To that end they developed a technical and aesthetic programme, manifested in the years between the two world wars, known then as the Modern Movement (now more commonly referred to as architectural and design Modernism). While acknowledging the important contribution made by that movement to the development of the modern interior this study surveys its subject through a wider lens, setting it in the context of a broader range of ideas emanating from the interior's engagement with modernity.

One of the key transformations brought about by the advent of modernity's main driver – industrialization – related to people's private and public experiences that affected the formation of both their self- and their collective identities. This study of the modern interior was partly triggered by an encounter with a scene from everyday life which raised a number of questions for me about the relationship of private interiors with the inside spaces of public buildings. Walking through a vast shopping mall in Calgary in Alberta a couple of years ago I encountered a small oasis of calm located in the midst of the hustle and bustle of mass shopping. The scene, which comprised a set of comfortable armchairs carefully positioned on an Oriental-style carpet and accompanied by potted plants, resembled a domestic living room – one, however, that had been removed from its more familiar private environment and repositioned in a public space that was utterly alien to it. Surrounded by enormous plate glass windows, fast-moving escalators and huge structural columns, that miniature scene seemed strangely out of place. What was that private stage set doing in an otherwise public environment? Like the Victorian parlour on which it modelled itself, it offered comfort and refuge, however temporary, from the world of work and commerce – a chance, that is, for a snatched moment of self-reflection and repose for its occupants, and for them to see themselves as individuals in an environment otherwise dedicated to the anonymity of the crowd.

Surprisingly, in spite of its location within a larger interior space with which it had no obvious relationship, that little setting had retained its historical relevance and meaning. Also, although seeming on the face of it so different, the two 'interiors' I had encountered – a private domestic parlour and a public shopping mall – had, I realised on reflection, something in common. While, back in the nineteenth century, the former had served as a sanctuary for middle-class Victorian men who had left home on a daily basis to work in factories and offices, the latter, a slightly later development, had developed as a covered space in which

Mrs Sarah Du Prau and Mrs T. Sebelin in the parlour of the Beaumont Hotel, Ouray, Colorado, *c.* 1905.

the mass-produced goods that emerged from those factories could be consumed. Both were essential components, therefore, of industrial capitalism and of the modern world. However, the dramatic contrast of meanings and values conveyed by their sharp juxtaposition, and the fact that the 'parlour' had been wrenched from its original setting and absorbed within the larger, enveloping space of the mall, caused me to reflect on the relationship between the worlds of the 'private' and the 'public' in the insides of our modern era buildings. This book is the product of that reflection.

The chapters that follow will expose the tensions, the ambiguities, the contradictions and the paradoxes that defined the relationship between the private and the public spheres in the period in question. That relationship was, I will suggest, central to the formation of the modern interior. Modern interiors could be clothed in period styles as well as in contemporary ones. They could also facilitate both private interiority and public mass behaviour. Nineteenth-century domestic parlours could be found in department stores, railway carriages and hotels, while, in the early twentieth century, the layouts of domestic kitchens were influenced by the interior spaces of factories. Ensconced as they are in a room which boasts a patterned carpet, heavy curtains, and floral upholstered furniture, the two women playing cards in the parlour of the Beaumont Hotel in Ouray County, Colorado in 1905 could have been sitting in their front room at home. On the other hand the stark simplicity of Walter Gropius's kitchen in his Dessau home of 1925–6 was a direct result of the fact that it had been organized according to the rational principles underpinning factory production. The apparent boundaries between private and public interior spaces were continually under threat, therefore, as they and the values they embraced constantly invaded each other's territories, taking with them as they did so the visual, the material and the spatial languages through which those values were expressed. In short the boundaries between the 'separate spheres' were fundamentally unstable and it was that instability, rather than the separation per se, that, I will suggest, defined modernity, and by extension the modern interior, reflecting the constantly shifting identities and the increasingly fragmented experiences of the inhabitants of the modern world.

Unlike the modern painting, the modern poem and the modern novel, all of whose high cultural forms are fairly easily identified by their rejection of one set of cultural traditions and values and their adoption of new strategies, the modern interior, which crossed the bridge between high and everyday culture, was a much more complex phenomenon. Its inherent complexity was further compounded by the fact that the modern interior can be understood in a number of different ways, that is, as an

The kitchen in Walter Gropius's house in Dessau, with furniture by Marcel Breuer, c. 1925–6, illustrated in Hans Eckstein's *Die Schöne Wohnung: Beispiele Neuzeitlicher Deutscher Wohnräume*, 1931.

image, as an assemblage of material objects or as a space. In turn it can be represented through architectural plans, drawings, photographs, ensembles of objects or constructed spaces.[1] Interiors are rendered even harder to discuss by the fact that they are constantly being modified as life goes on within them. In combination these characteristics constitute a significant challenge to the student of the interior and probably account for the paucity of serious literature on the subject. Unlike the multitude of widely available, visually-oriented books about interiors, *The Modern Interior* will not approach its subject primarily as a stylistic concept, nor will it limit its remit to the minimally-decorated interiors created or inspired by the architects and designers associated with European Modernism. Nor will it interpret 'modern' as simply meaning 'fashionable' or 'up-to-date'. It will aim, rather, to offer its readers an account of the complexity of the forces that were at play in the formation and development of the modern interior as it is defined in the pages of this book.

The era of industrial modernity was fully formed by the mid-nineteenth century and reached a level of maturity in the years around the First World War. Where the modern interior was concerned the two decades which followed saw a re-affirmation and a consolidation of the changes that had occurred in that earlier era, as well as a stylistic response to them. In the half century or so since 1945 the modern interior has depended, as the final chapter of this book will suggest, upon a continual reworking of the themes, ideas and tensions that were all in place by around 1914 and which, by 1939, were expressed through a number of alternative visual languages. The subject of 'modernity' – the historical and theoretical frame for this study – has preoccupied many writers. Like the interior it contains its own inner tensions and contradictions. For some it represents an experience of the world which, as a result of the accelerated expansion of mass communications; the loss of a single, unifying belief system; and the breakdown of familiar social structures, was rendered fragmentary, discontinuous, fleeting, incomplete and confusing. Others have defined it as an extension of the essential rationalism of mass production into all other aspects of daily life. Yet others have portrayed it as the result of the continual turnover of goods and images created by 'consumer desire'.[2] Most have seen it, however, as being characterized by its innate sense of progress, its 'forward-lookingness'.[3] For the German cultural critic Walter Benjamin, the advent of modernity coincided with the emergence of the private individual.[4] By extension the emergence of the private domestic interior, and its capacity to facilitate self-reflection, or 'interiority', on the part of its inhabitants, was also part of that same historical moment. Following Benjamin's logic to its conclusion, the interior itself was, therefore, an integral component of modernity and, by definition, modern.

Although some aspects of the development of the modern interior have been addressed by historians of modern architecture, and cultural historians have looked at the relationship of the 'outside' city streets to modernity, the interior's role in defining modern identities has, to date, received relatively little attention. Even some of the feminist scholars defining the moment of women's entrance into modernity have concentrated on their exit from their homes into the melee of the street, as, in the case of middle-class women, shoppers, or, in that of working-class women, prostitutes or shoplifters.[5] This study aims to fill that gap and to position the modern interior at the centre of the construction of the modern 'self', or 'subject'. Modernity was not just an abstract concept, however. It also existed physically and was experienced by real people. It was represented visually as a two-dimensional image; materially through the objects that went into it; and spatially through the architecture that contained it.[6] Another of modernity's key features, the continuing expansion of interior spaces, or 'interiorization', which helped create and control social and cultural distinctions and hierarchies, will provide a leitmotif through the pages of this book.[7]

To focus on the era of industrial modernity is, inevitably, to align the modern interior with the effects of industrialization. The advent of mass production clearly changed the nature and availability of goods destined for interior spaces. That dramatic socio-economic transformation had a much greater influence on the insides of buildings than the mere provision of new objects to go into them, however. One of its lasting effects, as Benjamin noticed, was the creation of a significant physical, psychological and aesthetic divide between the inside spaces of domestic life and those located within buildings dedicated to public activities, including work, commerce and communal leisure. The separate spheres – the gendered distinction, that is, between private and public life – emerged at the moment when most paid labour moved out of the home, and, as a direct consequence, middle-class men and women became physically separated from each other.[8] Although, inevitably, people of both sexes continued to venture out of their homes for a multitude of reasons – to worship together, to participate in leisure activities and so on – the notion that women's place was in the home became a pervasive ideological assumption within western, capitalist society. Reinforced as it was by the visual, material and spatial differences between the interiors in the two spheres, it also became a physical reality that, in turn, confirmed those distinctions.[9]

The simple idea that two different versions of the modern interior emerged in the middle years of the nineteenth century – one linked to the idea of 'home', and the other associated with the worlds of work and commerce – lies at the heart of this study. Both the structure and the key themes of this book have been determined by it. No sooner was this dualism articulated, however, than it was immediately challenged and the boundaries between the spheres became blurred. That instability was largely driven by the reluctance of what were understood as fixed categories of gender and class to remain in place. Firstly, like its middle-class female occupants, the domestic interior refused to be confined to the home. The advent of factories had put an end to much domestic manufacturing – the bottling of fruit and the making of clothing, for instance. Those goods remained domestic necessities, however, and women were compelled to purchase them outside the home. For the

Christmas window-shopping in turn-of-the-century New York.

middle classes, shopping also became a leisure activity, as the image of women window-shopping reveals. They stand gazing through the vast plate glass windows containing evocative displays of household textiles. Women's domestic interiors accompanied them on their shopping journeys. They were visible in the railway station waiting rooms in which they sat, the train carriages in which they travelled, and the department stores, clubs, cafés, restaurants, hotels and theatres they visited. These 'homes from home' provided them with a level of comfort when they ventured outside their homes, and helped them redefine themselves as consumers as well as home-makers.

The domestic interior also exposed itself to the public sphere through its developing relationship with the expanding mass media of the period. Along with the advent of mass production, mass consumption and the idea of the separate spheres, the expansion of the mass media was a key feature of industrial modernity. Like the development of 'homes from home' the relationship of the media to the domestic sphere served to facilitate and enhance the consumption of goods for the home. Through images in magazines, trade catalogues and other printed materials, as well as through room constructions at exhibitions and trade fairs, idealized domestic spaces stimulated desire and encouraged consumers to construct their own modish domestic interiors through the purchase of a new armchair or a piece of curtain fabric. Like the architecture which contained it, the modern domestic interior was defined by its engagement with the mass media.[10] Most significantly it was transformed through that engagement into an idealized phenomenon used to encourage the consumption of goods. In that idealized form the interior itself became a mass medium, a vehicle for the transmission of modern values of various kinds. Indeed, almost as soon as it had been created, the modern domestic interior became an 'object of desire', so widely represented that it rapidly became impossible to separate its idealized forms from its realized manifestations.

The idealized interior still features strongly in today's mass media. The magazines on stationers' shelves offer consumers a myriad of 'modern' options, from the country house style, to the Provençal look, to austere minimalism, to a rich, oriental aesthetic, and many more besides. Over the last few decades television has also embraced the design of the interior, hosting a vast number of programmes on the subject ranging from 'how to' and make-over shows, to voyeuristic glimpses into the homes of the rich and famous. One of the most popular interior-focused programmes, broadcast from 1996 to 2004, was *Changing Rooms*, which worked on the assumption that everybody's taste is equally valid as long as it is adequately expressed. It endorsed a pluralistic 'stage set' approach to interior decoration in which an eclectic range of fantasy environments are created as expressive backcloths in front of which the 'inner' lives of their inhabitants can be lived out. The strength of the feelings that individuals have for their interiors (linked undoubtedly to their fragile self-identities) was demonstrated by the number of tears shed when the 'make-over' proved to be a huge disappointment.

While the domestic interior was increasingly drawn into the public sphere through the second half of the nineteenth century, by the early years of the twentieth a pull in the opposite direction had also begun to be felt, which drew modern public sphere interiors into the home. That movement was effected by the group of architects and designers who aligned themselves with Modernism and who were deeply committed to eroding the boundaries between the spheres. Their efforts were partly driven by a shared distaste for bourgeois domesticity and partly by a desire to create a classless architecture that, they believed, would replace the values of middle-class Victorian domesticity (and indeed the interior itself) with the more democratic ones of efficiency and utility. They found those latter values in the modern, public interiors dedicated to commerce, industrial production and work.

At the heart of this book lies the proposal, therefore, that the modern interior was the result of the two-way movement between the private and the public spheres. Within that movement individual and group identities were formed, contested and re-formed. While the ideology of the separate spheres was enormously powerful, so too were the forces that determined to break down the divide between them. The dynamic tension created by that level of determination lay at the very heart of the modern interior and gave it its momentum. Visually, materially and spatially, the modern interior embraced a spectrum of possibilities. While its idealized manifestations often inhabited the two extremes of that spectrum, its lived-in expressions were usually hybrids. The levels of aesthetic purity or otherwise that were achieved, and the negotiation of the tensions that underpinned the creation of the modern interior, required a controlling hand, however. It was the role of 'design', implemented by the occupants of interiors themselves, by engineers, architects, space planners, upholsterers, interior decorators, or interior designers, among others, to play that determining role. In their hands design had the capacity to turn values, desires and aspirations into visual, material and spatial ideals and realities.

Industrialization, urbanization and an increased potential for social mobility – the defining features of modernity – encouraged ever larger numbers of people to regard the design of their interiors as an increasingly important aspect of their lives. Indeed within modernity the interior became a marker of people's changing identities, one of the only stable (if temporary) frameworks for the construction of the 'self' and social status. Design had the capacity not only to express social status and aspiration, but also to link individual identities – formed by class, gender and other cultural factors – to interiors and to focus on the meaning of the individual in the age of the crowd. At the same time it was also able to control large groups of people in public interior spaces, from shopping malls to sports stadia. The protagonists of the Modern Movement set out to further mobilize the potential of design in order to bring about social and political change. Above all it was through design that the tensions contained within the modern interior were managed and, when domestic interiors were reproduced outside the home and public interiors found their way into it, the necessary acts of negotiation and translation were performed. 'Designers', in their various guises, had, therefore, the ultimate responsibility of resolving the inner tensions within the modern interior, of defining its appearance and of constructing its meanings.

The Modern Interior is presented in two main parts. The first section, 'Inside Out', looks at a number of the ways in which values and ideas formed and developed within the domestic setting – the site of individual interiority and feminine modernity – and then moved out of the home and into the public arena. The socio-cultural and psychological faces of the modern interior are emphasized in this context, manifested through its relationships with mass consumption and the fashion system, and its role in facilitating individual and collective expression. In contrast, 'Outside In', the book's second section, focuses on the way in which the artists, architects and designers associated with the Modern Movement borrowed strategies which had been developed within the new, public sphere interiors, and the outside world in general – in particular those linked to the processes of rationalization and standardization, and to the artistic avant-garde – and injected them into the modern private residence. The final chapter offers some thoughts about the ways in which the themes which defined the modern interior as it developed between

1850 and 1939 were further played out in the years between 1940 and the present day. The conclusion offers a reflection on the ever-growing complexity of the relationship between the private and the public spheres in the contemporary context which could facilitate, among other strange phenomena, the bewildering presence of a living room in a shopping mall. However, with 'virtual' space becoming as influential in our daily lives as 'physical' space, the conclusion suggests, the concept of industrial modernity may have been stretched to its limits and the time may have come for us to think again about the meaning of 'the modern interior'.

Part One

Inside Out

A Victorian parlour in Manchester, England, *c.* 1890.

1 The Private Interior

The nineteenth century, like no other century, was addicted to dwelling.
It conceived the residence as a receptacle for the person and it encased him
with all his appurtenances so deeply in the dwelling's interior that one
might be reminded of the inside of a compass case where the instrument
lies embedded in deep, usually violet, folds of velvet.
Walter Benjamin[1]

The private face of the modern interior was formed in the middle-class Victorian home. That space performed a number of simultaneous roles, primary among them one of a comforting refuge from the worlds of work and commerce. As the nineteenth century progressed, however, the Victorian home also became a focus for aesthetic intervention, a destination for goods acquired through mass consumption and a focus for media attention. As well as offering opportunities for privacy, social activities and interactions also went on within the nineteenth-century domestic arena, providing possibilities for social display. Above all the ideology of the separate spheres made it a site where modern feminine subjectivity was largely negotiated, where women's sense of fashion could be demonstrated and where they could express themselves through their new role as 'decorators'.

The first five chapters of this book will focus on the domestic face of the modern interior, emphasizing the objects and spaces within it and the roles it performed. They will show how the language of the domestic interior reflected many of the key values underpinning modern life and how its replication outside the home transferred them into the public arena. Typically the spaces of Victorian domesticity were filled to the brim with items of comfortable, upholstered furniture, textiles on every available surface, bibelots on the mantelpiece, patterned carpets and potted plants. In this fairly typical late nineteenth-century middle-class living space in Manchester, England, for example, a crowded mantelpiece, multiple framed pictures suspended from the picture rail, prominently displayed plants in pots, an eclectic mix of chairs arranged semi-formally around little tables, and a large religious statue positioned in one corner combine to create an impression of an inward-looking home dedicated to comfort, self-reflection, social interaction and private spirituality. By the second half of the nineteenth century that language of Victorian domesticity had become a feature of the interior landscapes of a range of semi-public and public 'homes from home', including cafés, restaurants, women's clubs, hotels, the leisure areas of department stores, railway station waiting rooms, train carriages and mental hospitals. That replication challenged the separation of the spheres such that modernity, and by extension, the modern interior, were ultimately defined by the cross-over between the private and the public arenas rather than the distinction between them.

Not everyone believed that the Victorian domestic interior was 'modern', however. Several progressive architects and designers were already beginning to see the comfortable, bourgeois Victorian drawing room as antithetical to everything they were trying to achieve. The design reformer Charles Eastlake was especially vociferous on the subject. 'By that expression [knick knacks]', he wrote in 1868, 'I meant that heterogeneous assemblage of modern rubbish which . . . finds its way into the drawing room or boudoir.'[2] The art critic John Ruskin was equally dismissive of what he saw as the Victorian parlour's excesses. 'I know', he wrote, 'what it is to live in a cottage with a deal floor and roof . . . and I know it to be in many respects healthier and happier that living between a Turkey carpet and gilded ceiling, beside a steel grate and polished fender.'[3] Later, at the turn of the century, the Viennese architect and critic Adolf Loos was equally disdainful about the work of the Victorian upholsterer. 'It was a reign of terror', he wrote, 'that we can still all feel in our bones. Velvet and silk, Makart bouquets, dust, suffocating air and lack of light, portieres, carpets and "arrangements" – thank God we are all done with that now.'[4] The visual and material culture of Victorian domesticity, characterized by its love of clutter and its devotion to the bibelot, was linked in those men's minds with excessive materialism and a lack of aesthetic control. Above all they believed that Victorian domesticity was defined by its links with tradition and its resistance to the pull of modernity.[5]

Walter Benjamin, on the other hand, looking back from the perspective of the 1930s, understood the essential modernity of the Victorian home. For him it was the location in which the very idea of the interior – self-evidently, in his view, a modern phenomenon – had emerged. 'Under Louis Philippe the private individual makes his entrance on the stage of history', he wrote, adding that, 'for the private individual, the place of dwelling is for the first time opposed to the place of work. The former constitutes itself as the interior. Its complement is the office. The private individual, who in the office has to deal with reality, needs the domestic interior to sustain him in his illusions . . . his living room is a box in the theater of the world.'[6] In his short text Benjamin confirmed the idea that the separation of the worlds of the private and the public was a defining one for modernity, and by implication for the interior.[7] Nor was the representation of modernity by historical styles a contradiction for Benjamin. Rather it provided a confirmation of the way the domestic interior made it possible for its occupants to 'bring together the far away and the long ago', a necessary requirement, he felt, of life in the modern world.[8] For Benjamin, who looked beyond styles to the cultural meanings of the visual, material and spatial world, Victorian domesticity was intrinsically linked to modernity, rather than a marker of resistance to it. It did not emerge suddenly, of course, but was the result of the confluence of a number of earlier developments. Prior to the eighteenth century, for most of the populations of Europe, 'home' had been the place in which work, leisure activities, extended family relationships, the manufacture of clothes and food, and moral education had all co-existed. In the Renaissance Italy, for example, the *casa* had been 'a hub of activity – domestic, economic and social.'[9] By the eighteenth century a model of bourgeois privacy and domesticity, developed in the Netherlands, had spread across Northern Europe. It was joined at that time by the idea of 'comfort', which had originated in the aristocratic French interior. A century later the concepts of privacy, domesticity and comfort had converged to fulfil the needs of the new middle-class population which had arrived on the back of industrialization and urbanization – first in Great Britain and subsequently in Europe and the US.[10] The translation of those values into visual, material and spatial form resulted in the emergence of the nineteenth-century domestic interior.[11]

Rather than being an irrelevance in the modern world, the pull of the past in the domestic interior, in a context in which enhanced social mobility meant that change was increasingly the norm, could, as Benjamin understood, be seen to confirm its modernity. Materially, according to Benjamin, the interior held on to the past through 'an abundance of covers and protectors, liners and cases . . . on which the traces of objects of everyday use are imprinted.'[12] Nowhere was that attempt to capture the past for the present more evident than in the mid-nineteenth-century domestic parlour, where layers of textiles covered the walls, the furnishings, the mantelpiece and the windows. As one writer has explained, 'Tables would be covered with chenille cloths, hearths would be often dangerously draped with curtains hanging from a pelmet board

Al 'Bucky' Lamb's home in Aspen, Colorado, 1880s.

supported on the shelf of the chimney-piece. When there was no fire, the grate, which for some reason it was thought necessary to conceal, would disappear behind festoons of rep.'[13] In the 1880s home of an American, Al "Bucky" Lamb, for example, ropes and tassels were suspended in the doorways to create visual screens and to counteract the impression of openness created by the absence of doors. Many of the other familiar signs of Victorian domesticity were also present, including comfortable upholstery, a semi-casual arrangement of an eclectic mix of furniture items – velvet parlour chairs, straight-backed chairs, footstools, a chandelier and elaborate rugs among them – crowded surfaces, multiple patterned surfaces, and a sense of enclosure. There was no sense of aesthetic unity. Instead individual items were emphasized. Indeed the Victorian domestic interior was not conceived as a single visual entity but rather as an accumulation of artefacts.[14] The level of 'collecting' that went on in such spaces, manifested in Al Lamb's home by the wall paintings, the ceramic artefacts, the books and a number of other decorative objects, has been likened to activities more usually associated with the museum, the department store and the trade fair.[15]

The overwhelming emphasis placed on physical comfort in Victorian domestic spaces reinforced their roles as havens and as responses to what were perceived to be the less than comfortable public spaces of work and commerce. The idea of comfort emphasized the physical link between the bodies of the occupants of such spaces and the material objects within them. In Victorian England, as elsewhere in the industrialized western world, domestic family life took on a new significance at that time, as a symbol of Christian values, nationhood and empire. However, in response to the increasing complexity of public life, the threat from increased social mobility to hitherto stable identities, and the need, within modernity, for the individual to develop a concept of 'selfhood', privacy and the opportunity for self-reflection were demanded of the Victorian home above all else.

Inevitably the idea of the separation of the spheres was strongly gendered. By the end of the nineteenth century women had been given the responsibility for most the activities that went on within the home, most importantly for its appearance. In undertaking their tasks 'housewives' had to negotiate a subtle tension between the need to make the home a centre for fashionable living and display and the necessity of ensuring that it remained a comfortable 'haven' and a protection for the family from the realities of commerce and the capitalistic values of the marketplace. Gender differentiation was materialized and visualized in the choice of furnishings and decorative details in the Victorian home. In dining rooms, for example, usually seen as 'masculine' spaces, dark colours were frequently employed and the furniture items were often large and imposing. The dining room of a late nineteenth-century Manchester home, Sedgley New Hall, for instance, contained a number of such heavy furniture items, including a large mirrored sideboard (pictured overleaf). A male portrait on the wall above it reinforced that particular room's dominant masculinity. That focus was often contrasted by the decoration of parlours and boudoirs where lighter colours and more delicate, elegant furniture pieces were often included.[16] Both men and women had spaces in the home designated for their use which were both less and more private. Men, for example, invited others into their billiard and smoking rooms, but probably not into their studies, while women entertained in the parlour but undoubtedly less so in the bedroom or boudoir. Within their private spaces the codification of the furniture and décor served as an aid to the construction of men's and women's self-identities, while in the more public areas of the home it was their social identities that were being formed and reinforced.

Differences of social class and aspiration were also clearly embedded within the nineteenth-century home. The mid-century, middle-class European home modelled itself materially upon that of the aristocracy

The dining room of Sedgley New Hall, Manchester, *c.* 1880.

with many of its artefacts, framed mirrors surmounting mantelpieces, for example, clearly echoing noble dwellings. Nowhere in the late nineteenth century, perhaps, was the link between domestic interiors, social aspiration and material display more apparent, however, than in the late nineteenth-century US, where a generation of nouveau-riche clients, architects and decorators together created some of that era's most ornate homes. The hugely wealthy 'arrivistes' of Newport, Rhode Island had their vast summer homes, or 'cottages', as they called them, decorated like palaces. Richard Morris Hunt's design for Marble House, built between 1888 and 1892 for Mr and Mrs William K. Vanderbilt and given by the former to the latter as a birthday present, was decorated by the Paris-based decorators Allard and Sons. The extensive use of marble and gilt in its interiors reflected the huge sums of money that were poured into that house to create a visual, material and spatial representation of wealth or, more importantly, of refinement and class. Cornelius Vanderbilt, William's elder brother, displayed an even higher level of conspicuousness in his Hunt-designed summer house of 1895, The Breakers, some of the rooms of which were decorated by Allard and Sons and others by the American architect, Ogden

Dining room, The Breakers, Ochre Point Avenue, Newport, Rhode Island, 1895, photographed in *c*. 1950.

Codman, Jr. Once again the opulence of the materials used – marble brought from Tunisia and Italy, alabaster, onyx, ormolu, crystal, damask, leather and gilt in abundance – and its antique furnishings marked the wealth of the owner and his determination, in spite of the fact that the house was only used for between five to seven weeks a year, to create a glittering, Italian Renaissance-style interior. The dramatically scaled dining room in The Breakers boasted huge chandeliers, elaborate wall ornamentation, an enormous fireplace and a vast table used to entertain huge numbers of guests. The levels of conspicuousness and opulence notwithstanding, those 'cottages' were still 'homes' – sites, that is, dedicated to privacy and intimacy as well as to entertainment.[17] In her descriptions of the opulent interiors of a fictional house called Bellomont in her novel, *The House of Mirth*, the American writer Edith Wharton focused on the importance of domestic luxury for late nineteenth-century American society.[18] Indeed she equated the social aspiration of the book's main protagonist, Lily Bart, with that character's hatred of 'dinginess' and love of luxury, and she provided detailed descriptions of interiors and their objects showing how that luxury was manifested materially. In a passage describing Lily taking breakfast in bed at Bellomont, for example, the novelist wrote,

> Her maid had kindled a little fire on the hearth, and it contended cheerfully with the sunlight which slanted across the moss-green carpet and caressed the curved sides of an old marquetry desk. Near the bed stood a table holding her breakfast tray, with its harmonious porcelain and silver, a handful of violets in a slender glass, and the morning paper folded beneath her letters.[19]

As, from the late nineteenth century onwards, middle-class women increasingly entered the public arena in order to consume goods for the home, they acted as bridges between the private and public spheres. The clear ideological distinction that had existed a few decades earlier between the feminine and the masculine spheres was, as a result, significantly eroded. It was paralleled, and arguably facilitated, by the replication of the language of domesticity in interiors outside the home. That language quickly became a signifier of feminine modernity wherever it was located. On one level, therefore, the strong distinction between the private and public spheres observed by Benjamin was eroded almost as soon as it was formed. In inhabiting interior environments outside the home which were modelled on the domestic interior, the middle classes were, perhaps, protecting themselves from, and compensating themselves for, the realities of the world of commerce and production, as well as reinforcing and disseminating the values of the bourgeois lifestyle in the world at large. Domestic interiors could increasingly be found in many different semi-public and public spaces. British theatre foyers of the second half of the nineteenth century, for example, were 'public yet determined by private tastes [which] allowed for continuity of experience between the realm of home proper and the world of the theatre'.[20] This strategy was employed

The first class parlour in the Empire Music Hall, Newcastle upon Tyne, England, photographed by Beford Lemera, 1891.

to help make them respectable venues for middle-class audiences and to offset the 'sexual energy' potentially created by men and women mingling in crowds in dimly lit environments.[21] The first class parlour in Newcastle's Empire Music Hall undoubtedly performed a similar function. All the familiar signs of Victorian domesticity were in evidence, from the decoration on the carpet and wallpaper, to the eclectic mix of loosely arranged furniture items. The same desire for respectability undoubtedly underpinned the use of the domestic aesthetic in first class saloons in ocean-going liners and trains. The ornamented ceiling, draped curtains, patterned rug and comfortable, upholstered furniture in the mid-nineteenth-century drawing room car of the South Eastern and Chatham Railway Folkestone Express, served to align that interior with the domestic

The drawing room car on a late-19th-century British train.

parlour. Only the arrangement of the seating gave away the fact that it was a railway carriage. Even British mental asylums chose to employ the aesthetic of 'homeliness' at that time as it was linked to the preferred therapeutic treatments of the day.[22] In the turn-of-the-century female day room of the Northern Counties District Lunatic Asylum in Inverness in Scotland, the familiar upholstered armchairs, potted plants, side tables and patterned wallpaper and rug were all in place.

Along with many other cities, such as New York and Paris, London witnessed a huge growth in 'homes from home' for women in the last decades of the nineteenth century. Women's clubs were established to provide a facility for middle-class women, who travelled on the new forms of transportation, to take advantage of the shopping and other pleasure activities on offer.[23] They replicated the domestic environment and were experienced more as private, than as public, institutions. An article in *Queen* magazine of 29 June 1901 described the interiors of London's Empress Club, indicating that its decor had moved beyond the heaviness of the earlier Victorian style to embrace the lighter, more fashionable domestic idiom of that era. 'Walls, mirror frames, and ceilings are in

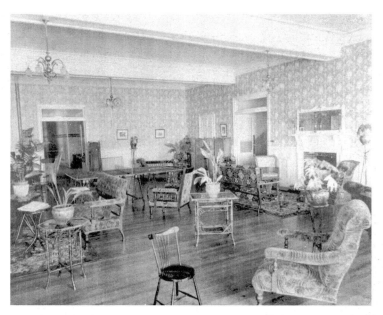

Female Day Room (Ward 7), Northern Counties Lunatic Asylum, Inverness, Scotland, 1902.

white', the journalist explained. 'The panels of the walls, the hangings, and coverings of the furniture are in crimson Beresford brocade, and the comfortable chairs and lounges, tall cool palms and tasteful screens make this withdrawing room the ideal of comfort for the rapidly increasing race described by our transatlantic cousins as club women.'[24] New York's first all-female club, the Colony Club, the interior of which was designed by the pioneer interior decorator, Elsie de Wolfe, was opened on Madison Avenue two years later. The decorator herself described the socially aspirational, yet eminently domestic atmosphere of the entrance hall: 'The first impression', she explained, 'is that which one receives in the old Virginia mansions, so dignified is the treatment of the panelled walls, the selection of old mahogany furniture, the color scheme of green and white and mahogany.'[25] In the club's garden restaurant, de Wolfe created a fashionable inside/outside space, complete with ivy-clad terracing and a decorative fountain, such as might be found in the conservatory of an early twentieth-century country house.

Other urban sites of modernity for women in the period – restaurants, tea-shops, museums and art galleries among them – offered a variety

Trellis Restaurant, Colony Club, New York, decorated by Elsie de Wolfe, 1905–7 and illustrated in Elsie de Wolfe, *The House in Good Taste*, 1913.

of interiors which complemented a trip to the department store. In London's Piccadilly the Criterion pleasure complex, designed by the architect Thomas Verity in 1871 and built three years later, combined an underground theatre with a lavish restaurant, the walls of which were decorated with tiles and gilt mosaic patterns. The theatre, originally planned as a concert hall within the restaurant complex, was constructed with a neo-classical street level façade.[26] Whether within the department store or the adjacent tea rooms, taking afternoon tea quickly became an integral feature of the female shopping experience. In London Mrs Robinson's tea-shop contained a library and a reading room in which shoppers could recuperate, while Toronto's Little Blue Tea Rooms, established in 1906, was a highly domesticated space. It promoted the fact with the phrase 'We Bring Home into Town'. For both men and women who did not stay in clubs, hotels provided an alternative. Although the idea of the hotel went back several centuries it wasn't until the nineteenth century that the modern idea of the grand urban hotel came into existence. Early examples included the Grand Hotel in Paris, the Fifth Avenue Hotel in New York and the Palmer House Hotel in Chicago.[27] Many others followed in the principal cities of Europe and the USA. The modernity of

The Little Blue Tea Rooms, 97 Yonge Street, Toronto, Ontario, c. 1920.

those buildings, with their grand, usually neo-classical, interiors, lay in their relationship with the new railway and road systems that had opened up Europe and the USA to travellers and shoppers. From the perspective of their guests, hotels were idealized replicas of the domestic interiors of the affluent. While hotels did not strictly sell things they nonetheless played an important role in the consumption of goods inasmuch as, in collaboration with the railways, they helped to ensure that consumers could access them.[28]

For a variety of reasons, therefore, the language of the nineteenth- and early twentieth-century private, domestic interior moved outside the home, rendering ambiguous the spaces of feminine modernity as it did so. In addition to their new role as consumers, however, middle-class women also continued to perform their roles as domestic producers, especially in the areas of household textiles and decorative objects.[29] Once again this served to blur the boundaries between the spheres. From the 1870s onwards, the increasing popularization of the 'artistic home' – of, that is, a home that was visually unified and that focused on its appearance above all else, confirmed the role of women as amateur home decorators. Eastlake's *Hints on Household Taste*, published in Great

'A Drawing Room Corner', frontispiece to Robert Edis's *Decoration and Furniture of Town Houses*, 1881.

Britain in 1868 and in the USA four years later, provided them with information about the fashionable styles of the day. It was followed by an avalanche of advice books published through the 1880s and 1990s, aimed at less affluent households, which increasingly addressed themselves to, and were written by, women. By the last years of the nineteenth century the strongly moral focus of the domestic sphere of a few decades earlier had been subtly replaced by a more overtly aesthetic preoccupation with the home. The shift from the eclectic, mid-Victorian, morally-oriented, domestic interior to the 'artistic home' was hugely significant in the evolution of the modern interior. It demonstrated an understanding that the interior's aesthetic had become a significant marker of taste and social status for an increasingly wide sector of society. Impelled by social pressures to participate in the creation of 'artistic homes', middle-class women learnt how to engage with the rules of taste and fashion and to translate that engagement both into the clothes they wore and into the domestic spaces they inhabited and controlled. Although the emphasis was increasingly upon visual harmony and control this did not lessen the desire to acquire large numbers of domestic goods. Rather it has been suggested that a new clutter, made up of 'an indiscriminate mix of women's handiwork, rattan furniture, peacock's feathers, beaded curtains and Japanese fans', simply replaced the old one.[30] In the frontispiece to his 1881 book *Decoration and Furniture of Town Houses* (illus.14), Robert W. Edis confirmed that this was indeed the case. The space he depicted contained all the necessary components of a fashionable 'aesthetic' interior, from the classically inspired frieze above the picture rail (depicting a peacock, the aesthetic icon par excellence), to decorated china in a dresser, a Japanese screen, an Oriental vase and a number of light, cane-seated chairs.

The emergence of the self-consciously aesthetic domestic interior brought with it a new emphasis upon visuality over materiality and spatiality. The dominance of the eye within modern consumer culture has been noted by a number of writers.[31] Its arrival also coincided with the emergence of the idea of a 'modern lifestyle' and its effects on the way spaces were used, and in which occupants developed their identities through their homes. By the turn of the century the parlour had been replaced by the living room, the latter seen as a much more informal space in which the notion of 'personality' rather than of 'character', could be expressed.[32] The former was linked to morality and to a world which recognized fixed principles of conduct while the latter 'connoted magnetic attraction, fascination, aura and charm.'[33] Twentieth-century 'personality' broke down the distinction between private and public as the former became increasingly visible in the latter.[34] Within this transformation it was clear that the home was sensitive to the changes that occurred within modernity over the period in question, and that it was responding to them through the reconfiguration of its interior spaces. Also, as the character of modernity grew more complex and the imperatives of fashion more demanding – in addition to the existence, in Britain, of what came to be called 'the servant problem' – the need to simplify one's interior spaces grew apace. Thus the early twentieth-century living room emerged as 'a product, in part, of the post-Victorian revulsion from the riotous materialism of the late nineteenth-century parlor'.[35] On one level it represented 'an attempt to control matter out of place'.[36] On another it was simply a response by female consumers to the changing fashion of the day.

Between 1850 and 1914, in response to the modernizing forces of mass production and consumption, secularization, urbanization and suburbanization, the democratization of the fashion system, women's changing self-identities and roles, enhanced levels of social aspiration and social mobility, and the growing importance of the concept of taste, the domestic interior underwent a number of significant transformations. All those forces had a dramatic transformative effect upon it in its manifestations both inside and outside the home. On a number of levels the modern values that had come to be represented by the domestic interior in that period – those, that is, that were linked to its relationship with mass consumption and with commerce; with the modern concept of 'fashion' that, to a considerable extent, drove mass consumption; and with the important role it played in providing an expressive outlet for women and a means through which they could form their modern identities – were no longer limited to the private arena of the home. The following four chapters will focus on the journey that took them from 'inside out' and which, in the process, helped form the modern interior.

2 The New Interior

The shattering of the interior occurs via Jugendstil at the turn of the century.
Walter Benjamin[1]

The emergence of the aesthetic interior in the last decades of the nineteenth century marked a new interest in the appearance of middle-class domestic spaces and, most significantly, in the need for them not only to be modern but also to look modern. Not everybody suddenly threw out their old belongings and brought in interior decorators to modernize their domestic spaces of course, nor were period styles (especially those like the French revival styles, which facilitated a lighter, brighter, more unified approach towards domestic spaces) completely rejected. However, the ideas of the 'new', the 'modern' and the 'fashionable' increasingly penetrated popular attitudes towards the design of the domestic sphere. Like its mid-nineteenth-century antecedents, the new turn-of-the-century interior also developed within the context of private domesticity but moved quickly into the public arena. That momentum was increasingly driven by the reforming ideals of architects, however, as well as by the more conservative practices of upholsterers and decorators working with middle-class housewives.

The new interior emerged in a number of guises in the years between 1890 and 1914. Manifested through the simple forms of Britain's Arts and Crafts Movement, the sinuous curves of French and Belgian Art Nouveau, or its rectilinear Northern European equivalent, Jugendstil – or, a little later, the undecorated, standardized, machine-inspired forms created by a group of designers based in Germany – it sought above all to address its own era. Most significantly, whatever their preferred style, a number of architects located in Europe and the US began to think of the interior as an integral feature of their projects and to develop the idea of a *Gesamtkunstwerk*, a 'total work of art', in which a sense of visual unity brought together every element of their buildings and their inner spaces. They aimed to bring together architecture and the decorative arts into a new synthesis that would not only facilitate modern life but that, through the use of non-historicist forms inspired by the contemporary worlds of nature and the machine, would actually embody it.

In the daring experiment that was Art Nouveau or Jugendstil, depending on where and how it manifested itself, many architect-decorators began to search for a new language for the interior.[2] The term 'the New Interior' came to be widely used to characterize the striking results of their experiments. In that its designers sought to create a modern interior style which would cross the divide between the private and public spheres, to be as at home in an exhibition hall and a department store as in a living room, Art Nouveau was the first modern style to fully recognize the permeability between the spheres. The architect-designers recognized that women were increasingly replicating the interiors they saw outside the home in their domestic settings and that, conversely, the creators of interiors in exhibitions and stores were working hard to ensure that women felt 'at home' in the settings in they consumed.

Ultimately however, according to Walter Benjamin, although the architects' intentions were to individualize and personalize their creations through the level of control that they exerted over all the elements of their buildings, inside and out, the result was to undermine the subtle qualities of domesticity and privacy that had been embodied in the mid-nineteenth-century domestic interior. For Benjamin this meant the death of the autonomy of the 'interior' itself.[3] Indeed the totalizing effect of Art Nouveau in the interior was to prove its ultimate undoing as a successful style for the domestic interior. In that context it was really only fully successful in the highly idealized homes that architects created for themselves and their families, and in those of a relatively small number of 'far-sighted' wealthy clients who were prepared to live with a high level of aesthetic control in their homes in exchange for the cultural capital they gained from it. For the most part, however, Art Nouveau was successful – albeit, given its innate fashionableness, for a limited time period only – in public interiors dedicated to culture, leisure and commerce. It featured in department stores, museums, world exhibitions, cafés and restaurants and in a number of other inside spaces outside the home, especially those inhabited by women.

The New Interior had its roots in the 1890s when a number of architects began to seek innovative interior design solutions to what they perceived to be the 'problems' of the historicism and eclecticism of mid-nineteenth-century domesticity. In the face of what they saw as the chaotic proliferation of mass-produced goods for the home, the problem of 'taste' created by the democratization of consumption, and the emergence of the amateur, usually female, home decorator whom they believed to be ignorant of architectural principles and driven solely by the dictates of fashion, the Art Nouveau architect-decorators sought to gain complete control over their architectural constructions. Because of its visual, material and spatial complexity, its psychological density, its multi-layered relationship with modernity and its stylistic possibilities, the interior increasingly became the focus of their intentions. The New Interior architect-decorators first directed their gazes on the private spaces of domesticity. By that time, the English Arts and Crafts definition of 'home', as formulated by C. R. Ashbee, C.F.A. Voysey, M. H. Baillie Scott and others, had not only repudiated display in favour of simplicity, privacy, comfort and family life, but had also encouraged many others to readdress the subject of the domestic interior. In France, for example, 'the ... importation of the word "home", evoking the Arts and Crafts conception of the domestic sphere as a place of both beauty and comfort', was widespread.[4] Following on the heels of those developments a new generation of international architect-decorators began to use the domestic interior as a test-bed in which to try out new ideas about the relationship between architectural structures and the spaces within them and, for a period of less than a decade around the turn of the century, in spite of Benjamin's fear that it had been 'shattered', the interior became the focus for a number of key debates about the nature of modernity itself.

As a means of promoting the principle that the domestic interior environment should be created in sympathy with the architecture that housed it, several architects chose to design their own houses and interiors for themselves and their families. Once again the inspiration came from England, specifically from William Morris's commission to Philip Webb to create a house for himself and his new wife which he filled with his own furnishings and those of his associates. The Red House in Bexleyheath, Kent, marked a turning point in the emergence of the modern interior. When the Belgian architect, Henry Van de Velde, decided to create a complete home for himself in the Brussels suburb of Uccle, he inevitably looked to Morris for inspiration. The exterior of Bloemenwerf, the house he created for his family, owed much to Arts and Crafts neo-vernacular designs. Inside the walls of his little cottage Van de Velde created a set of spaces, the structure, furniture and furnishings of which were conceived and designed as a whole. The set of chairs around his

Henry Van de Velde's Studio in the Villa Bloemenwerf, Uccle, Brussels, 1895–6.

dining table, for example, featured softly curved backs which flowed into their gently curving legs. Even the flowing forms of his wife's dress, designed by the architect from Morris fabric, were echoed in the interior spaces she inhabited. Van de Velde's studio, was also subjected to the same unifying process. He covered its walls with his own paper designs, placed one of his own chairs in the space, filled the shelves with vases he had created himself and hung one of his own paintings on the wall. Van de Velde described his forms and decorations as organisms, a metaphor that helped him explain the way in which he conceived of the exterior and the interior as a single entity. In this way he linked the structural aspects of his interiors with the non-structural, the practical with the decorative and the two-dimensional with the three-dimensional.

Unlike Morris, Van de Velde was working in a new era in which, through the expansion of the mass media and the growth of mass consumption, the boundaries between the public and the private spheres were being rapidly eroded. As a result he crossed over from the domestic sphere to the commercial arena with ease, seeing no boundary between them. This flexibility was reflected in an 1899 design for an office interior for the Havana Tobacco Company in Berlin. The space he created featured arches, the forms of which were repeated in stencilled patterns on the walls and in the arms of the chairs he positioned within the space. Two years later Van de Velde decorated the interior of a hairdresser's

Henry Van de Velde, interior of the office of the Havana Tobacco Company, Brussels, 1898.

salon in Berlin for François Habry fitting it out with a row of mirrors from which electric lights, suspended from strips of metal designed to look like organic stems of plants, were cantilevered. He also worked in the cultural arena, designing the interior spaces of the Folkwang museum in Hagen in 1902 and transforming those of the Weimar museum in Germany six years later.

When the German architect, Peter Behrens, set out to create a home for himself and his wife Lilli in Darmstadt in 1901–2 he was following in the footsteps of Van de Velde. The unified exterior and interior which Behrens created was much more luxurious and decorative than that of his Belgian predecessor, however. The effect of that unity was achieved through the architect's repeated use of geometrical motifs on the windows, the walls, the floors and the surfaces of furniture pieces, all of which were created especially for the rooms of the house. In his

The daughter's bedroom in Peter Behrens's House in Darmstadt, designed by Peter Behrens, 1901, illustrated in *The Studio*, 1901.

daughter's bedroom, concentric circles were inlaid into the wooden head and foot of the bed. They were also applied to the back of a side chair and to the mirror of the dressing table, while a suspended lamp, the bed-linen and the curtains also featured the same motif. Little side tables were built into the bed-head. In the music room a built-in sofa was fitted against

Part of the drawing room in the studio flat of Charles Rennie Mackintosh and Margaret Macdonald, designed by the couple, Glasgow, 1900, illustrated in a special summer edition of *The Studio*, 1901.

one of the walls, a furnishing strategy widely used by many members of this generation of architect-decorators and which later became a leitmotif in numerous Modernist designs. Behrens extended the same approach to the fitted shelves in his study and to a small guest's bed built into the eaves. The gentle curves on the back of the dining room chairs were repeated as motifs on the glass doors of fitted cupboards in the same room, while metal candelabras and a porcelain dinner service featured the same forms, in three dimensions in the case of the former, and in two dimensions in the latter. Behrens proudly proclaimed that his house was a combination of 'practical utility and abstract beauty'.[5] Like those of van de Velde, Behrens's decorating principles were as applicable to the commercial sphere as they were to the domestic arena. In 1902 he designed a complete dining room for Berlin's Wertheim department store which brought together into a single, unified environment, a fully set dining table and chairs, a geometric light suspended over the table, a painted frieze around the top of the containing walls, porcelain on the dresser and pictures on the walls. His 'theatre set' approach to the interior took on a new significance in the modern context.

When the Scottish architect Charles Rennie Mackintosh married Margaret Macdonald in Glasgow in 1900 he decorated the interior of their first home, the first floor flat at 120 Mains Street. The project arrived just at the moment when the architect was turning his attention to interiors and furniture, when, that is, he was entering 'an intimate and largely domestic world . . . it was as if Margaret Macdonald took him by the hand and they went in together.'[6] Although Mackintosh had to work with the room of an existing Victorian house, he intervened into their proportions by introducing a frieze which had the effect of lowering the ceilings. Thwarted by not being able to build furniture into the structure of this rented property he created a form of micro-architecture within it. The hanging lamps in the drawing room were made of silver and had purple glass ornaments set into them. The white writing cabinet, decorated with panels and lock-plates of beaten silver, had rose-coloured jewels on the outside and four painted panels within. The white, cream, light grey and purple colours Mackintosh used in the room served to integrate its components into a single decorative scheme. The flat's dining room, following the convention of the day, was decorated in darker colours. In the bedroom, Mackintosh created a remarkable interior within an interior through the construction of a hardwood bed frame with curtained sides. Once again a sense of aesthetic unity was created. The walls and woodwork were treated in the same tone of white, relieved by green panels in the broad frieze rail, by richly embroidered bed hangings and window curtains, and by the glass jewels used in the ornamentation applied to the bed, the mirror and the wardrobe. When Mackintosh and his wife subsequently moved to their new home at 6 Florentine Terrace in Glasgow they took their bed with them and reinstalled it in their large L-shaped bedroom in that house.

Mackintosh was preoccupied with the creation of an integrated interior aesthetic through a deliberate use of contrasts, light with dark, floral with rectilinear motifs, structure with decorative surfaces, and masculine with feminine spaces. In his creation of the interior as an aesthetic space first and foremost he was indebted to Japanese art, in which floral and geometric patterns and shapes often coexisted. In the entrance to one of his most successful domestic interiors, The Hill House, built in Helensburgh between 1902 and 1904 for the family of the publisher Walter Blackie, he introduced a motif that combined a geometric grid pattern with the curved profile of a tulip.[7] Underpinning the important shift in that period from curvilinear to rectilinear design, the influence of

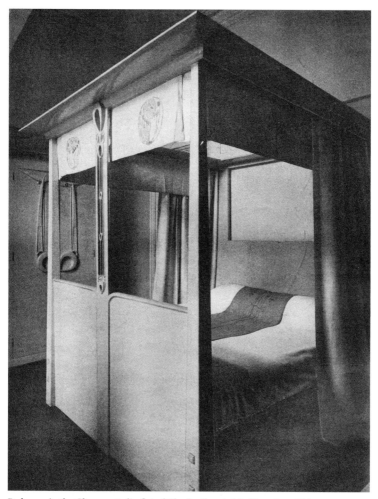

Bedroom in the Glasgow studio flat of Charles Rennie Mackintosh and Margaret Macdonald, designed by the couple in 1900, and illustrated in the special summer edition of *The Studio*, 1901.

the art of Japan was all-important, especially in helping architects to justify their interventions in the interior. In the 'formal expression of Zen', one writer has explained, 'interior and exterior were allowed to flow smoothly one into the other by means of simple design and thoughtful use of materials.'[8] Mackintosh was well aware of the license that gave him to move from architecture into the interior.

An umbrella- and coat-stand in the Ingram Street Tea Rooms, Glasgow, designed by Charles Rennie Mackintosh, *c.* 1900, illustrated in *The Studio*, 1903.

Mackintosh's ease in moving between the domestic and the public spheres was manifested most clearly in his designs for Miss Catherine Cranston, who opened a chain of tea rooms in Glasgow at the turn of the century. Influenced by the temperance movement, the sophisticated, artistic spaces they created together rapidly became fashionable places where middle-class women could take tea in the afternoons during their shopping trips. The rooms also provided lunches for office workers of both sexes. Mackintosh began working with Miss Cranston in 1896 on the Buchanan Street rooms, where he created a number of stencilled murals. Next, at Argyle Street, he created the furniture. Between 1900 and 1911 he worked with his wife on the Ingram Street rooms, where they created a number of striking interiors combining his talent for rectilinear form and Margaret Macdonald's for floral, symbolist-inspired, decorative work. The level of his attention to detail was manifested in his design for a coat rack and umbrella stand, created for the 'White Room' in Ingram Street. Its rectilinear form mirrored the aesthetic used throughout the interior. The bright white spaces, dark oak chairs and the variety of materials employed – from beaten tin to stained glass to painted wood – combined with Mackintosh's eye for proportion and harmony to create a strikingly modern space which must have evoked considerable excitement in industrial Glasgow.[9] Mackintosh's other interventions in the public arena in those years included a design for the city's department store, Pettigrew and Stephens, for a lace display stand at Glasgow's 1901 International Exhibition.[10]

Many other architect-decorators working at that time also created their own interior living spaces. Otto Wagner designed the interior furnishings for his abode at Rennweg 3 in Vienna, while Koloman Moser created a highly unified interior for himself in the same city. Adolf Loos designed the interior of his own flat in Vienna in 1903. Creating a fitted or aesthetically unified domestic interior, in which no modifications or personal additions were possible for oneself or one's next of kin, was one thing, but creating such a set of domestic spaces for a client was another. It meant an almost absolute adherence to a set of lifestyle rules and the commitment of occupants to lead their lives as part of a work of art. It was a brave client, therefore, who took on an Art Nouveau architect-decorator. A number of international clients proved willing, however, to commission a New Interior. They included the Heiseler family, for whom Hermann Obrist created an interior in 1898; the textile manufacturer Herbert Ash and his wife Johanna, for whom Van de Velde created a house in 1902–3; Dr Aderhold Froese, for whom the same architect designed a house in Hanover in 1909–10; the Glasgow provisions merchant for whom Mackintosh created Windyhill in 1900–1; the publisher, Walter Blackie, the owner, as we have seen, of Mackintosh's The Hill House of 1902–4; Dr Hermann Wittgenstein, Josef Hoffmann's client of 1906; and the banker, Adolphe Stoclet, the owner of Hoffmann's Palais Stoclet of 1905–11. They were united by their wealth, frequently newly acquired through manufacturing, and their professional standing but, above all else, by their commitment to modern art as a marker of social status. Although they were prepared to live in a New Interior, some clients reached compromises with their architects. Walter Blackie, for example, insisted on using his own, traditional furniture in the dining room of The Hill House, limiting Mackintosh's intervention in that room to the fireplace and the light fittings.[11]

Stoclet and his fashionable Parisian wife, Suzanne, went the whole way, however. They commissioned a building and an interior, which were

A sitting area in the Palais Stoclet, Brussels, designed by Josef Hoffmann, 1905–11, illustrated in *The Studio*, 1914.

conceived as totally unified and which, more than most, aspired to the status of a luxurious work of art. Hoffmann achieved that goal through a repetition of the delineation of the joints between the planes of the building and of its contents, and through a unified approach towards the manipulation of the proportions, the lighting, the colours, the materials, the decorative details of the internal structural elements, and the furniture and the furnishings. So visually and materially rich and complex was Hoffmann's interior composition, the walls of which were covered with original artworks by Gustav Klimt, that it was almost impossible to distinguish between the container and the contained. Hoffmann acted as the choreographer of the whole ensemble, commissioning many of his colleagues to create items for it as well as designing many of them himself, including the silverware, porcelain and glassware. In the sitting area in the house depicted, the texture of the marble used for the walls almost merges with the pattern on the fabric used to upholster the chairs. The vases of flowers and the statue on a plinth serve to complete the artistry of that rich interior.

In addition to working on many residential projects for clients, like his contemporaries Hoffmann also designed for the commercial sphere. In 1900 he created a striking rectilinear interior for a barber's shop in Vienna, demonstrating that men could also be pampered in fashionable spaces and become part of modish display. In 1903, with Koloman Moser, the same architect-decorator designed a dramatic, rectilinear reception space, complete with a table, high-backed chairs and flowers, for the salon of the Flöge sisters. In the same year the two of them also created an interior for the Wiener Werkstätte's showroom in Neustiftgasse in Vienna.

While the impetus for the New Interior undoubtedly began in the domestic context, its public arena manifestations were not afterthoughts but conceived, rather, as continuous spaces in the same modern world. Mirroring to a significant extent the exodus of middle-class women from the home into the commercial sphere in that period, the New Interior was 'at home' in the commercial and cultural spaces of the metropolis, especially in those locations in which women could increasingly be found entertaining themselves and shopping. Linked to fashionable taste and emphasizing the commodity, the New Interior undoubtedly posed less of a threat in those temporary spaces as it could be experienced by itinerant women, in their capacity as *flâneuses* in the city, as fleeting encounters. Its fashionableness and desirability were heightened by its presence in public spaces and it encouraged women to become consumers of its small component parts – ceramics, glass objects, jewellery, even small pieces of furniture – which could easily be added to existing domestic spaces without transforming them beyond recognition.

A few hotels embraced the fashionable interior styles of their day, among them the Hotel Metropole in Brussels (1904), the interior of which was created by Alban Chambon; the Palace Hotel also in Brussels (1904); the Palace in Lucerne (1906); and the Hotel and Pension Eden au Lac in Zurich (1909).[12] Other hotels, among them the Grand in Melbourne, embraced the equally fashionable Moorish style as an alternative. Fearful that they would alienate their more cautious visitors who came for luxury and comfort rather than for high fashion, most hotels preferred to stick to more conservative idioms however, neo-classicism and revived eighteenth-century French styles among them. Fairly typical was the interior created by the firm of Mewes and Davis for the Carlton hotel in London. The 'Palm Court' look they created in the early 1890s rapidly became a familiar sight in a range of early twentieth-century luxury leisure interiors, including luxury ocean liners. Thomas Edward Collcutt, the designer who carried out much interior work for the P&O line, was also commissioned by Richard D'Oyly Carte to create interiors for London's Savoy Hotel in 1893, demonstrating the close links between these two interior spaces.[13] Hotels, liners and other luxury leisure spaces of the era depended on communicating an image of an aspirational lifestyle to attract a nouveau riche clientèle. While both hotels and liners embraced the same modern, luxury, domestic aesthetic, the former took their lead from the latter rather than directly from the home.[14]

Ironically, although it was born in, and given its meaning within, domesticity, the New Interior ultimately failed to transform the popular home, except through the inclusion of small decorative artefacts. It thrived, however, in the public urban setting as a fashionable style, or set of styles, which successfully evoked modernity for middle-class women and enhanced feminine consumer desire. Between the mid-1890s and the outbreak of the First World War the public, commercial interior was transformed. This was especially the case in department stores, many of whose interiors were decorated in the modern style, florid Art Nouveau, evident in the displays of the French stores at the 1900 Paris Exhibition. In Brussels Victor Horta created a striking new Art Nouveau interior for the Waucquez store in 1906. Consumers were shown modern interiors within modern interiors, the suggestion being that as well as bringing domesticity outside with them they could also take a piece of the public arena back home. The latest fashions, equally expressed by interior settings as by dress, could be embraced outside the home as well as within it. Adolf Loos's strikingly modern interior of 1908 for the menswear shop, Goldman & Salatsch, showed the way forward where fashion salons were concerned. The interior of that shop, with its dramatic geometric forms, shiny surfaces, glass display cabinets and 'functional' hanging lights, was hugely influential on many store interiors that came after it. The New Interior also permeated cultural spaces, among them art galleries, theatres

A sales room on the ground floor of the Michaelerhaus, designed by Adolf Loos for Goldmann and Salasch, Vienna, 1908, photograph *c.* 1912.

and museums. Van de Velde designed both the private office and the front of house for Meier-Graefe's La Maison Moderne in Brussels, for instance, while Moscow's Art Theatre was decorated by Fyodor Shekhtel in 1902 in the Art Nouveau style.

Restaurants, cafés and tea rooms also embraced the New Interior, becoming sites of fashionable display in the process. While, as we have seen, in Glasgow it was linked to tea-drinking, in Vienna it was focused on the coffee house, a traditional public space for men and increasingly, in the late nineteenth century, for women as well. The Viennese Secession itself had been formed in the Griensteidl coffee house in 1897 and six years later the Wiener Werkstätte were also established in a similar setting. Loos's Café Museum of 1899 retained a number of traditional features, however, including standard bentwood chairs which evoked a classless

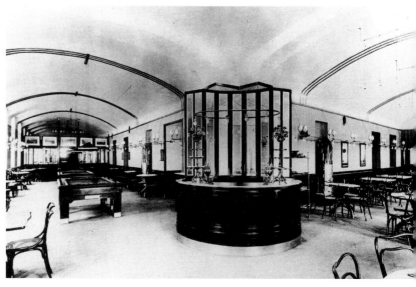

The Café Museum in Vienna, designed by Adolf Loos, 1889.

modernity. As in his menswear shop, Loos used his interior fittings to great effect. In the café a circular counter was added to create a sense of drama. In stark contrast to the underplayed aesthetic of the Café Museum, Hoffmann's Café Fledermaus, attached to the cabaret and bar of the same name and created eight years later, could not have been more decorative. With its black and white chequerboard floor, colourful walls and purpose-designed and -made furniture it offered Viennese coffee-drinkers a totally new experience of modernity.

The new forms of public transportation also presented a challenge to architects in the years leading up to 1914. Otto Wagner's work on the Viennese railway stations of the mid 1890s, Hector Guimard's dramatic additions to the Paris metro system in 1900 and Alfred Grenander's 1901 Jugendstil entrance to the Berlin electric railway showed how it was possible to bring decorative art and the public environment together. Designers also sought to expand their sphere of influence to other forms of transport. That was especially the case in Germany, where Bruno Paul created a set of interiors for the new ocean liners, among them the *George Washington* of 1908. By 1914, the year of a major German Werkbund exhibition, the architect-decorators, August Endell among them, had included the interiors of railway compartments as well. By that date there were few traces of Jugendstil left however, as it had been overtaken by a more simplified, machine-inspired aesthetic which was to become much more widespread after 1918. Otto Wagner, a pioneer of the new simplicity in design, made a significant impression in the design of interiors in the semi-public and public sphere in these years. Committed to a highly rational and functional approach towards construction and to the use of new materials such as aluminium, his interiors and furniture designs for the telegraph office of the newspaper, *Die Zeit*, of 1902, and for the Austrian Post Office Savings Bank of 1904–6 indicated a direction of travel that went beyond the social elitism of Josef Hoffmann's work and the transient fashionableness of Art Nouveau. Together with the German architects and designers, who began to embrace industrial manufacture and to understand the need to create low-cost sets of furniture, Wagner's approach offered a way out of the impasse of the inherent elitism of the New Interior.

Although the New Interior was an ephemeral phenomenon it provided many lasting lessons which went on to underpin the development of the modern interior through subsequent decades. The debates it engendered were especially interesting. Josef Hoffmann's determination to control every detail of the Palais Stoclet was, for example, strongly criticized by his fellow countryman, the architectural critic Adolf Loos. In his essay 'The Poor Rich Man' (1900), Loos described the way in which a wealthy man brought in an architect to create a sumptuous artistic interior for his apartment and pointed out the possible enslavement of the individual by the artistic interior. Not only did the architect that Loos described supervise all the tradesmen he used to create the impressive space, he also had to educate his client into knowing where everything went.[15] The heated discussion held in 1914 between Van de Velde and Hermann Muthesius grew out of the encounter between the New Interior and ideas about standardization. While the former believed in the concept of individualism, which had been born in the years of the Enlightenment and sustained through the development of the idea of the 'modern self' in the nineteenth century, the latter defended the collective principles underpinning industrial mass production and standardization.[16]

Although as a fashionable style Art Nouveau was short-lived, its impact on the development of the modern interior was highly significant. It established the idea of a link between the exterior and the interior of a building, and it supported the dominance of the architect over the upholsterer and the decorator. It also suggested the importance of fitted furniture as an enhancement to the architectural frame, and it proposed the possibility of interiors becoming works of art. In addition it confirmed the significance of the links between the interior, dress and lifestyle. All of those themes were to resurface continually in the modern interior's journey through the twentieth century. Probably the New Interior's most significant contribution, however, derived from the role it played in breaking down the barriers between the separate spheres and in showing that, within early twentieth-century modernity, it was the continuities between them, rather than their differences, that were all-important.

3 The Mass-consumed Interior

The more the manufacturer or dealer arranges model rooms or representa-
tive exhibits, or practices ensemble room selling, the more help and suggestion
it will be to the consumer.
Christine Frederick[1]

From the moment the manufacture of large numbers of domestic goods
was transferred to factories, and middle-class home-makers were forced
to leave the comfort of their homes to purchase them, mass consumption
and the interior developed an intimate relationship with each other. As
the domestic interior came to be seen as the destination for consumed
goods, its replication in the public sphere (in idealized forms) as a frame
for displaying those products became increasingly widespread. We have
seen how Peter Behrens created a dining room for Berlin's Wertheim
department store in 1902 which contained a fully laid table. A later commercial display, mounted in Bowman Brothers' London store in the
1930s, set out to be even more 'authentic', comprising, as it did, a table set
for breakfast complete with boiled eggs and toast. The dinner service
being promoted was designed by the English ceramics designer Susie
Cooper. Increasingly, represented interiors, or components of them such
as these, were used as the frames for objects of desire in commercial settings. Through the process the domestic interior was itself transformed
into an object of mass consumption.

Mass consumption, it has been claimed, was one of modernity's
defining features.[2] That same claim could also be made for the domestic
interior, as it became absorbed by the world of mass consumption. The
model of consumption that used the interior as a selling tool was highly
dependent upon the creation of consumer desire. Through an engagement with the evocative design of interiors in commercial spaces in
which goods were displayed, the desire to purchase was encouraged. As
women came out of their homes to purchase domestic goods, the modern interior's relationship with mass consumption had an 'inside out'
push built into it. The evocatively designed interior became, therefore,
both a means (of selling) and an end (the location for the consumed

A breakfast table set with a service designed by Susie Cooper, displayed in the Bowman Brothers' Store, London, late 1930s, illustrated in C. G. Holme, ed., *The Studio Year Book*, 1939.

goods) in this context. Gradually, as the power of the marketplace expanded the means came to dominate the end and the idealized public sphere interior became as important as, if not more so than, its realized counterparts. Indeed, in that form, the modern interior became an accomplice in the construction of the 'irrational' desire which under-pinned the mass consumption of goods intended for 'real' interiors. The result was that it became increasingly difficult to view them independently and yet another level of ambiguity between the private and the public spheres was created.

Another effect of the interior's expanding relationship with mass consumption was felt in retail spaces themselves. Arcades were covered over to make the conditions for consuming more acceptable, and as a consequence the idea of spaces within spaces, of rooms within rooms and of stores within stores became increasingly widespread. The experiences that took place within those retail spaces – from department stores to shopping malls – were ones of continually enhanced 'immersion', of being increasingly shut off from the outside world and contained within safe, unthreatening and (when the technology became available) temperature-controlled spaces. Commercial branding also played a key role in those constructions helping the flow of people through them. Gradually, as the process of interiorization increased its pace it became increasingly hard to distinguish 'inside' experiences from 'outside' ones, and more and more difficult to understand where the boundaries between what previously had been separate spheres were located. The same thing was happening in the domestic arena. In the interior of Adolf Loos's Moller House, created in Vienna's Starkfriedgasse in 1927–8, for example, the designer combined oriental rugs, parquet floors and wood panelling with a subtle use of different levels, thereby developing, in a domestic setting, the idea of insides within other insides – a layering of inside spaces a bit like Benjamin's layers of envelopment within the compass case. 'It is no longer the house that is the theatre box', one writer has explained in connection with Loos's complex interior design, 'there is a theatre box inside the house, overlooking the internal social spaces . . . the classical distinction between inside and outside, private and public, becomes convoluted.'[3] In locating spaces within other spaces Loos could have been anticipating the shopping mall of the early twenty-first century.

The work that went on behind the scenes in the construction of idealized interiors was inevitably hidden from consumers. Model domestic interiors were presented as static images and spaces, complete with puffed-up cushions.[4] Real lives, in that context, were replaced by the modern, mass media-dependent notion of 'lifestyles', the idealized versions, that is, of the lives that people actually lead.[5] An abstract, totalizing concept created by the sum of consumers' possessions, activities, aspirations and desires, the concept of 'lifestyle' emerged largely as a result of the mass media's engagement with the modern interior. It filled the gap left by the loss of the home's economic and productive role and linked it more firmly with the processes of mass consumption and identity formation. That, in turn, led to the absorption of interior decoration into the fashion system and to the ensuing presentation, in mass market women's magazines, of a mix of different kinds of information related to interiors, fashion and leisure activities in a single publication. Rapidly, however, the idea of lifestyle began to take on an existence of its own, above and beyond the individual elements upon which it was dependent.

A couture dress by Paul Poiret in an interior with fabric also designed by the couturier, illustrated in *La Revue de La Femme*, May 1927.

Various forms of the mass media were quick to represent the idealized domestic interior and to use it as a mechanism for stimulating desire and mass consumption. Viewed inside the home the printed pages of magazines, mail order catalogues, advice books, exhibition catalogues and newspapers played important roles, while outside the domestic arena world exhibitions, department stores, restaurants and museums began to contain constructed interiors which were also intended to stimulate consumption, or at least the desire for it.[6] The late nineteenth and early twentieth centuries witnessed a number of ways in which the mass media, in its various manifestations, helped to construct relationships between consumers and interiors. Developments in lithography and photography made it increasingly easy to represent whole interiors in two dimensions and to reproduce those images in large numbers. The problems of early flash photography and the long exposures that were needed to capture the interior meant that it took longer than other areas of the environment to photograph. By the last decades of the century, however, those technical obstacles had mostly been overcome. Women's magazines extended their promotion of fashionable clothing items to include components of the interior and complete interiors. An image of a woman wearing a Poiret dress from the 1920s, for example, was published in the French women's magazine *La Revue de La Femme* in May 1927. She was framed by, and depicted gently caressing, a pair of curtains designed by the same couturier, suggesting a unity between her body, her dress and the interior in which she was located.[7] By the early twentieth century interiors had become an important component of a wide range of women's magazines, including the 'upmarket' *Vogue*, then as now a fashion-oriented magazine in which sumptuous interiors created by interior decorators complemented the fashionable images of modern luxury evoked by the couture clothing which graced most of its pages. It was sharply contrasted with the 'pseudo-rationality' of other, more 'downmarket' magazines such as *Good Housekeeping*, which targeted home-makers and the work that went on in the home. It claimed to undertake laboratory tests of many of the items it featured as a means of ensuring their scientific validity, their reliability and their value for money.

Magazines, read and looked at in the home for the most part, attempted on a number of different levels to focus women's attention on idealized versions of the very interiors in which they were frequently sitting while they read. Magazine culture was very important in nineteenth-century England. 'The magazine', one writer has explained, 'bought by an upper middle-class woman, might be read by her daughters, her servants and friends, then swapped for another through the exchange pages of the first magazine before being thrown out or sent to a second-hand bookshop.'[8] Advertisements for items of furniture and other decorative domestic objects were the most obvious way in which the housewife was targeted as a consumer of, and for, the interior. They frequently showed their 'subjects' within interior settings. An advertisement in the March 1914 edition of the American magazine, *Ladies' Home Journal*, for example, which was promoting a brand of floor polish, depicted a housewife and her maidservant busy polishing while a group of children played happily on the floor. The conventional, cosy, middle-class interior setting that was represented, complete with its solid wood dining table, piano and patterned curtains, was intended to make the product seem 'real' and appealing. In an article titled 'How You Can Furnish a Five-room Apartment for $300' the same journal once again focused housewives' attention on the interior. 'A careful shopper', the author suggested, 'can furnish her apartment both inexpensively and tastefully'.[9] Colour drawings and a list of prices were included. Editorials represented a much softer, and possibly more effective, sell than advertisements. The same idea was also appropriated by advertisers, however, as a Harrods' advertisement in a 1920 Ideal Home Exhibition catalogue, headed 'Harrods Furnish a 6-Room Flat Complete for £500', clearly demonstrated.[10] Blurring their promotional and editorial content, magazines played a role in reinforcing their readers' ambiguous identities as readers/home-makers/consumers. Mail order catalogues provided another means of consuming interiors at home. In the USA, where greater distances made them more necessary than in Europe, the Sears, Roebuck and Company and Montgomery Ward catalogues dominated the field.

Consumers of the interior did not always remain in their homes, however. From the late nineteenth century onwards, as we have seen, people (mostly women) came out of the home to buy household goods to take back into it. A wide range of shopping options for direct purchasing were on offer – from market stalls, to fixed shops, to chain stores, to department stores. The last, however, were most linked with modernity in those years and addressed themselves to middle-class female consumers most directly. Those modern 'cathedrals' or 'palaces', as they have been called at different times, played a key role in that context.[11] Much has been written about the ways in which, in the late nineteenth and early twentieth centuries, department stores employed varying levels of

An interior of the Bon Marché department store, rue de Babylone, Paris, 1880.

spectacle to entice customers inside them and to stimulate desire and pleasure so that consuming, for the middle-class women who were their first customers, was perceived as a leisure activity rather than work. In the French department stores, Galeries Lafayettes and Bon Marché among them, consumers were given a sense of being practically exposed to the sky but nonetheless enclosed with a fantasy world.[12] This engraving of an interior in the Bon Marché store in Paris reveals an open, multi-storey, iron and steel structure. The cold, industrial nature of those materials was visually offset, however, by the presence of a variety of goods – items of clothing, lengths of fabrics and rugs among them – which were suspended from the balconies of the different floors and on lines hung between the building's structural columns. One writer has described some of the ways in which that sense of being in a fantasy world was achieved visually. 'Display managers learned the new color theory and exploited color, often in the most adroit ways', he has written. 'They decorated with puffed archways of colored silk; they hung garlands of flowers, draperies of colored plush, cages of colored birds. The biggest stores designed rooms . . . around a single color scheme. Green in all its tints and shades prevailed from basement to roof at William Filene's Sons Company in Boston in 1901.'[13] By that time furniture sets and room settings were beginning to be used both inside American stores and in their windows to achieve an exotic, luxurious look.[14] 'To obtain the desired effect of "Parisianism", store managers imitated French salons . . . and even copied the complete interior of a "real Parisian boulevard *appartement*"', one writer has explained, demonstrating, in anticipation of the hotels and shopping malls of Las Vegas several decades later, just how effective evocations of the interior could be in stimulating the imaginations and fantasies of consumers.[15] The evocation of the private sphere in the public context satisfied the requirements of familiarity, voyeurism, curiosity and wish-fulfilment. However the 'spectacularization' of the department store applied equally to restaurants, hotels, theatres and dry goods stores.[16]

By the end of the 1920s the furniture sections of American department stores had fully embraced the modern interior design style, known as Art Deco, that had become popular in Europe following the 1925 *Exposition Internationales des Arts Décoratifs et Industriels Modernes*, and they had begun to display complete modern room sets, sometimes in partnership with museums. A mixture of modern French and American designs in room settings were shown at both John Wanamaker and Macy's in New York in 1927. Macy's cleared its floor of traditional pieces

A backcloth for a store window display of furniture, illustrated in a store window display manual, 1925.

and showed only modern designs at that time.[17] The president of New York's Metropolitan Museum of Art, Robert W. de Forest, became the chairman of the store's advisory committee, thereby giving that commercial project a level of cultural validation.[18]

Many other American stores were quick to follow Macy's lead and displayed rooms filled with designs by European 'masters', such as the German Bruno Paul, and the Italian Gio Ponti. The appeal of the room setting over individualized items of furniture undoubtedly lay in its strong visual impact and its ability to evoke an idealized version of 'reality'. It also suggested a lifestyle. The idea of the *Gesamtkunstwerk*, so beloved of early twentieth-century designers, had, by the 1920s, been transformed by store designers into a selling tool. In the 1930s Mary, the wife of the designer Russel Wright, devoted limitless energy to selling her husband's aluminium ware. She undertook live demonstrations in stores using real food as props, thereby sustaining a commercial tradition that had been in place in American stores since the early century. In 1950 the Wrights published a book together titled *Guide to Easier Living* in which they explained that 'Good informal living substitutes a little headwork for a lot of legwork. It doesn't need wealth, but it does take thought, some ingenuity and resourcefulness, and more than a little loving care to create a home that is really your own.'[19]

Displays of furniture ensembles and of complete interiors were not only visible inside the bodies of stores, they were also installed in shop windows which could be viewed from the street. By the early twentieth century the three-walled interior frame had become a familiar sight in department store windows. It had its origins in the theatrical stage set and the domestic dramas of the decades around the turn of the century. A 1925 American manual for 'mercantile display' advised that 'the installing of a design of this character is well worth the effort as it lends itself to the display of a varied line of merchandise'.[20] The same manual also included a display of living-room furniture, explaining that, 'The furniture is arranged in a manner to show [it] off to good advantage, using the necessary accessories such as the lamp, book rack, pictures etc.', reinforcing the, probably tacit, knowledge of professionals in that field that consumers needed to be shown just enough of an interior for their imaginations to be stimulated and their desires evoked.[21] The neo-classical simplicity of one model shop window interior in the manual, intended for a display of furniture, provided a fairly neutral backcloth (p. 63). Draped curtains added a level of theatricality, a chequered floor a suggestion of Viennese modernity, and a fringed standard lamp a counterpoint to its otherwise strict symmetry.

While department stores provided an urban means of consuming the interior, the shopping mall became its suburban equivalent. With the advent of the automobile in the us, demand grew for out-of-town shopping places where there was plenty of parking space.[22] Thus the shopping mall, a collection of individual shops brought together into a single unit, was born. In 1916 the Chicago architect Arthur Aldis created one of the first shopping complexes of that kind, Market Square in Lake Forest, a wealthy suburb of Chicago. He integrated twenty-eight stores, twelve office units, thirty apartments, a gymnasium and a clubhouse, and added landscaping around them. His aim was to position everything in one place so that the consumer could combine shopping with leisure activities. Through the twentieth century the idea of the suburban mall gradually displaced that of the urban department store. Targeting a range of social classes, it offered consumers a very different interior experience, one which was usually less consistent, less spectacular, less luxurious, less glamorous and more utilitarian. By the end of the century shopping malls had taken over from the department store for the most part, offering, through their more nuanced and complex 'inside' spaces, an even more ambiguous retail experience than their predecessors.

Although the direct purchasing of objects for the interior did not usually take place at exhibitions on a significant scale, they played a crucial role, nonetheless, in the development of the representation of the mass-consumed interior in the public sphere.[23] Walter Benjamin described the world exhibitions as 'places of pilgrimage to the commodity fetish' intended 'to entertain the working classes'.[24] It wasn't until the last decades of the nineteenth century that complete (or at least two- or three-sided) 'room sets' were exhibited in those settings. Prior to that isolated items of furniture had been displayed either in elaborate cabinets or in roped-off areas. At Philadelphia's *Centennial Exhibition* of 1876, for example, finely carved wooden display cases containing free-standing items of furniture had stood looking rather lost under the vast iron trusses and plate glass of that vast exhibition hall.[25] Full-scale models of workers' houses had been shown at the 1867 exhibition in Paris, but the emphasis at that time had still been upon their exteriors rather than their interiors.[26] The Austrian critic Jacob von Falke, the author of the first German language book on interior design, *Art in the House* (1871), was among the first designers in Germany or Austria to create a complete 'ensemble' interior display in an exhibition.[27] By 1880 it had become a fairly common strategy used by curators in applied arts museums and by designers at trade fairs. A William Morris exhibit at *The Foreign Fair* of 1883–4, for example, held in Boston's Mechanics Hall, was divided into six compartments, or rooms. A pamphlet describing the display cautioned that 'the rooms must not . . . be taken to represent the rooms of a dwelling, nor is the ordinary decoration of a house attempted. Morris and Company are exhibiting here as manufacturers only, and the arrangement of goods is that which seemed best for showing them in the ways most accordant to their actual use.'[28] That caveat could have been applied equally well to all the exhibition room sets that came after it.

By the time of the Paris *Exposition Universelle* of 1900, room sets were being extensively used. That exhibition set out to celebrate modern art, industry and commerce and for all the exhibiting countries the integrated interior represented a level of achievement in all of those three areas. It also demonstrated the degree of progressiveness, or modernity, embraced by the countries in question. Examples of exhibited interiors at *Paris 1900* included those designed by German exhibitors, Richard

Georges Djo-Bourgeois, study for the 'Studium Louvre' Pavilion, exhibited at the *Exposition Internationale des Arts Décoratifs et Industriels Modernes*, Paris, 1925.

Riemerschmid among them, and the famous Art Nouveau settings created by Eugène Gaillard, George de Feure and others which were displayed in the Samuel Bing pavilion. Austria also made its presence felt with, among other displays, the *Viennese Interior*, a *Gesamtkunstwerk* designed by Joseph Olbrich, and an *Interior of a Pleasure Yacht* created by the same designer.[29] Other interiors were sponsored by the Parisian department stores, Bon Marché among them, again in the Art Nouveau style. (The pioneer American interior decorator, Elsie de Wolfe, later recounted in her autobiography that the last had been purchased by her friend, the Marchioness of Anglesey, who, in turn, had passed on to her the eighteenth-century wooden wall panelling which it had displaced.)

    Through the twentieth century the exhibition room set increasingly became a commonplace, at least until the late 1950s. At the Turin 1902 exhibition the Italian designer Carlo Bugatti showed his dramatic interior based on a snail's shell, while Charles Rennie Mackintosh and Margaret

Marcel Guillemard, dining room for the 'Pavillon Primavera', exhibited at the *Exposition Internationale des Arts Décoratifs et Industriels Modernes*, Paris, 1925.

Macdonald's *Rose Boudoir* was widely admired at the same event. The 1925 Paris *Exposition Internationales des Arts Décoratifs et Industriels Modernes* depended heavily upon its spectacular exhibited interiors to entice its visitors into its buildings. Although actual shopping was not possible anywhere in the exhibition, many of the displays reinforced the fact that Paris was the city in which consumption took place on a spectacular scale.[30] A number of room sets were constructed in a group of pavilions which were created to promote the interior decorating sections of Paris's leading department stores. One such room, an office designed by Georges Djo-Bourgeois, was installed in the Grands Magasins du Louvre's *Studium Louvre* pavilion. Featuring leather armchairs, a piece of sculpture by Léon Leyritz and lacquered panels by Pierre Demaria, it was a rich, masculine space offset by a number of feminine touches including vases of flowers and patterning on the curtains and carpet. A dining room was designed by Marcel Guillemard as part of Au Printemps' *Primavera* pavilion. The rich woods and modern furniture forms in Guillemard's room set were intended to persuade visitors that employing *Primavera* to decorate their homes would bring a high level of elegant luxury and modernity into their lives.

It was not only the large international exhibitions that employed the concept of the constructed interior as a display strategy, however. At a more local level, events such as Britain's *Ideal Home Exhibition*, established by the *Daily Mail* newspaper before the First World War, and the annual exhibition held in Paris, *the Salon des Arts Ménagers*, also used room sets.[31] Their aim was less to present a display of national prowess in an international context but rather to inspire the public, fulfil their dreams and aspirations and to encourage them to consume. As the century progressed the messages conveyed by constructed interiors in exhibitions became increasingly complex and their audiences more sophisticated. At the *Britain Can Make It* exhibition, held at London's Victoria and Albert Museum in 1946, a range of room sets were presented as representations of class, age and gender. Examples included 'a technical office for a television research engineer', 'a secondary school classroom', 'a cottage kitchen for a miner', and a 'bachelor's bed sitting room'.[32] The exhibition curators aimed to encourage a more reflective response from its audience than that of consumer desire alone. A notice on a wall at the exhibition instructed visitors to 'view the rooms as if the family has just vacated it'. The intention was to move one step nearer to the occupant than had been achieved at earlier exhibitions, and in so doing, to engage the audience's imaginations as completely as possible. Several reviews were critical of the strategy, however, and one commentator wrote that, 'we feel bound to remark that in most cases the rooms bear no relationship to the imagined families and the class-distinction in naming the rooms appears utterly meaningless . . .

A period room from Cane Acres, an eighteenth-century house on the Perry Plantation, Summerville, South Carolina, exhibited in the Brooklyn Museum, New York.

This is an exhibition, and therefore it is no criticism to say that most of these rooms lack reality. It is important that the public should realise this. Otherwise they may feel that it is all rather outside their powers of attainment.'[33]

Museums played a crucial role in collecting and displaying period interiors through the twentieth century and, indeed, many of the strategies used in the more commercial contexts of exhibitions and department stores had originated in the context of the 'period room'. The Victoria and Albert Museum acquired its first complete interior in 1869 while New York's Metropolitan Museum of Modern Art began to collect rooms in 1903.[34] The Brooklyn Museum also engaged in acquiring period rooms. One of its exhibits, an eighteenth-century dining room from a plantation house in South Carolina, called Cane Acres, contained a number of tasteful, English-influenced items of furniture. Visitors to the museum were encouraged to believe in the 'authenticity' of the setting by the presence of wine in the glass carafes. The original motivation behind what came to be known as the 'period rooms' phenomenon had been to educate the public in historical styles at a time when historicist eclecticism

Raymond Loewy and Lee Simonson, reconstruction of Loewy's office for an exhibition held at the Metropolitan Museum of Art, 'Contemporary Industrial Art: 1934', New York, 1934.

was the taste of the day. The Cane Acres room set out to do just that. At one of its exhibitions, held in 1934, instead of showing the usual domestic period interiors, the Metropolitan Museum of Art focused on the contemporary workspaces of well-known industrial designers of the day as a means of educating the public about the design profession and it contribution to modern life. Raymond Loewy and Lee Simonson recreated a version of the former's office as a 'frame' in which to display his design skills and their wide application to boats and cars as well as interiors themselves.

Popular films, or 'movies', provided another important means through which the interior was mediated and a desire to consume stimulated on a mass scale through the twentieth century. Movies were created to entertain, distract and provide a level of fantasy and escapism from the realities of everyday life. They offered, therefore, an ideal vehicle for

The second-floor drawing room of Hope Hampton's residence at 1145 Park Avenue, New York, designed by Elsie de Wolfe Inc., *c.* 1934.

A still from Jacques Feyder's 1929 film *The Kiss*, starring George Davis and Greta Garbo.

commercial and ideological messages and product placements.[35] In the 1930s the idea of Hollywood 'celebrities' homes' acquired media appeal. Elsie de Wolfe's decorating firm created several home interiors for movie stars, including one for Hope Hampton in New York and another for Gary Cooper in California. The former contained a multitude of luxurious materials. 'It's all white and gold and shimmering', a journalist explained in 1938, 'with a kind of lighthearted dignity about it. The oyster-white furniture is trimmed with gold, the draperies are white satin; and the marble floor is quite sumptuous, with its inlay of gray, oyster-white and yellow. A French window and a scrolled iron gateway lead out to a terrace for al-fresco dining.'[36] The glamorous atmosphere of that sumptuous apartment was mirrored in the countless 'fantasy' sets created for Hollywood films in that decade. In *Grand Hotel* (1932) the cinematography, sets, costumes and the slim figures of Greta Garbo and Joan Fontaine all contributed to a glamorous representation of modernity in which the 'moderne interior' played a star role.[37] In *Dinner at Eight* of the following year a 'moderne' setting was used to represent 'arrivisme' and to contrast with a more 'tasteful' classical setting which stood for upper class tradition.[38] A 1929 film, *The Kiss*, directed by Jacques Feyder and starring George Davis and Greta Garbo, also wooed its audience through its use of stylish 'streamlined moderne' sets. Film interiors were hugely influential. A bedroom set in *The Kiss* reappeared, for instance, in a bedroom design created by John Wellborn Root which was shown at the *Architect and the Industrial Arts* exhibition held in New York's Metropolitan Museum of Art in the same year the film was released.[39] The level of spectacle employed in those films, as in many others, evoked high levels of consumer desire.[40]

The idealized modern interior made an impact in many different contexts and fulfilled a number of different purposes. Through its proximity to consumers' everyday lives and its role in helping to form the concept of 'lifestyle' it was able to perform a powerful communicative function which could only be equalled by dress or food. Providing a level of familiarity for consumers outside the home, it tapped into their desires and succeeded in stimulating their dreams and aspirations. Arguably, as a result, in its idealized and mediated forms, the modern interior was one of the key drivers of mass consumption in the twentieth century as well as, in its realized versions, the destination of many of its objects.

4 The Fashionable Interior

Who doesn't know the woman who goes to a shop and selects wall papers as she would her gowns, because they are 'new' and 'different' and 'pretty'?
Elsie de Wolfe[1]

By the late nineteenth century the requirement to be 'fashionable', especially but not exclusively for women, had spread beyond the social elite to embrace the new middle classes. Not only was it important to be seen to be wearing fashionable clothes, it was equally important to live in, and to be seen in, fashionable interiors, both inside and outside the home. Indeed for consumers of the interior and its objects 'fashionableness' became a key criterion underpinning many of their purchases and, as interiors began to wear out more quickly stylistically than physically, they contributed to the accelerated consumption of those years.

The idea that fashion was a defining component of modernity preoccupied several writers and theorists in the second half of the nineteenth and the first decades of the twentieth centuries, from Charles Baudelaire to George Simmel to Walter Benjamin. In 1863 Baudelaire aligned fashion with his view of modernity, which he saw as being characterized by the increased fragmentation of the experiences of everyday life, describing it as the 'ephemeral, the fugitive, the contingent'.[2] His abstract definition of fashion as a symptom of the modern condition facilitated its transference from dress to a range of other goods and environments which enjoyed a close relationship with the female body, including the interior. By the end of the nineteenth century fashionable dress and interior decoration had also acquired the status of modern 'art' forms which undoubtedly compensated for the increasingly overt, and much derided, commercialism of both practices.[3] The emphasis on 'taste' in the negotiation between artistic practitioners and clients in both areas concealed the large amounts of money that passed hands, as well as the fact that both class status and an engagement with modernity could be bought in the marketplace.

The close relationship between fashionable dress and the modern interior was manifested in numerous ways. Firstly, there was a strong psychological link between them. Both played a key role in identity formation, especially in the creation of (particularly feminine) modern identities. In their capacity as material and spatial layers around the body dress and the interior both played a role in the process of 'interiority' through which modern subjects developed a notion of 'themselves'. That link developed first within the private sphere but, as women went into the public arena, moved out with them into the marketplace. Secondly, there were strong professional links between fashionable dress and the interior as the commercial practices developed by couturiers from the mid-nineteenth century onwards were adopted by interior decorators when they began to establish their own professional framework in the early twentieth century. As the self-identities of both couturiers and decorators became important parts of their commercial brands, those practices crossed the private and public divide. Thirdly, fashionable dress and the interior came together in the public context of mass consumption, in the physical spaces of the theatre, department stores and exhibition halls, as well as in the representational spaces of women's magazines. Such were the workings of the fashion system as it engaged with both dress and the interior that, as the values formed within the context of domesticity were taken out into the marketplace, the idea of the separate spheres was, once again, challenged.

The link between fashionable dress and the modern interior was also facilitated by practitioners in one area openly embracing the other. Fashion designers engaged with the interior as a setting for fashionable dress, as a site for the formation of their own identities and as an extension of women's relationship with modernity. In addition, dress was frequently linked to specific locations within the domestic interior.[4] Light airy cottons and linens were worn in the breakfast room, for example. A strong sense of theatricality pervaded that practice.[5] Middle-class women of that era also went as far as 'dressing' furniture items with ruffles and fringes, transforming them, in the process, into extensions of themselves.[6] The concept of 'interiority' assumes a blurring of the inner, mental activities of occupants and the material and spatial environments they occupy. That psychological reading of the interior has been explored by a number of literary scholars interested in the relationship between writers' work – especially those who emphasized the concept of modern interiority – and the spaces in which they were written.[7] Some have focused on Walter Benjamin's phrase 'the phantasmagoria of the interior', used to refer to the reverie of the subject experienced within private, interior space.[8] Building, also, on Sigmund Freud's emphasis on interiority as a starting point for psychoanalysis, and on his notion of the compartmentalized house as a model, or metaphor, for interiorities which have been constructed over a number of years, literary scholars have discussed the idea of the fusion of 'literal and the figural space'. The specifically 'modern' context of interiority has also been acknowledged and its rise seen as paralleling the separation of work from home, the increased privacy of the domestic setting and the emergence of the 'modern subject'.

At the level of the social elite, dress and the interior have had a relatively long history of interconnectivity. Female members of the eighteenth-century French court – Madame de Pompadour among them – had themselves painted in their interiors adorned in stylish clothing. Fashionable dress first acquired its link with the notion of democratized feminine modernity in late eighteenth-century Europe with the demise of the sumptuary laws which had outlawed the wearing of dress beyond one's station. The gates opened at that time for people to acquire dress suggesting membership of a social class which was not that of their birth.[9] In mid nineteenth-century France, an era of increasing wealth in that country, the idea of fashionable dress was reinforced and encouraged by a new interest in sartorial elegance inspired by the wife of Napoleon III, the Empress Eugénie.[10] With the birth of haute couture at that time, the relationship of fashionable dress with the interior took on a new incarnation which was inextricably linked to the notion of modernity. Indeed fashionable dress and interior decoration became the visual, material and spatial expressions of women's engagement with modernity, both of them offering ways in which, through consumption, women could acquire a stake in the world of 'taste'. Both dress and interior decoration became, at that time, forms of modern luxury empowered to act as signs of social status, whether inherited, acquired through consumption, or aspired towards.

It was within the changing climate of the middle years of the nineteenth century that the Englishman, Charles Frederick Worth, became one of France's first and most successful modern couturiers. His numerous commercial innovations included the construction of showrooms furnished to resemble the drawing rooms of well-appointed houses (hitherto dressmakers had usually visited the homes of their clients). The interiors in his dress establishment were extremely elegant and could be accessed via staircases lined with exotic flowers.[11] For Worth the decorated interior performed a double role, however. It was both a backcloth for his creations and a marker of his own artistic identity, which, in turn, became inseparable from his commercial brand. He decorated the interior spaces of a house he had built for himself in Surêsnes in an eclectic mix of Gothic, Indian, Old English and Moorish styles and posed as an artist within them. Late in his life he dressed to look like Rembrandt with a beret, a cloak and a tied scarf.[12] Other commercial strategies developed by Worth included his use of a live model (his wife Marie), an early version of the fashion mannequin; his encouragement of his wife to wear his clothes at social occasions, such as the races; mixing with the aristocracy; the introduction of the idea of seasonal models; and the use of a brand label sewn on to the bands inside the waists of his garments.

Several of the French couturiers who followed Worth built upon his commercial practices. They also consciously engaged with designed interiors as both sites in which to show their creations and through which to define their own artistic identities.[13] The couturière Jeanne Paquin, for example, sought to extend her interest in the interior beyond its role as a backcloth for her fashionable designs when, in 1914, she asked the architect Robert Mallet-Stevens to create a house for her in Deauville. Sadly the project was never realized. A little later Paul Poiret also commissioned Mallet-Stevens to create a house for him. The flat-roofed, white-walled Modernist home created by the architect for the couturier was built in Mézy-sur-Seine between 1921 and 1923. The work the Irish interior decorator, Eileen Gray, undertook in the homes of the couturiers Jacques Doucet and Madame Mathieu-Lévy (the second proprietor of the fashion house of Suzanne Talbot) in the first decades of the twentieth century also served to bridge the worlds of fashion and interior decoration. For the latter client she created a highly decorative interior with lacquered walls inlaid with silver. The *Pirogue* chaise longue, upholstered in salmon pink, was created by Gray for that space. In her early career Gray was committed to the use of decoration in her interiors and to the link between interior spaces and the identities of their occupants. Like Worth, both Gray's clients understood the importance of the relationship between their roles as creators of fashionable dress, the private spaces within which they defined and communicated their own modern self-identities, and the more public spaces within which they showed and sold their fashion items. Doucet's salon was an elegant, domesticated, eighteenth-century-styled space, featuring a patterned carpet, panelled walls and a chandelier, which undoubtedly made his clients feel simultaneously

The sales room in Jacques Doucet's Couture House, illustrated in *L'Illustration*, 1910.

comfortable and fashionable. The modern role of interior decoration as a constructor of identities was reinforced by Doucet, both within the private spaces of his home and the more public environment of his fashion house.

The early twentieth-century French couturier, Paul Poiret, was not enamoured with the idea of the *Gesamtkunstwerk*, the concept which had played such a key role in early twentieth-century debates about the interior, describing it as a 'substitution of the taste of the architect for the personality of the proprietors [which] has always seemed to me a sort of slavery – a subjection which makes me smile'.[14] Like Adolf Loos and others, Poiret was unconvinced by the way in which a number of turn-of-the-century architects – Henry Van de Velde, Peter Behrens and the members of the Wiener Werkstätte among them – had sought to unite architecture, the interior, furniture and furnishings, and dress into a stylistic entity. In their attempts to distance themselves, and the modern interior, from what they perceived to be the superficial world of fashion and fashionable dress, those architects had aligned themselves with the dress reform movement, thereby embracing the idea of 'rational dress', and rejecting the notion of fashion entirely. That is not to say that Poiret

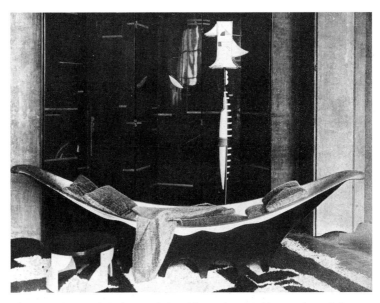

Eileen Gray, *Pirogue* chaise longue, designed for Madame Mathieu-Lévy's rue de Lota Apartment, 1918–22, shown in the window of the designer's Paris shop, Jean Desert, in the early 1920s and illustrated in *Wendingen*, 1924.

was not interested in constructing a bridge between fashionable dress and the interior. On the contrary, he simply did not see architecture as the starting point. From his fashion-centric perspective he sought to transfer the values of fashionable dress into new areas, including the interior.

Poiret had trained as a fashion designer in the couture houses of Doucet and Worth where he had come to understand the complex meanings and operations of the late nineteenth- and early twentieth-century fashion system, which was predicated upon the idea that modern women were in search of luxurious, material means of expressing their modern identities. In 1911 Poiret formed his Atelier Martine, an interior design-oriented initiative, and two years later he created a set of brightly coloured rooms for a Berlin exhibition. The walls of a dining room he showed there were covered with painted plant stems and leaves which blended with the floral pattern on the fabric used for the curtains and as upholstery for the little chairs that Poiret had introduced into his space. A 'bedroom for a French house in the country' was also displayed at the same exhibition.[15] That interior was characterized by the juxtaposition of the dark patterning of the wallpaper and floor covering with the white

A dining room in an exhibition held at the Hermann Gerson department store, Berlin, designed by Paul Poiret in 1913 and illustrated in *Deutsche Kunst und Dekoration*, 1914.

of the lace of the bedcover and of the fur rug placed at the foot of the bed. In 1925, as part of the Paris *Exposition Internationale des Arts Décoratifs et Industiels Modernes*, the Atelier Martine decorated the interiors of three barges: the *Amours*, intended as a comfortable resting place complete with perfume dispensers to create another sensory dimension; the *Délices*,

A bedroom for a French house in the country, designed by Paul Poiret in 1913, shown at an exhibition at the Hermann Gerson department store in Berlin, 1913, illustrated in *Deutsche Kunst und Dekoration*, 1914.

dedicated to gastronomy and the *Orgues*, a location for spectacles and dancing. The studio's nautical interest also extended to the interiors it created for the French liner, the ss *Île de France*, which was launched in 1926. As part of the 1925 exhibition the Atelier Martine's boutique was on show in the Grand Palais. Velvet couches, tasselled cushions, and elegant built-in furniture combined to create the same mood of modern sumptuousness and exoticism that characterized the couturier's dress designs.

A group of professional female interior decorators emerged in the us in the first decades of the twentieth century. Led by Elsie de Wolfe, they saw themselves as operating within the same fashion system as Worth and his followers, and they consciously emulated a number of their commercial strategies. Many links existed at that time between the us and France as wealthy American women were enthusiastic customers of the French couturiers. De Wolfe was among the first of her generation to understand the workings of the fashion system and its relevance to the interior, largely due to the fact that she had moved into interior decoration, as an amateur, from an earlier career in the theatre. As an actress she had liked to wear couture gowns onstage. The picture on p. 82 shows her in an elegant gown posed against a highly decorative backcloth. In the years before the English couturier Lucile (also known as Lady Duff

1920s Art Deco dining room, designed by the Atelier Martine, in the French liner *Île de France,* 1927, illustrated in Paul Frankl's *New Dimensions: The Decorative Arts of Today in Words and Pictures* (1928).

The Salon of the Boutique Atelier Martine, decorated by Paul Poiret, shown in the Grand Palais at the *Exposition Internationale des Arts Décoratifs at Industriels Modernes,* Paris, 1925.

Elsie de Wolfe in a couture dress, *c.* 1900.

Gordon) used live catwalk shows, the theatrical stage had been the only place where couturiers could display their wares on live models. Like Worth, de Wolfe mixed with America's aristocracy and new rich; like him she opened a showroom; she also socialized with artists so that their image would rub off on to her; and, like Worth, she presented herself as a brand. That last commercial strategy was especially apparent in the

pages of her widely read advice book, *The House in Good Taste*, on the first page of which she included an elegant portrait of herself accompanied by her signature. She chose as the location for that photograph the living room of her East 17th Street, New York home, which she redecorated herself in the late 1890s and which she shared with her close companion, the literary agent Elisabeth Marbury. Just as Worth had been able to dictate the course of fashionable dress in France in the second half of the nineteenth century by adding his personal artistic 'genius' to an item of clothing, so de Wolfe and her followers set out to persuade wealthy clients that the association of their names with interiors had the potential to make their occupants appear more fashionable. Like Worth, Paquin, Poiret and others, de Wolfe understood the importance of dress and the interior to modern women's search for self-identity in a world in which flux was the only constant. She was particularly adept at creating private boudoirs for her female clients where personal identity, rather than social status, was at stake. The suite of rooms she created for her close friend, Anne Morgan, for example, comprising a bedroom, a sitting room and a dressing room, were intended for private use only. The dressing room was filled with mirrors, fixed to the doors of fitted wardrobes, enabling Miss Morgan to see herself from all angles.[16]

The model of the fashionable 'signature-decorator' established by de Wolfe was emulated and built upon by several other female decorators through the first half of the twentieth century, among them Ruby Ross Wood, Frances Elkins, Rose Cummings, Dorothy Draper and Syrie Maugham. Maugham was the only Englishwoman among them and her most influential design was a striking all-white living room which she created for her own house in Chelsea. In reality it brought together a number of shades of off-white, cream and beige: the settee and chairs were upholstered in beige satin, and the rug, designed by Marion Dorn, was composed of two tones of cream. A folding screen, comprising mirrored glass panels, stood behind the settee. Like their dress-oriented counterparts, those twentieth-century interior decorators presented themselves as fashionable beings first and foremost. By extension, their work was perceived as fashionable and their clients as fashion-conscious, modern and discerning. Just as couturiers created exclusive items for replication by department stores, although most of the interiors created by decorators were for individual clients, their fashionable spaces also became widely accessible through their presence in mass media publications. Furthermore, the decorators stocked their showrooms with items resembling those they had used in individual settings, thereby enabling a wide range of customers to purchase them.[17]

By the end of the nineteenth century the idea of the seasonal model, promoted by Worth and others, had become the norm in the world of fashionable dress. Similarly in the world of interior decoration certain furnishing and upholstery colours and styles came regularly in and out of vogue. While surface changes to the interior – paint colours and textile patterns among them – could be made quite frequently, other transformations were necessarily more infrequent as some interior items represented a considerable investment. Often fashions began in the world of dress and moved, albeit usually with a time lag, into interior decoration.[18] In France, bourgeois families moved home more frequently than the aristocracy because they were not limited by inherited homes and bulky items of furniture.[19] In New York, also, from the 1860s onwards, the

An 'all-white' living room designed by Syrie Maugham for her house in Chelsea, 1934, illustrated in Derek Patmore's *Colour Schemes and Modern Furnishing*, 1945.

custom of the middle classes was to move house on an annual basis, thereby accelerating the need to continually redecorate and refurbish their homes. By the end of the nineteenth century the social messages of fashionable dress were becoming less clear, however, and the interior was increasingly taking over the role previously performed by dress.[20] Even more than fashionable dress, which had taken on a somewhat frivolous connotation by that time, interior decorating came to be defined as an art of everyday life, a genuinely modern art form.[21]

While the haute couture profession offered much that was useful and relevant to the new interior decorating profession of the twentieth century, the close links that existed between fashionable dress and the interior were also understood by housewives who decorated their homes as amateurs, this having been made possible by the availability of advice literature and the new opportunities offered through mass consumption. In spite of the transference of much domestic manufacture to factories in the nineteenth century, some hand-making survived in the domestic context, focused for the most part on home dress-making and interior decoration. Many of the small artefacts that were made at home, crocheted antimacassars for example, were often combined, in interior settings, with purchased items, such as sofas. By that time the 'crafting' of the interior covered a spectrum of activities, from making objects to employing taste values in the selection and consumption of artefacts, as well as arranging them in a setting which may also have included self-made artefacts. The modernity of that practice lay in its enhanced significance for increasing numbers of women who undertook such work both as a form of self-expression and as part of their newly acquired responsibility for its interior decoration.

Home-makers were helped in their task by an expanding body of interior decoration advice books which were published from the 1870s onwards to assist those women who had not had the necessary skills passed down to them. Many of those texts embraced the idealistic, Arts and Crafts-oriented visions of John Ruskin, A.W.N. Pugin, William Morris and others, while others were more practical. Editions of key texts appeared on both sides of the Atlantic. As we have seen, Charles Eastlake's misogynistic *Hints on Household Taste* of 1868 appeared in the US four years later and was enormously influential, while the American writer Clarence Cook published his manifesto about aestheticism in the household, *The House Beautiful* (1878), on the heels of the appearance in Britain of the *Art at Home* series published by Macmillan. In the US Janet Ruetz-Rees's *Home Decoration* (1881) opened that decade, while the reforming zeal of other American Aesthetic Movement enthusiasts filled the pages of a series of publications titled *Artistic Houses*, in 1893 and 1894.[22] While each individual text had a slightly different agenda, the publications of the 1870s and '80s, on both sides of the Atlantic, shared a commitment to the concepts of good taste, good workmanship and the importance of 'art' in the home. In the US a series of journals including *Godey's Lady's Book*, *Petersons* and *The Household* added their contributions to that programme of reform in the domestic interior.[23] In 1897 novelist Edith Wharton and architect and decorator Ogden Codman, Jr shifted the emphasis away from what had by then degenerated from an initial commitment to taste reform into a promotion of the house as a site for fashionable statements, towards a plea for respect for the architectural context and, above all, for a return to classicism.[24]

Many more household advice books appeared in the early twentieth century, Elsie de Wolfe's *The House in Good Taste* (1913) being among the most popular.[25] The years after 1914 saw the emergence of a vast quantity of published material focusing on advice for amateur 'craft' in the home. They included articles in popular woman's magazines, manuals for male artisans (carpenters and house-painters among them), domestic economy and management books containing chapters on home decoration, from both practical and taste perspectives, and more specialized, 'upmarket' books about interior decorating styles and strategies. Each one addressed a particular sector of society, defined usually (although not always overtly) by class and gender. A sense of the existence of the modern world and of the need to embrace it in one's private interior became increasingly clear in those years and was addressed from a wide range of perspectives. Numerous possible models of modernity were represented and suggestions made about ways in which readers could negotiate them, either through an engagement with 'hand-making', or through the application of taste in the consumption of goods for the interior.

As well as sharing styles and cultural meanings, fashionable dress and interiors also had a number of commercial strategies in common and they shared many of the same settings in that context. As has already been mentioned, the theatre provided an important mediating role for both of them. Most nineteenth- and early twentieth-century couturiers designed clothing for the stage. Worth, for instance, created a dress for Eugenie Dich who played Marguerite in a production of Alexandre Dumas, fils' *La Dame aux Camélias*. He also created costumes for the actress Sarah Bernhardt in 1867 as well as for the popular French playwright, Victorien Sardou, who was a close friend of Elsie de Wolfe.[26] Several couturiers dressed actresses both on and off stage. That early use of 'stars' to endorse products and brands had, by the early years of the twentieth century, become common practice. Jeanne Paquin also designed dresses for actresses and Poiret often dressed actresses at no cost.[27] As has been noted already, in the days before the live catwalk fashion show became a widespread phenomenon, actresses wearing couture dresses on stage had performed a similar function and de Wolfe frequently wore Worth, Paquin or Doucet gowns for her performances. The stage set itself also became a means of propagating fashionable interior styles, and many domestic dramas of those years were set in fashionable, eighteenth-century French interiors. Lucile's early catwalk shows took place in an interior into which a small stage had been added in recognition of the pioneering role of the theatre in that context. The idea of the stage-set also encouraged an understanding of the modern interior as a 'psychic backcloth' for which the architectural frame was unimportant but for which the identity and self-expression of the character being enacted were paramount. The idea was transferable to the domestic setting and became an important component of the modern interior in those years.

While the theatre provided one means of bringing fashionable dress and the interior into a single frame of reference in the public sphere, department stores also recognized the important relationship between them. In the 1850s and '60s, as we have seen, a number of such stores were established, including the Bon Marché, the Louvre store and the Printemps store in Paris, as well as Macy's and Lord and Taylor, among others, in New York. In 1869, at the time of the opening of its new store in Paris, the Bon Marché department store focused on a range of cheap goods which would appeal to women – *nouveautés* – from clothing to fabrics to sewing goods to interior furnishings. Beds were available from the 1850s and rugs from the 1860s, while the following decade saw the introduction of tables, chairs and upholstery. Eventually room sets were constructed in the store. Some displayed deluxe cabinet-work and others country furniture. Kitchen wares came into the store in 1900.[28] A decade later complete modern kitchen installations could be found there.

The stores provided bourgeois women with complete material environments. They could purchase a range of goods – from dresses to furnishing fabrics to lamps. The process of shopping for dress and the components of the interior in a single store served to reinforce the links between them.[29] In the last years of the nineteenth century and the early years of the twentieth, the stores also began to take over the earlier role played by theatres in that context. The French couturiers were keen to show their work on live mannequins on American soil and the department stores gave them the opportunity to do so. In the 1890s Lord and Taylor imported designs by Doucet (possibly the source of de Wolfe's gowns) while Poiret undertook a tour of American department stores in

1913, orchestrating fashion shows for eager customers. A handful of couturiers also established their own individual outlets across the Atlantic.
Madame Paquin, for example, opened a shop for furs in New York in 1913
(the source, very probably, of the coat worn by de Wolfe in the frontispiece to the *House in Good Taste*). At around the same time American
stores began to establish departments dedicated to interior decoration.
The journalist-turned-decorator Ruby Ross Wood directed the Wanamaker
store's first 'atelier' Au Quatrième, which opened in 1913, just a year after
the fashionable French store, Au Printemps, had established its Atelier
Primavera. (Other French stores, as we have seen, followed in the early
1920s: Galeries Lafayettes with La Maîtrise, the Louvre department store
with its Studium Louvre, and Bon Marché with its Atelier Pomone).[30]

World exhibitions provided yet another important shop window
for the public's simultaneous encounters with fashionable dress and interiors. Worth exhibited designs at the French universal exhibitions of
1855, 1889 and 1900, while, at the Paris 1900 exhibit, as we have seen, the
department stores Bon Marché, the Grands Magasins du Louvre and
Au Printemps created pavilions in which to exhibit a wide range of their
wares. They did so again at the 1925 *Exposition Internationale des Arts
Décoratifs et Industriels Modernes* in Paris, where the emphasis was on
complete interior assemblages created by the leading decorators of the
day. Women's mass circulation fashion magazines also provided an
important means of taste dissemination which embraced both dress and
the interior. When Condé Nast first launched *Vogue* magazine in the US
in 1909, for example, he was, as we have also seen, deeply committed to
showing interior decoration alongside couture fashion. At the level of the
market at which he was directing his publication, the assumption was
that *Vogue* readers would be able to buy couture clothes and employ an
interior decorator. Architectural and decorative arts magazines of the
period, the *Studio* among them, also included interiors within them but
their fashionable face was less in evidence and dress was rarely included.

The close alliance between dress and interiors that developed
through the nineteenth and early twentieth centuries was sustained, therefore, through their common cultural meanings, the shared commercial
strategies of their creators, and the commonality of the commercial sites
that framed them. Dress led the way for the most part, defining the
nature of the fashion system, but interior decoration followed swiftly
after it. Their relationship served to emphasize the psychological function of the interior and its close links with feminine subjectivity, identity

and modernity. It also highlighted the breakdown of the boundaries between the private and the public spheres. That both dress and the interior could play such a key role in identity formation and in the transmission of the experience of modernity depended, to a significant extent, upon their shared potential for personal, and collective, expression. That level of expression was facilitated by the commitment, on the part of both couturiers and decorators, to the expressive function of their products, which was made possible, to a large degree, by their understanding of the role of decoration both of the body and of the spaces that contained them.

5 The Decorative Interior

It is essential to realise that our decoration is as much a characteristic product of our civilisation as our newspapers, our poems, our dances and our morals.
Dorothy Todd and Raymond Mortimer[1]

One of Elsie de Wolfe's most memorable proclamations was made in 1913. 'You will express yourself in your home whether you want to or not', the decorator explained.[2] In the era of industrial modernity the use of decoration in interiors enabled large numbers of occupants to express themselves within them. Although the idea of 'decorating' the interior had become commonplace by that time the words 'interior' and 'decoration' hadn't always denoted a single concept. The term 'interior decoration' was in fact a French invention, but it had entered the English language soon afterwards.[3] It first appeared in print in the title of Charles Percier and Antoine Fontaine's *Receuils de decorations interieures*, which was published as articles in 1801 and as a book in 1812.[4] In the English language the term was first used in 1807 in the title of Thomas Hope's publication *Household Furniture and Interior Decoration*. At that date the concept was linked exclusively to the household and did not extend to the public sphere. Its emergence coincided with that of industrial modernity coming at the moment, that is, when the middle classes either began to 'hunt out their own wallpaper, much in the modern manner', or to seek the services of an upholsterer, or 'upholder', as they were called then, who could supply them with all the necessary components for their interior schemes.[5] An 1829 publication defined interior decoration as 'the planned co-ordination for artistic effect of colours and furniture, etc., in a room or building', demonstrating that aesthetic self-consciousness was a defining feature of the concept of interior decoration at an early date.[6] However, the idea that a room's decoration necessarily expressed its occupier's modern personality, mental life and emotions, emerged a little later in an 1841 publication by Andrew Jackson Downing in which he discussed the idea of a 'permanent dwelling that we can give the impress of our own mind and identify with our own existence'.[7] By the middle of the nineteenth century, therefore, all the components of modern interior decoration were in place and it was understood that the decorated interior provided its occupants with an expressive frame. While its role was undoubtedly at its most intense in the privacy of the home, it was quickly extended, along with many other values engendered within the context of domesticity, to work and public leisure environments as well where the thoughts and feelings of communities of users could be expressed. In the process the separate spheres were, once again, blurred.

The desire to embellish interior spaces has, of course, characterized the entire history of civilization. For centuries people have applied patterns, colours, and textures to structural surfaces, and arranged non-fixed items within their interior spaces. In the modern era, however, decoration moved from being a communally understood symbol of shared values – familial, religious, political, national and civic among them – to have the potential of becoming an expression of individualism. Prior to industrialization decoration had communicated through sets of visual languages, or styles, which had expressed fairly consistent messages and reinforced established social hierarchies. As representations of power and wealth, shared decorative languages had acted as forms of control, marking and sustaining fixed social structures.[8] With the high level of social mobility that came with industrialization, however, interior decoration gradually moved away from confirming stable social structures to actively seeking to renew or transform them.

Interior decoration was also linked to personal memory and identity. Walter Benjamin frequently referred to the role of the collector in that context, while much has been written about the significance of the collection of artefacts that filled Sigmund Freud's consulting room in Vienna.[9] Many of the nineteenth-century design reformers realized that decoration was an important means of linking people to their environments and of making them feel 'at home' in a modern world which was characterized by increasing levels of social flux and psychological alienation. In their search for a link between decoration, tradition and spiritual values, William Morris, Owen Jones, Christopher Dresser and others, for example, looked both to the medieval past and to the exotic world of non-western decoration.[10] With the advent of Art Nouveau the emphasis turned to the world of nature, to, that is, a contemporary source of decoration that would suit the requirements of the modern age.

Stylistically the Art Nouveau experiment led to two distinct paths of development for the modern interior. The first built on the abstract,

The living room in the Villa Jeanneret-Perret, designed by Le Corbusier (then Charles-Edouard Jeanneret), 1912.

universalizing and rationalizing aspects of the movement, focusing primarily on its architectural achievements. A second trajectory, more visible in France than in Germany, emphasized the decorative aspects of the movement and the quest for an appropriate modern form of decoration for the modern age. A couple of decades later the Modernist architects and designers were to reject decoration, however, seeing it as synonymous with nineteenth-century bourgeois domesticity and social aspiration. Ironically, though, given their clear and frequently articulated distaste for the interior, several of them had begun their careers in that field. Le Corbusier, for example, had worked as a decorator in his native Chaux-de-Fonds, when he was still known as Charles-Edouard Jeanneret.[11] The salon he created for the Jeanneret-Perret residence in 1912 was highly dependent upon the language of nineteenth-century bourgeois domesticity featuring, as it did, patterned rugs and wallpaper, draped curtains, items of antique furniture and ornaments on the mantelpiece. The German Modernist architect, Walter Gropius, had also worked on a number of interior projects in his early career, among them an advocate's consulting room in Berlin in 1910. His introduction of leather-upholstered, padded furniture gave that space the appearance of a traditional

An advocate's consulting room designed by Walter Gropius, 1912.

gentleman's club. Also, as we have seen, the early work of Eileen Gray, who became best known for the Modernist interiors she created for her own home, E1027, in Roquebrunne, France, between 1926 and 1929, comprised sumptuous interiors which acted as containers for her luxurious and highly decorated lacquered artefacts.[12]

However hard those Modernists, among others, sought to reject it in their later careers, so deeply rooted was decoration's relationship with 'inside spaces' that, by the twentieth century, it had become a defining

Otto Wagner, The Post Office Savings Bank, Vienna, 1906.

characteristic of the interior. The establishment of a modern architectural movement was inevitably followed by a search for an appropriately expressive form of modern interior decoration to accompany it. In the years between 1900 and 1939 many attempts were made to address that challenge. The intense interest in the modern decoration of the interior that characterized artistic activity in Vienna in the first decade of the twentieth century proved to be hugely influential. The programme of urban renewal in that city focused not only on the home but also on the interiors of public sphere buildings. As we have seen they included coffee houses and restaurants where the protagonists of the modern decorative style met to exchange views and develop their ideas. As we have also seen, the new Viennese interest in the interior was architectural in origin, rooted in the concept of the *Gesamtkunstwerk*. The interiors and interior artefacts created by men such as Otto Wagner, Josef Hoffmann, Dagobert Peche and Koloman Moser represented attempts to fuse the rationality of architectural structure with a new, geometric decorative language which both grew from it and was integral to it. Wagner's famous interior for Vienna's Post Office Savings Bank, one of the most rational architectural designs of those years, depended, nonetheless, on a use of decoration. His employment of small, geometric, decorative details included carefully positioned rows of covered rivets on the supporting side columns. Some were genuinely structural while others were added for decorative effect. Hoffmann adopted a similarly restrained, abstract, geometrical approach to his interior designs for the Purkersdorf Sanatorium, created between 1904 and 1906, while, as we have seen, in the private spaces he created for the Stoclet family in Brussels between 1905 and 1911, he pushed his modern decorative language much further, letting the texture of the marble and the patterned surfaces of his specially designed fabrics and other items of household equipment combine to create a luxurious, harmonious and sumptuous whole.[13] In a room used for entertaining guests in the Palais Stoclet, the architect employed pattern, texture and other decorative details. The inclusion of a piano and a small stage for domestic performances reinforced the theatricality of the space recalling Adolf Loos's use of spaces within spaces in the Moller house. Some of the more intimate spaces of the Palais Stoclet were less elaborate, however. 'The

An entertainment room in the Palais Stoclet, Brussels, designed by Josef Hoffmann, 1905–11, illustrated in *The Studio*, 1914.

wall cupboards, fittings, carpet and upholstery' of the lady's dressing room, for example, were 'restricted to black, white and light grey, in order to provide a subtle foil for the clothes donned by the lady of the house'.[14] Such was the depth of Hoffmann's understanding of the occupier's presence in his spaces. However, while he was committed to the total unification of the interior in the houses he created for his clients, in his own homes the architect allowed himself a more eclectic approach, mixing older pieces with new furniture items he designed himself.[15]

The decorative schemes developed by the Viennese designers were disseminated through the pages of *Deutsche Kunst und Dekoration* and quickly became popular internationally. In *The House in Good Taste* Elsie de Wolfe recorded her awareness of the Werkstätte's interiors. 'Black and white', she wrote, 'is always a tempting combination to the decorator, and now that Josef Hoffmann, the great Austrian decorator, has been working in black and white for a number of years, the more venturesome decorators of France, England and America have begun to follow his lead and are using black and white, and black and color, with amazing effect'.[16] Hoffmann also exerted a strong influence on many of his students. Lillian Langseth-Christensen, for example, who had studied under him at the Kunstgewerbe School, explained in her 1987 autobiography that '*Deutsche Kunst und Dekoration* had shown me how a bedroom should look. It was no longer a place for a bed, a night table, a chiffonier that was too high to look into the top drawer, a dresser and a chair. It was, instead, a place of glossy white enamel, of flush-fronted, built-in cabinets, a built-in-the-niche bed, and a cozy sitting corner'.[17] A branch of the Wiener Werkstätte opened in New York in the 1920s. The interior of its showroom was designed by the Viennese émigré architect, Josef Urban, who had already established himself as an interior and exhibition designer prior to his arrival in New York in 1911. Urban went on to design sets for the Metropolitan Opera and the Ziegfeld Follies, as well as numerous film sets for William Randolph Hearst. His theatrical approach, with its emphasis on the effects of light and colour and its sympathetic relationship with the costumes worn by the occupants of his interiors, had its roots in Viennese interior decoration. He relied heavily upon the role of modern decoration to express modern identities and to provide suitable backcloths for the 'performers' of modern life. In 1933 he applied his theatrical skills to the overall colour scheme for Chicago's *Century of Progress* exhibition.

In 1916 an American writer, Hazel H. Adler, published her book, *The New Interior: Modern Decoration for the Home*. Adler took a more

A dining-room in a Small Town House in golden yellow, blue, violet and dull green, designed by the Aschermann Studio and illustrated in Hazel H. Adler's *The New Interior: Modern Decoration for the Home*, published in 1916.

'inside' focus than her architectural contemporaries and aimed her advice at 'that large body of intelligent people who are seeking to create for themselves expressive and individual environments of life.'[18] Rather than hiring a professional interior decorator she advocated letting homes evolve to embrace the 'new taste'.[19] The illustrations to her text revealed a strong Austrian influence, several of the schemes – ironically, given her views on decorating professionals – having been created by Paul Zimmerman and others by E. H. and G. G. Aschermann, who had also studied with Hoffmann.[20] The chequered floor, patterned wallpaper, repeated vases of flowers and built-in furniture featured in one of the Aschermann interiors illustrated in Adler's book recalled Werkstätte designs. The Aschermanns were part of the same generation of immigrant decorative designers which also included Winold Reiss and Alfons Baumgarten, who had left Munich and arrived in the US in around 1913. Reiss went on to create modern, decorative interiors for numerous commercial buildings in the US, including the Busy Lady Bakery, designed in 1915, which was later described as 'the first modern store in New York'.[21]

The Viennese movement also influenced modern decorative Swedish interior design. Josef Frank had been active as an architect in Vienna before moving to Sweden in 1932. In 1925 he had opened an interior decorating shop, Haus und Garten, with Oscar Wlach, and in the same year his firm had exhibited a small niche containing furniture items at the 1925 Paris *Exposition Internationale des Arts Décoratifs et Industriels Modernes*. Striking for its lack of unity – Frank, like Poiret before him, rejected the idea of the *Gesamtkunstwerk* – its eclecticism, and its embrace of the past. Frank's work prefigured a new approach to the domestic interior which opposed that promoted by the hard-line Modernists. Frank was open about his rejection of the Modernist interior, especially the use of tubular steel for furniture and standardization in the interior, but, in their self-conscious response to the demands of modern life, his proposals for the domestic interior were no less modern. 'The modern person', he explained, 'who is increasingly more exhausted by his job requires a domicile cozier and more comfortable than those of the past'.[22] Later he explained that 'coziness' could be achieved through a mixture of furniture items, some old and some new, the inclusion of comfy sofas and cushions and the use of patterned surfaces. 'The monochromed surface', he wrote, 'has an unsettling effect, the patterned surface is a calming one because the beholder is involuntarily affected by the slow, calm mode of production'.[23]

Josef Frank, a large living room designed for the Weissenhof Siedlung, 1927, illustrated in Hans Eckstein's *Die Schöne Wohnung*, 1931.

An interior Frank created in Vienna for the Weissenhof Siedlung of 1927, which featured cushions and patterned curtains at the windows, was heavily criticized by Theo van Doesburg, who described it as 'feminine'.[24] Through the 1930s, from his base at Stockholm's elegant furniture store, Svensk Tenn, and in conjunction with the shop's owner Estrid Ericson, Frank developed an interior idiom combining references from the past (the eighteenth century in particular) with white walls and modernized versions of traditional patterns. Ironically, given his Austrian roots, by the late 1930s his interior aesthetic had been dubbed 'Swedish Modern' and had become inextricably associated with that country's bid to lead the way in the formulation of a mid-century, modern decorative interior style.

By the mid-1920s the pre-eminence of the Viennese designers in the formulation of a modern decorative language for the interior was being taken away from them, however, by the French 'ensembliers'. A 1915 article in *International Studio* magazine caricatured the difference between the German/Viennese developments and those of the French claiming that, 'the German and Austrian work [is] the result of intellectual activity, and the French work [is] instinctive, intuitive.'[25] From the early years of the century the ensembliers had been developing an approach towards the modern interior which was rooted in the eighteenth century, and which had sought to bring the benefits of the past into the present. Moving away from the ambitions of the Art Nouveau designers to break completely from the past, André Mare, Francis Jourdain, Emile-Jacques Ruhlmann, André Groult, Maurice Dufrêne, Leon Jallot, Louis Sue and others, inspired by the progressive designs they had seen at the German exhibition at the 1910 Salon d'Autumne, had begun to develop a more holistic approach to the decoration of the interior, with an emphasis on the 'ensemble', and to combine the Empire style with French provincial references. As Katharine Kahle pointed out two decades later, 'the decorators began to make drawings of complete interiors and the architect was forced into second place.'[26] The ensembliers developed a soft, decorative, feminine, brightly coloured interior aesthetic which was at its best in small spaces such as studies, small salons, boudoirs and bedrooms. In that respect Art Nouveau's commitment to modernity, privacy and interiority was sustained.[27] Like the Art Nouveau protagonists as well, however, the French ensembliers aligned themselves enthusiastically with the commercial sector, several of them joining forces, as we have already seen, with the new department stores. In addition Ruhlmann, Louis Sue and André Mare formed *La Compagnie des Arts Français*, Joubert and Petit formed DIM (Décoration d'Intérieures Modernes) and Robert Block established the *Studio Athelia*.

The Exposition of 1925 had been anticipated for many years but it was postponed because of the advent of the First World War. When it finally happened it showcased the achievements of the ensembliers, signalled their pre-eminence to the rest of the world, and made a clear statement about France's commitment to a luxurious, craft-based, highly eclectic, but eminently modern approach to the interior. It received mixed reviews, however. Looking back from 1939 Emily Genauer recalled it as a moment when 'decoration was at last unloosed from the bands of period slavery', whereas a decade earlier Dorothy Todd and Raymond Mortimer, in search of a 'satisfactory modern idiom of ornament' had found it 'as brilliant, as noisy and as disconcerting as a parrot show'.[28] In Paris the decorators found an outlet for their new aesthetic which combined

Emile-Jacques Ruhlmann, the living room in the Pavillon du Collectionneur, shown at the *Exposition Internationale des Arts Décoratifs et Industriels Modernes*, Paris, 1925.

references to the eighteenth century with exotic materials acquired from France's imperial pursuits, sumptuous patterns, rich colours and modern, often geometric, forms. The result was an aesthetic of refinement that spoke of modern luxury, glamour and opulence.

The interiors of the buildings constructed for the 1925 event were inward-looking and unresponsive to the spaces outside them. They evoked fantasy lifestyles and a world towards which most visitors could only aspire. The bedroom in Ruhlmann's magnificent Hôtel du Collectionneur, for example, which also contained a *grand salon*, a dining room, a boudoir and an office, brought together the grand proportions and wood panelling of an eighteenth-century space with a soft colour scheme, ivory damask wallpaper, an elegant, tapered-legged dressing table veneered in amboyna and inlaid with shagreen and ivory, and a wall lamp with an alabaster shade. A classical simplicity pervaded the room aided by the simple, geometric lines of its low wooden bed. The seamlessness and level of craftsmanship in the interior added a level of fantasy and a luxurious sense of comfort. With its crystal chandelier and wall lights, its use of Macassar ebony, its dramatically draped curtains, the highly patterned wallpaper on its curved walls, designed by Stéphany, its rugs and tapestries created by Gaudissart, its grand piano, its items of lacquered furniture designed by Jean Dunand, in addition to other pieces by Jallot and Rapin, and its works of contemporary art, the hôtel's *grand salon* was possibly even more luxurious.

The international impact of what came to be called the 'Art Deco' interior was unprecedented and lasted right up to the outbreak of the Second World War. Its strong message to all social classes about the possibility of participating in what had become by the mid-1930s a mass-produced modernity, which valued the experience of the individual and offered the potential for modern luxury, glamour, leisure, pleasure and escape (and which was, above all, accessible), was hugely appealing in those years. It quickly found its way into cinemas, hotels, clubs, beauty salons, small select shops, leisure centres, cafés, restaurants and ocean liners across the world.[29] It was especially well received in the US, where department stores made it available to almost everyone who wanted it.[30] In that country it encountered the indigenous streamlined style and the term 'streamlined moderne' began to be used. The film industry inevitably recognized its appeal and, as we have seen, Art Deco sets featured in countless Hollywood movies (see p. 71).[31]

More than any other modern decorative interior styles, French Art Deco and the American 'streamlined moderne' aesthetic penetrated the mass market and, for the first time, made 'modern' a real choice for many home decorators. That was facilitated and encouraged by a vast number of decorating advice books which demonstrated ways in which the modern look could be achieved. An English publication of the mid-1930s, for example, *The Home of Today*, illustrated a 'delightful' modern kitchen which featured a 'novel "porthole" window', clearly influenced by the glamorous liners of the era – the French *Normandie* leading the way – as well as an 'unusual hall' with a dramatic black and white striped floor and 'new propeller lights'.[32] An American book from 1936, *What's New in Home Decorating?*, contained an image of a modern bedroom-cum-office, which also showed signs of Art Deco treatment. Decorated by Hazel Dell Brown the room was described as 'one of those rare rooms which seem to have everything – decoratively speaking. From the smart, cork-veneered furniture to the checked upholstery material and such up-to-the-minute details as the white porcelain mask and unframed circular mirror, it is the perfect setting for the dashing young Modern for whom it was designed.'[33] A

An American young woman's bedroom-cum-office, decorated by Hazel Dell Brown and illustrated in Winifred Fales's *What's New in Home Decorating*, 1936.

French magazine from the same period, *La Decoration de la Maison*, revealed, however, that although 'Moderne' *was* a real choice – images of *Une Salle a Manger Moderne*, *Un Salon Moderne* and *Un Studio Moderne* appeared in its pages exhibiting the familiar Art Deco style – French home decorators could also choose *Une Piece Rustique dans L'Esprit Moderne* (a hybrid interior featuring a ladder back chair and a sofa covered in a rustic fabric); *Une Salle a Manger Béarnaise* (which featured solid wooden furniture and ceiling beams); or *Un Salon xviii Siècle*. In that pot pourri of possibilities the Art Deco-inspired 'moderne' interior was just one option – albeit the only ostensibly modern one – among many other traditional alternatives.

Several other attempts were also made in the first decades of the twentieth century to define modern decoration. In their 1929 book *The New*

The library in the London flat of Clive Bell, decorated by Duncan Grant and Vanessa Bell, 1920s, and illustrated in Dorothy Todd and Raymond Mortimer's *The New Interior Decoration*, 1929.

Interior Decoration: An Introduction to its Principles, and International Survey of its Methods, Dorothy Todd and Raymond Mortimer made a substantial claim for the socially elite work of the English 'Bloomsbury Group' – that of Vanessa Bell and Duncan Grant in particular.[34] The couple's use of intense, hand-made decoration was visible in the library they worked on in Clive Bell's London flat. Their predilection was for interiors which combined the application of colourful, abstract patterns on to as many surfaces as possible with artworks – their own and of others – and personal items, from books to memorabilia. The result was a charming, highly personalized set of modern spaces. New descriptive names for other variants of the modern decorative style emerged in the 1930s, among them *Swank Modern*, which was used to describe the work of the American lady decorators. Emily Genauer coined the terms Rustic Modern, Baroque Modern and Directoire Modern, an indication of the variety of contemporary interior

105

styles available at that time.[35] Gradually the distinctions between those overtly decorative modern styles and the minimal, machine aesthetic of the Modernist interior were eroded and numerous hybrid modern interiors were engendered. In addition, the national distinctions that had characterized the new styles that had emerged in the 1920s were also replaced by a new internationalism, driven by the increasing globalization of the mass media. However stylistically hybrid it became, however, the modern decorative interior never lost its promise of modernity and of the opportunity for occupants to express themselves through their engagement with a modern lifestyle. As Todd and Mortimer perceptively observed in their 1929 study, echoing the earlier words of Elsie de Wolfe, 'The extraordinary recent increase of interest in interior decoration has largely resulted from a more acute need for self-expression.'[36]

Although the concept of 'interior decoration' was well understood by the early twentieth century, the debate about whose professional role it was to decorate interiors remained unresolved for many years to come. In the previous century the tension had been mainly between architects and upholsterers, but with the emergence of professional interior decorators, the situation had become more complicated by the end of the century. One of the last group's selling points was its awareness of the need to be sensitive to their clients' requirements for individual self-expression. Not surprisingly, given women's enhanced role in the household in the last decades of the nineteenth century, many members of the new profession were female, as indeed were their clients. At the turn of the century increasing numbers of middle-class women moved into the workplace, taking up jobs that reflected their domestic and nurturing skills. The role of decorating other people's homes was an obvious one for them to take on board. In England the Garrett sisters, Agnes and Rhoda, were among the first women to make a living by providing complete decorative schemes for interiors. Up until that point, at least for members of the social elite, such schemes had frequently been created by architects. Men such as R. Norman Shaw had worked on both the exteriors and interiors of houses. In his Old Swan House in Chelsea of 1877, for example, Shaw had created an 'aesthetic' sitting room complete with a decorated cornice, a fancy over-mantel and eighteenth-century chairs. Less wealthy householders had relied on the combined efforts of upholsterers, cabinet-makers, and painters and decorators. In Liverpool, a wealthy English city at that time, the decorator S. J. Waring employed 500 staff in his St Anne Street workshop.[37] In the US the 1880s and '90s saw architects, including Richard Morris Hunt and Stanford

White, working on the interiors of their buildings, while, for the very wealthy, European firms, such as Allard and Sons of Paris and Allom, White of London, were brought in by architects and clients to create interiors which combined antique furniture pieces with new furnishings in the eighteenth-century French style.

The vogue for antiques, which had become widespread by the 1890s, increasingly brought art and antique dealers into the frame of interior decoration. In the US, during the era of the aesthetic home, artistic teams such as *Associated Artists*, led by Candace Wheeler, Augustus Saint-Gaudens and John La Farge, supplied work for interiors. In 1895 Wheeler, a textile designer who had worked for Louis Comfort Tiffany, published two influential articles entitled 'Interior Decoration as a Profession for Women'.[38] She advocated a solid training in the field and discouraged amateurs. A number of women heeded her advice, among them Mary Jane Colter, who designed the interior of the Hopi House in the Grand Canyon as well as interiors for dining cars for the Santa Fe Railroad.[39] Others did not and plunged into the profession with only a 'good eye' and lots of entrepreneurial zeal to draw upon. Elsie de Wolfe was among the first of the latter group, having, as we have seen, moved from a career in acting to decorating her own home in New York, to being asked to design the interiors of the Colony Club, to creating, with the staff members of her design studio, interiors for hundreds of nouveau-riche clients over the next forty or so years.[40]

Female professionals sought to align the taste of their clients with their interiors through the selection of appropriate decoration. Wharton and Codman's 1897 book, *The Decoration of Houses*, led the way with its depictions of decorative interiors from the eighteenth century, French, English and Italian for the most part.[41] The styles of the eighteenth century, those of France in particular, were fully embraced by the lady decorators and their clients. Not only did they provide a route out of Victorian gloom and the possibility of injecting lightness and air back into interiors, they also offered a direct link with the history of feminine interventions in the interior, from that of Madame de Pompadour onwards. The lady decorators' use of period styles reflected a new age in which women embraced modernity. Theirs was no less 'modern' a strategy than that of the Modernists, who turned to the 'rationality' of the machine for their inspiration. While the formulation of the machine aesthetic offered a 'masculine' solution to the modern interior, the return to the styles of eighteenth-century France arguably represented its 'feminine' equivalent. In that context women took control of the construction of their own modern identities even though they were still defined domestically for the most part. De Wolfe's stage set approach, which involved unproblematically combining antiques with modern reproduction pieces, was emulated by most of her fellow decorators.

Before the First World War the eighteenth-century French styles were most frequently embraced in that context, although, for certain projects, those of the English Renaissance, or the furniture of Thomas Chippendale, seemed more appropriate. In nearly all cases, however, the emphasis was upon the modernizing process of creating a frame for social mobility and, at the same time, enabling women to develop their private selves in their homes, especially in its most private areas, the bedroom and the boudoir in particular. The emphasis was on lightness, elegance, comfort and taste. Chintz was used widely, both as a means of recalling English country houses, which inspired so many projects in those years, but also because of its unpretentiousness and its patterned surfaces complementing the use of plain, light colours on the wood panelling which was frequently used to cover the walls. De Wolfe evolved a soft colour palette which combined light grey with pale blues, pinks, yellows and creams. Flowers were used liberally, in de Wolfe's case with an emphasis on roses and lilies.

Between the two world wars the influence of the new European decorating idioms – especially those of Art Deco and that developed a little later in France by a group of artists and decorators associated with the Surrealist movement – was felt across the Atlantic.[42] As a result more overtly modern elements began to make an appearance in interiors.[43] Frances Elkins, for example, introduced objects designed by Alberto Giacometti, Jean-Michel Frank and Jean Dunand into her otherwise traditional spaces. She also took the chintz theme to surreal extremes, using the fabric on multiple surfaces in a single interior to dramatic effect. Dorothy Draper also modernized the period room by playing around with the scale of its components. In a scheme for the lobby of 770 Park Avenue executed in 1929, for example, she placed a huge clock on a yellow chimney breast over a 'moderne' fireplace. In her book *Decorating is Fun* Draper explained that, 'the big electric clock is fine in scale and is made of white plaster with a carved black wooden eagle over it. By putting all the emphasis on the clock it was unnecessary to have any more decoration.'[44] In the lobby of the Hampshire House apartment hotel on Central Park South – the largest commercial commission ever awarded to a woman in the mid 1930s – she positioned a huge mirror with a rococo frame made of plaster over the fireplace.[45] Such strategies served to align those interiors much more closely with European developments and to radicalize the idea of the period room in the US.

In spite of those striking innovations the tensions that had existed in the years before 1939 between architects and interior decorators over the right to design and control interior spaces in buildings, in both the private and the public spheres, reached a climax in the 1940s. The tension was caused by architects' fears of becoming feminized and of being linked to trade rather than to a profession. They sought universal solutions and dismissed the lady decorators as untrained and working through intuition alone.[46] By the mid-twentieth century the idea of facilitating self-expression and of constructing feminine identity through the interior was well established, however. It placed the work of the lady decorators in direct opposition to the male architectural approach to the design of the interior. As a result, in the words of one writer, 'by the 1940s [interior] design was professionalized and colonized by architects and the emerging brand of industrial designer. A new model emerged which was opposed to . . . the feminized amateur practice which dominated interior decoration in the inter-war period.'[47]

The abundance of mass-mediated, modern decorative interior styles available in the marketplace by the middle years of the twentieth century provided consumers, at most levels of society, with an opportunity to select from a range of modern identities and to follow de Wolfe's 1913 advice. Given that they were nearly all made up of mass-produced and mass-disseminated components, and reproduced in mass circulation magazines, the move from individual self-expression in the home to collective expression in leisure and other public sphere activities did not involve a huge transformation. Whether in the home or in public spaces, interiors were very likely to be have been influenced by the aspirational styles depicted in Hollywood films and in the pages of home-oriented magazines. Through the agency of the mass media, therefore, self expression was rapidly transformed into a more collective expression of the age, and what had once been private became overtly public.

As the first section of this book has demonstrated, by engaging so profoundly with so many of modernity's defining themes, bourgeois domesticity played a fundamental role in the formation of the modern interior, although it was visually transformed by the plethora of modern styles it embraced in the period between 1850 and 1939. It also infiltrated the public arena to a significant degree – particularly spaces dedicated to modern commerce and leisure. Through its engagement with fashion-ableness, its ability to express modern personality, its proximity to mass consumption and its link to the idea of lifestyle, a new psychological, symbolic and cultural role for the interior was established as a representation of industrial modernity. The strength of bourgeois domesticity did not deter the Modernists from attempting to reject it by opposing as many of its values as they could. Their radical programme of reform sought to establish a set of alternative values for the interior and, beyond that, to deny its very existence, so corrupted, in their view, had it become. The second section of this book will focus on the strategies adopted by the Modernist architects to wage war on the interior, and to create buildings which had no interiors in the conventional sense of the term, modern or otherwise. Ironically however, not only did the Modernists provide the modern interior with a set of alternative values, it also generated some of the most beautiful and lasting modern interiors of the twentieth century. Modernism also rejected the interior decorator and spawned the professional interior designer. Given the strong links that the Victorian domestic interior had already forged with the commercial forces of modernity, however, Modernism's political and ideological ambitions were not easily fulfilled. In the end bourgeois domesticity did not disappear but, rather, took on a new mantle linked to the visual and spatial language of architectural Modernism.

Part Two
Outside In

The Passage de l'Opéra, Paris, *c.* 1880–1900.

6 The Public Interior

Others talk about the street, the café, the gallery.
Virginia Woolf[1]

The public face of the modern interior was formed in the second half of the nineteenth century in the new inside spaces of commerce, culture, work and public leisure. Like its private, domestic counterpart, which was reproduced in a range of semi-public and public spaces, the public modern interior developed its own visual, material and spatial language which, in this case, found its way back into the home. Early signs of the emergence of a new, public sphere interior aesthetic were visible from the early nineteenth century onwards in a range of buildings from shopping arcades, exhibition halls, museums, railway stations to department stores. From a 'separate spheres' perspective, that development could be seen as a form of anti-domesticity. Its primary relationship was with commerce and its light, airy, neutral forms were made possible by new building technologies and new materials. Glass, iron and steel facilitated the construction of those large, open plan interior spaces and the high levels of transparency which helped to emphasize the objects frequently located within them. In search of a new architectural aesthetic to represent the modern age the Modernist architect-designers of the first decades of the twentieth century adopted those highly engineered commercial buildings, and their interior spaces, as models for a modern architecture which sought to side-step the values of Victorian domesticity. As Le Corbusier proclaimed, 'Our engineers produce architecture, for they employ a mathematical calculation which derives from natural law, and their works give us the feeling of HARMONY.'[2] Twenty-five years later the Modernist apologist Siegfried Giedion echoed that same sentiment when he wrote that, in contrast to the upholsterer who in his view 'debased the cabinetmaker's craft', in 1850s and 1860s America, 'inventive fantasy and the instinct for mechanization were the common property of the people'.[3] Unwittingly, however, by injecting the methods and materials employed by nineteenth-century engineers into their residential buildings, the Modernists also brought commerce into the home.

In the second half of the nineteenth century the public face of the modern interior determined many people's experiences of the modern world as well as playing a key role in the dramatic transformations of many urban spaces.[4] Most accounts of the late nineteenth-century metropolis, and of modernity, have ignored those new public interior spaces, choosing instead to emphasize the outside, visual spectacle of the urban streets which was experienced by men for the most part.[5] Walter Benjamin's famous *flâneur*, for example, first observed by the nineteenth-century French poet Charles Baudelaire, defined modernity as an essentially outside, masculine experience. Free to wander the streets of the modern metropolis, he looked in shop windows, but had no intention of purchasing goods. His was an undirected wandering of the city streets.[6] Benjamin wrote extensively about the making of the modern metropolis, focusing on the roles played by commodification and display and highlighting features like the shift from gas to electrical street illumination. In his work on the Parisian arcades, however, he captured an in-between world which was half inside and half outside.

Created between the eighteenth and the mid-nineteenth centuries, and building on the idea of covered markets, Benjamin's Parisian arcades were covered rows of shops, constructed in the gaps between other buildings, created to accommodate the increased production of goods, especially textiles, and to make shopping a more pleasant experience in a city which, at that time, had no sewers or pavements. In the *Passage de l'Opera*, what had been the exterior walls of buildings were suddenly transformed, through the addition of an iron and glass roof, into interior walls. *The Journal des Artistes* of 1827 described the arcades as a solution to the 'ingenious need to increase the number of shops in order to increase capitalists' profits'.[7] Those pedestrian-focused alleyways allowed *flâneurs*, and later *flâneuses* as well, to wander without the discomforts that had hitherto been created by horse-drawn carriages, crowds, dust and mud. Dining and drinking, bathing in public baths, playing billiards, attending the theatre and prostitution were also undertaken in those new inside/outside spaces. The early arcades had had timber roofs with skylights inserted into them. Iron- and glass-domed structures were built over the later ones, however, allowing more light to penetrate their interior spaces, thereby reinforcing the sense, for the shoppers and crowds within them, of being both outside and inside at the same time. Walter

Benjamin described them as 'a city, a world in miniature', emphasizing their strong relationship with the 'outside'.[8] He also saw them as the 'forerunners of department stores'.[9] Top lighting, which had also transformed the Grande Galerie in the Louvre Museum, was widely used.[10] Gas lighting was introduced into the arcades in the early nineteenth century.[11]

The Parisian arcades, and others which appeared subsequently in cities such as Brussels, Berlin, Naples and Milan, established a new type of commercial interior space made possible by new materials and building technologies. The combination of materials used proved to be eminently transferable to other commercial spaces created at that time to provide shoppers with a sense of freedom from the claustrophobia of home and protection from the elements. In the first half of the nineteenth century iron and glass had most frequently been employed in the construction of greenhouses, which had required the maximum amount of light to enter into them. It is not surprising, therefore, that the first international exhibition, held in London in 1851, was mounted within a giant greenhouse. The *Great Exhibition of the Works of All Nations*, held in London's Hyde Park, has been widely heralded as the first of the modern exhibitions. Its interior spaces provided a third of the British population with an opportunity for an encounter with modernity. Joseph Paxton's dramatic iron and glass building was modelled on the concept of a greenhouse and, in sharp contrast to the middle-class domestic parlour which sought to exclude the outside world, aimed to bring in as much light as possible. The interior view of the 'Crystal Palace' (shown overleaf) depicts the opening of the Great Exhibition with two heralds awaiting the arrival of Queen Victoria. The trees that were left on site are in full view. That same strategy was to be emulated later by the Swiss modernist architect, Le Corbusier, in his Pavillon de L'Esprit Nouveau, exhibited at the 1925 Paris *Exposition Internationale des Arts Décoratifs Modernes et Industriels* (see illus. on p. 141). The transparency of the Hyde Park building, created by the extensive use of glass, and the feeling of openness made possible by the use of iron as a structural material, are also visible. The building was little more than a shelter, albeit one executed on a monumental scale. Visitors to its expansive inner space must have felt that they were as near to being outside as it was possible to be, short of actually being so. It was also an experience that allowed them to become part of the modern world, which was increasingly characterized by the dominance of the visual experience of goods to be consumed. Objects could not be purchased at the exhibition, however, but simply

A print of an interior view of the Crystal Palace in London's Hyde Park, 1851.

admired, a strategy on the part of the exhibition organizers which served to augment the visitors' (unrequited) levels of desire. Benjamin fully understood the commercial impact of that event, and others like it, when he wrote that, 'World exhibitions glorify the exchange value of the commodity. They create a framework in which use value recedes into the background. They open a phantasmagoria which a person enters in order to be distracted.'[12]

Paxton's earlier experiences of designing buildings had been in the world of garden design. In the 1940s, a writer described his 'great conservatory' of 1851 as being 'an acre in extent, and it was considered by the early Victorians to be almost one of the wonders of the world. One could drive a carriage through its vast expanse, while fern and palm and cedar waved amongst its girders.'[13] Paxton's vast interior was defined by the visible, structural iron columns around its edges, an inner balcony created by more iron pillars, and its vast open space. The Hyde Park building was, on one level, an enormous shop window, its simplicity and neutrality serving to enhance the spectacle of the highly decorated objects displayed within it. As well as acting as an inspiration for Modernist architects later on in the twentieth century, the Crystal Palace provided a model for several other types of commercial interiors built in the latter half of the nineteenth century, above all those of department stores. Whiteleys store was, among others, a direct descendant of it.[14] William Whiteley had visited the Crystal Palace many times and been impressed by the way in which the exhibition 'made goods available to the eye but ultimately unattainable'.[15] The department store turned the *flâneuse* into a consumer.[16] It built on women's experiences at exhibitions where idealized domestic interiors were often displayed. By the first decade of the twentieth century stores had begun to introduce 'sets' into their windows complete with life-size mannequins. The stage set nature of those displays introduced a strong link between public interiors created for commercial ends and the theatre.'[17] When the Selfridges store had its ceremonial opening in London in 1909 the watching crowds were stunned by its windows which, rather than being filled with goods, contained 'mannequins [which] held lifelike poses in front of painted backgrounds'.[18]

By allowing in as much light, and creating as much open space as possible so as not to detract from the visual effects of the goods on sale, as well as being fantasy environments, the interiors of department stores emulated the visual strategies of the exhibition hall. Although the late nineteenth century/early twentieth century department store has been the subject of numerous studies, the appearance of its interior spaces has received relatively little attention. The architect of Paris's Bon Marché store was L. A. Boileau, the engineer of the famous Gustave Eiffel, and its founder, Aristide Boucicaut.[19] Built of iron and glass, its interior consisted of spacious open bays, glass skylights and a series of open inner courts.

> Inside the monumental and theatrical effects continued. The iron columns and expanse of glass provided a sense of space, openness and light. Immense gallery opened upon immense gallery and along the upper floors ran balconies from which one could view, as a spectator, the crowds and activity below. Three grand staircases, elegant and sweeping, conveyed the public to these floors as if they were climbing to loges at the opera ... Part opera, part theatre, part museum, Boucicaut's eclectic extravaganza did not disappoint those who came for a show.[20]

The interior of the Parisian store was a vast open space, similar to the interior of the Crystal Palace, with a glass roof which had a huge chandelier suspended from its centre. Walkways around the periphery of the iron-structured space provided customers with vantage points from which to view the stock which lay beneath them. Side lighting and fabrics were, as we have seen, suspended in swags from the columns to complete the effect. The central staircase of the store emphasized the vertical nature of its cavernous space while the salon was an equally vertically-oriented space of enormous scale but with ceilings painted in the classical manner and paintings covering the walls. Away from the commercially driven shop floors that last space was more historical in style, offering the store's customers a more domestic experience. The potential threat of the commercial world was softened by that more overtly cultural space which reassured female consumers in what was otherwise an unfamiliar modern interior.

Selfridges, which opened in London in 1909, was the only British department store to equal Paris's Bon Marché and the Marshall Field's store in Chicago. It had 'wide aisles, electric lighting, crystal chandeliers and a striking colour scheme – all-white walls contrasted with thick green carpet.'[21] Typically of that early Edwardian era the interior was at once, in its negation of the darker Victorian spaces of earlier stores, both novel and, with its crystal chandeliers, traditional at the same time. That 'cathedral' of modernity had to strike a delicate balance between representing a post-Victorian world in which women were free to enter the public arena without fear, while simultaneously providing them with an aspirational, luxurious space which would stimulate the consumption of the new goods on offer. The department stores were undoubtedly the most striking of the commercial interiors of nineteenth-century modernity to build on the language established by the Great Exhibition. Their restaurants, lounges and tea rooms were, however, part of the network of domesticated public spaces that belonged to the same era and that played an important role in the female experience of modernity. Marshall Field's store in Chicago had an equally spectacular interior consisting of an open central atrium which could be looked down upon from the open balconies of the building's four floors. The whole interior was covered by an enormous domed ceiling covered with mosaic tiles, which was designed by Louis Comfort Tiffany, one of the US's most fashionable decorators of the period. Garlands of flowers were suspended from the ceilings to soften the repetitive arrangement of rows of horseshoe-shaped glazed counters and storage cabinets with multiple drawers which covered the store's floors. Once again the rational, open structure which exposed the goods on sale was offset by decorative features, adding a level of domestic comfort.[22] Museums and art galleries were also affected by the advent of iron and glass. Edinburgh's Royal Museum building on Chambers Street, built between 1861 and 1888, contained behind its Venetian façade a dramatic iron and glass main hall that had much in common with the open spaces of department stores.

While the exhibition space, the department store and the museum were public spaces dedicated to commerce and culture, the work spaces of the factory and the office, which were equally important to the creation of economic capital but not accessible to the general public in the same way, also went through a radical modernization process at that time. This was based, in these cases, on the need for enhanced productivity and efficiency. In the spaces of the factory and the office visuality was subordinated to utility and the process of rationalization was applied to that end. Rationalism had been one of modernity's driving forces from the era of the Enlightenment onwards, given momentum by the increasing secularization of society and the growing importance of science. It affected society and culture in a number of different ways, including the manner in which industrial work was organized. Driven by the profit motive underpinning economic capitalism, factory work practices, such

The interior of the National Museum and Art Gallery, Edinburgh, 1861–8, photographed in 2007.

as the division of labour which cut across the holistic process of the craftsman, were rationally conceived and organized. Inevitably the spaces in which work was undertaken had to be designed to facilitate them. Little or no thought was given to the appearance of those spaces, however, nor to the physical and psychological comfort of their occupants. Factory engineers and space planners, rather than architects, decorators, upholsterers or amateur 'home-makers', determined the lay-outs of the machinery that went into them. The 'automatic' machinery being used in the illustration opposite is laid out following the consecutive procedures of the manufacturing being undertaken.

In the early twentieth century the desire to enhance the rationality and efficiency of factory production processes was particularly evident in the manufacture of complex, high-technology, engineered goods, such as automobiles. Two significant rationalizing forces emerged to influence that area, one centred around the work of Frederick Winslow Taylor and the other led by Henry Ford in his Highland Park factory. Ford's engineers pushed the concept of mass production several stages forward through, among other initiatives, the introduction of the moving assembly line which replaced the craft workshop in which several men had worked simultaneously on a single static car. Taylor adopted a different approach, however. The purpose of 'Scientific Management', which was fully developed by around 1900, was to ensure that the tasks given to workers in factories were as fully rationalized and as efficiently undertaken as possible.[23] To implement that objective he undertook time and motion studies of factory workers and proposed alternative procedures. Taylor's theory was premised upon the existence of a divided labour process and the principle that work could be made more efficient. It was analysed and reorganised rationally in terms of the space and time in which it was undertaken. It involved, for example, ensuring that workers did not waste time by taking too many steps or by unnecessary repetition. As Sigfried Giedion subsequently explained, 'everything superfluous had to go.'[24] Taylor's approach emphasized the importance of the physical arena in which work was undertaken but he conceived it purely in terms of a space/time continuum. Importantly, he was also keen that his approach should be implemented not only in factories but also in 'homes, farms and governmental departments'.[25]

The look of the spaces inside nineteenth- and early twentieth-century factories emerged, therefore, as a direct result of a focus on the rationalization of the activities that went on within them, rather than, as

A San Francisco can-making factory with automatic machinery illustrated in *American Machinist*, 14 July 1883.

was increasingly the case in the home, of a self-conscious interest in the aesthetic deployed inside them. Factories resembled large, open sheds, made possible by the structural use of metal pillars. Although they had much in common with the large, open spaces dedicated to commerce they were essentially production rather than consumption oriented and they did not need to demonstrate the same commitment to transparency. The interior of Wheeler and Wilson's sewing machine factory in Bridgeport, was a large open space supported by metal pillars, filled with undisguised pulleys and machines, and with high level windows as the only source of light. Several straight rows of work benches were positioned within that open space, an arrangement that facilitated 'the Colt way' of manufacture which involved the use of interchangeable, standardized components in products, the division of labour with sequential tasks, and of specialized machine tools.[26] That cavernous internal space was exclusively dedicated to efficient production. Its lack of decoration contrasted dramatically, however, with I. M. Singer & Co.'s showroom in New York, an equally large space but one that, because it was accessible to customers, also boasted a patterned carpet on its floor, an intricately moulded ceiling and ornate arches over the windows. The sharp contrast between the two spaces emphasized the importance of the language of domesticity in retail spaces where customers needed to feel 'at home'.

The Wheeler & Wilson Sewing Machine Factory, illustrated in *Scientific American*, 3 May 1879.

Views from around 1913 inside Ford's Highland Park factory show that the rationality and efficiency of the work process remained overriding preoccupations. In that context the appearance of the interior, like those in Benjamin's arcades, was achieved as a solution to a problem. Only at the managerial level did domestic details make an appearance in the factory at that time. The superintendent's office at Highland Park, for example, revealed the addition of a few personalized details – a photo on the wall and a clock among them – which offset the otherwise basic austerity and functionality of that overtly masculine workspace.

The office was scrutinized in a similar way to the factory in the early twentieth century. Indeed it has been claimed that the changes made to the office environment as a result of the process of rationalization were 'more profound than those in factories'.[27] Another work-based space determined almost exclusively by function, rather than by aesthetics or taste, the office resembled the factory in many ways. It did not focus on the production of manufactured goods, however, but rather on the processing of administrative tasks, which were, of course, no less important to local and national economies. Office work was seen as being ripe for potential rational reorganization as a means of increasing efficiency. By the late nineteenth century the office helped men and women to engage in a relationship with the modern world, less (as in the public context of consumption) through the creation of theatrical fantasies or idealized modern interiors than through a forced proximity to new machines which transformed the nature of work in that particular environment. Going out to work was men's primary means of entering the public sphere. They encountered there a set of newly rationalized work practices and standardized routines that rapidly became part of modern living and that determined the nature of the interior spaces they occupied. It took some time, though, for the appearance of the office to overtly reflect the fact that it had become an important site of masculine modernity. In the middle years of the nineteenth century it was still a dark dingy place with high wooden desks that allowed individuals a high level of privacy, stools and dark panelled walls.[28] Lights, adjusted by weight and pulley systems (like those used in factories) were introduced as soon as electricity became available, replacing the candles and gas lights that had preceded them. Visitors to an office usually encountered a wooden counter serviced by an office boy. Office work could even be undertaken in railway carriages, either with the assistance of a small writing desk suspended from the luggage rack above or within an appropriately modified carriage which came complete with a lady typist.[29]

The expansion of commercial activity in the latter half of the nineteenth century brought with it the formation of large companies demanding more expansive spaces. In addition the introduction of typewriters and adding machines created the need for departmentalization in the office. As a result small, mixed purpose offices gave way to regimented typing pools and accounts sections. As in Ford's Highland Park factory, management increasingly distinguished itself by inhabiting offices that, complete with family photos, ornate furniture, patterned wallpaper and decorative objects arranged on the mantelpiece, resembled the gentleman's study in the middle-class home. Indeed the distinction between areas designated for middle-class occupation in a number of public spaces – including those in trains and ocean liners – and those destined for the working classes was frequently made through the contrast of comfortable domesticated spaces with more utilitarian and regimented interiors, the latter emphasizing the uniformity of the masses and characterized by an absence of bourgeois comfort. As has already been demonstrated in the very different social context of the 'cottages' of Newport, the design of the interior was an important agent in class formation.[30]

Like work in the factory, office activity was divided into a number of discrete tasks, each of which had an 'optimum method' for its implementation, and, like the factory employee, the clerical worker gradually ceased to be a craftsman in charge of a complete process from beginning to end. Departmentalization flowed naturally from those developments and the application of scientific management ideas followed. Efficiency was controlled by the addition of the time clock. New items of furniture were added to deal with the new 'divided' tasks, filing cabinets, for example, and with the adoption of standard systems, standardized flat top desks allowing for none of the privacy for individual office workers that had been provided by the earlier roll-top desks. Their introduction enabled easier supervision of the work being undertaken. An impression of efficiency was frequently enhanced by the presence of straight rows of desks, closely resembling those of the work benches in factories. In his design for the interior of his Larkin Administration Building of 1904, for example, the American architect Frank Lloyd Wright created an impression of efficiency through the disposition of the furniture items within it. The interior of the building contained five stories (see overleaf). Balconies on each floor looked down into the courtyard below, and the open space was topped by an iron and steel roof similar to those which crowned exhibition halls and department stores. Air conditioning and radiant heat controlled the temperature within the space and Wright designed special metal furniture to go in it. The use of metal in office furniture reinforced the modern look of the spaces they occupied, serving to align them more closely with the factory than the domestic interior. From the 1890s onwards the production of mass-produced metal furniture items became increasingly widespread in the US. A company called A. H. Andrews & Co., for example, created metal furniture for offices, restaurants, factories and hospitals, among other places.[31]

The last decades of the nineteenth and the first decades of the twentieth centuries saw the arrival of women into the office in significant numbers. In the 1880s typists worked on large machines placed on iron framed tables resembling those which supported treadle sewing machines in the same period. Women's entrance into the workplace was one of the most dramatic and immediate ways in which they embraced modernity and they brought elements of domesticity with them into their work

The Central Court of the Larkin Building, designed by Frank Lloyd Wright, in Buffalo, New York, 1902–6.

The typing office of the Society for the Employment for Women, illustrated in *The Quiver*, 1889.

spaces, as a means of softening the abruptness of the shift in identity that they experienced. In the typing office of the Society for the Employment of Women, female employees brought their artistic home interiors into work with them in the form of Japanese prints and fans that they displayed on the walls. In yet another public environment the working-class women – originally called 'Gladys's' but later known as 'Nippies' – who worked as waitresses in the Lyons tea houses saw a more rational side of the business than their middle-class, leisure-seeking counterparts, who merely dined there.[32] Bentwood chairs reinforced that impression, as they had in Loos's Café Museum, although a hint of the 'artistic' interior was also present in paper lanterns that were suspended from the ceiling.

By 1914 the new inside spaces dedicated to modern commerce, work and leisure were fully formed. They were the result of technological

Lyons Tea Shop and waitresses, London, 1890s.

advances, the work of engineers and planners, and of new rational thinking about ways of improving productivity and efficiency. Above all they
had emerged as solutions to problems, and as responses to opportunities
presented by the advent of industrial modernity. Over the next two decades
a new generation of architects and designers was to embrace the ideas and
the forms offered to them by these new spaces and to integrate them into
a new architectural movement which, in turn, dramatically transformed
both the nature and the appearance of the modern interior.

7 The Rational Interior

Around this time the real gravitational center of living shifts to the office.
Walter Benjamin[1]

For many Modern Movement architects the interior had become so inextricably linked with Victorian middle-class domesticity, fashion, personal expression and mass consumption that they felt compelled to develop an architecture which minimized its existence. They found an alternative model, which they believed to be both rational and functional, in the spaces inside the new public sphere buildings – factories, stores and exhibition halls among them. They were also inspired by the functional spaces in new objects of transport, including Pullman train kitchens and ships' galleys.[2] Several of them focused on social housing projects and developed the idea of the 'minimal dwelling', but many of their commissions came from progressive, middle-class clients who wanted a taste of what was rapidly becoming a new, clutter-free lifestyle.

In spite of the numerous hesitations expressed about it a Modern Movement domestic interior inevitably emerged. Unlike its nineteenth-century predecessors which had been dominated by materiality, however, it was primarily spatially defined. Its roots lay in what the Modernists believed to be the unconscious, utilitarian, 'engineered' aesthetic of the new public sphere interiors and they introduced it into modern residential spaces in their efforts to address what they saw as the 'problem' of bourgeois domesticity. Rapidly, however, it was recirculated back into the public arena and applied to a wide range of building types – restaurants, shops, leisure centres, schools, hospitals and churches among them – some of which were new and others of which were being 'modernized' for the first time. In that new context it became a highly self-conscious aesthetic which openly declared its alliance with modernity. In effect, therefore, once it had been reformulated within the Modernist dwelling, the modern public interior was transformed into a metaphor of and for itself. The Modern Movement architect-designers also embraced the idea of the *Gesamtkunstwerk*. Architecture took the lead, therefore, while the so-called 'decorative arts', a catch-all term which embraced the interior, followed meekly after it. For the Modernists the interior was simply the space within buildings, an inevitability which, in order for daily life to take place, had to be 'equipped' – albeit as minimally as possible.

By the 1920s the international Modern Movement in architecture and design, part of a more broadly based cultural response to modernity also encompassing literature, music and drama, was fully formed. It embraced new materials and building techniques – reinforced concrete, plate-glass and steel-frame construction in particular – which had a dramatic impact on the development of the interior spaces of its buildings. Above all, the Modernist architects transferred the key characteristics of new commercial interiors – large open-planned spaces, high levels of transparency and porosity and, perhaps most importantly, a sense of inside/outside ambiguity – into the domestic arena. By taking those features into private spaces they set out to eradicate the domestic interior's role as an overt expression of beauty, as a space for interiority and identity formation, and its links with fashionableness and social status. In their place they emphasized its utilitarian features and the efficiency of the processes undertaken within it. That latter ambition had first emerged, as we have seen, in factories and offices as well as in a number of other public sphere workspaces such as commercial kitchens and laundries. Of the three main drivers of modernization – industrialization, rationalization and standardization – the first two came together in that context. No sooner had they been implemented in the public sphere, however, than Modern Movement architects sought to transfer them into the home, hoping in the process to dedicate that arena to rational production and social equality.

The Modernists' rational approach to space planning inevitably impacted most strongly on those areas of the home dedicated to work rather than to leisure, display, social relations or interiority. That was especially the case as household servants became increasingly scarce and the housewife had to take on more household tasks. In its early formulation, the domestic rational interior focused exclusively on process rather than aesthetics. In the hands of Modernist architects, however, a new aesthetic for the interior also began to emerge. In line with modernity's prioritization of the visual, by the inter-war years the idea of the modern interior had become increasingly associated with a simple, abstract, geometric, undecorated interior style, often referred to as the 'machine aesthetic'. It denoted a high level of functionality and came to be seen by many as *the* modern interior aesthetic of the twentieth century. Although the style was initially only applied to domestic kitchens, bathrooms and other work-oriented areas, as it increasingly came to represent modernity itself, and, by extension, the modern lifestyle, it quickly spread to other areas of the house as well, the living room and dining room among them. The effect was yet another blurring of the distinction between the appearance of interiors outside and inside the home. That function-driven, rational, essentially non-domestic – or, as it became in the hands of the Modernists, 'anti-domestic' – approach to home interiors appealed, at one and the same time, to housewives seeking to put their domestic role on a professional footing, to a group of early twentieth-century feminists who sought to develop collective housing as a means of supporting a way of life that rejected the Victorian ideology of domesticity, and to politically-motivated Modernist architects and designers who set out to develop standardized social housing projects that would provide large numbers of people with access to basic living standards.

By the first decade of the twentieth century the principles of scientific management that had transformed the factory and the office were also beginning to have an impact in the home. Particularly in the US, where acquiring servants was especially difficult, many middle-class women sought to professionalize their domestic activities by comparing them to work undertaken in the factory or the office.[3] They also sought to reorganize their household work and to apply rational principles to it. Aided by new technological developments both inside and outside the home – the advent of sewing machines, refrigerators and factory food processing among them – many housewives, or 'home-makers' as they increasingly called themselves, began to engage with the infatuation with efficiency that was becoming increasingly widespread in the workplace. By the end of the nineteenth century women such as Ellen Swallow Richards – the first woman to enter the Massachusetts Institute of Technology and the founder, in 1910, of *The Journal of Home Economics* – had helped turn what was called, alternatively, 'domestic economy', 'domestic science' or 'home economics' into a discipline capable of being taught.'[4] The title of Richards's 1882 article, 'The Chemistry of Cooking', demonstrated her uncompromisingly scientific approach to her subject.

Back in the middle of the nineteenth century a number of female advocates of household efficiency had already begun to articulate ideas about its effects on the workspaces of the home. It was the American,

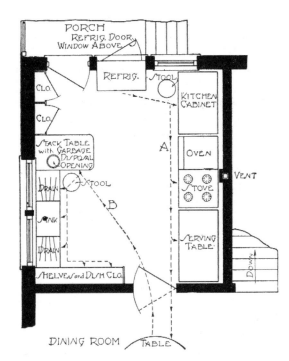

An 'Efficient Grouping of Kitchen Equipment' from Christine Frederick's *Efficient Housekeeping*, 1915.

Catherine Beecher, who had first 'made the art of housekeeping a scientific study'.[5] In her 1869 publication *The American Woman's Home* she had declared her belief in the idea that a more rational way of working would give Christian women pride and satisfaction in the creation of an efficient home. She had also outlined the concept of the 'rational kitchen' which, at that time, was situated at the heart of the house.[6] Beecher's attempt to create new names for rooms in the domestic context also indicated her desire to renew the meaning of the home and to rid the dominant Victorian domestic ideal of its power to control women's lives.[7] By 1912, the year in which Christine Frederick became the household editor of *Ladies' Home Journal* and started to publish a series of articles that were published in book form the following year with the title *The New Housekeeping*, the effects of scientific management were being directly felt in the domestic arena. In 1912 Frederick documented the moment when she made her decision to apply the new ideas she had been hearing about efficiency in factories to the home. 'After Mr. Watson had gone', she wrote, 'I turned eagerly to my husband. "George", I said, "that efficiency gospel is going to mean a lot to modern housekeeping, in spite of the doubts I have. Do you know I am going to work out those principles here in our home! I won't have you men doing all the great and noble things! I'm going to find out how these experts conduct investigations, and all about it, and then apply it to my factory, *my* business, *my* home.'"[8] Frederick focused on the idea of 'step-saving' in the kitchen and drew diagrams showing good and bad kitchen arrangements. In her well organized spaces (see left), the number of steps needed to perform the tasks of preparing, cooking, and cleaning up after a meal were reduced to a minimum. She relegated the kitchen to the back of the house, creating a small but efficient 'laboratory' in which the housewife, clad in a white overall, and seated on a high stool from which she could reach everything she needed for the preparation of food, was destined to spend most of her time. In separating the kitchen from the rest of the house Frederick was taking her cue from the non-domestic arena, as 'hotels and men's clubs had separated the kitchen from the living quarters long ago'.[9]

Frederick's advocacy of grouping kitchen equipment and tools in line with the craftsman's workshop and tool bench revealed her dependence on undivided labour and the skilled craft process in the domestic setting. Her idea that the home should become a site of efficient production was novel, however, and, to that end, Frederick sought to rationalize, and make more efficient the activities that went on in it. Her ambitions

'Sitting down to wash dishes', from Christine Frederick's *Efficient Housekeeping*, 1915.

were linked to a general desire at that time to grant the housewife a new professional status, to make her the equivalent of a scientist working in his laboratory. Not only was the housewife to be seen as an efficient worker, she was also expected to have considerable managerial responsibility in the home making her 'an executive as well as a manual labourer'.[10] Although its effects were felt much more strongly in the kitchen than in the other spaces of the house, Frederick's advocacy of scientific management in the home had a significant impact on the development of the modern interior. It confirmed the movement away from the home as a place ruled by moral, spiritual, ideological and aesthetic values, and the 'irrational' forces of feminine consumption, and towards it becoming one in which the emphasis was on its occupants undertaking household tasks and which recalled the public spaces in which they worked. Frederick's attempt to transform the home into an arena dominated by reason opened the way for a completely new way of thinking about domestic equipment and furniture and their spatial arrangements in the home. It served to undermine Victorian domestic ideology and the idea of the separate spheres, and to align the home with the public, rational face of industrial modernity.

In their desire to raise the status of the housewife, Frederick and others, including Lillian Gilbreth, the wife of Frank Gilbreth, a colleague of F. W. Taylor, aimed to rethink the bases on which the concept of modern domesticity and, by implication, its interior spaces, were conceived. An even more radical idea was embraced by another group of American women, described as 'material feminists', however. They sought to reject not only the Victorian domestic ideal but also the idea of family life that underpinned it. Above all, like the European Modernists who came after them, they understood the potential of interior space not only to reflect social ideals but actually to embody them and make them a reality.[11] Even more actively than Frederick, women such as Charlotte Perkins Gilman, the author of the *The Home: Its Work and Influence* (1903), challenged the physical separation of household space from public space and looked to the latter as a model with which to transform the former. Gilman was concerned about the psychological effects of bourgeois domesticity on women. Her 1892 novella *The Yellow Wallpaper* described a woman descending into mental illness through being forced to take a rest cure at home. 'It is not', wrote Gilman, 'that women are really smaller-minded, weaker-minded, more timid and vacillating, but that whosoever, man or woman, lives always in a small, dark place, is always guarded, protected, directed and restrained, will become inevitably narrowed and weakened by it. The woman is narrowed by the home and the man is narrowed by the woman.'[12] The material feminists advocated the introduction of cooperative housing, kitchenless homes, public kitchens, community dining clubs, day-care centres for children and communal laundries. Borrowing ideas from hotels, restaurants and factories they sought to challenge the idea of the separate spheres and to end women's isolation in the home, their dependency on men, and their old-fashioned 'craft' approach towards housework.[13] Theirs was a total rejection of the traditional domestic ideal. In search of alternative ways of living and bringing up children they advocated a radical revision not only of the way of life built around the Victorian concepts of the family and the home but also, most importantly, of the visual, material and spatial environments which had both engendered and supported it.[14]

Gilman and her co-workers went a significant way towards redefining the relationship of the private with the public sphere in the name of radical feminism. They understood the relationship between interior spaces and the lives that were lived in them and that a radical transformation of those spaces was the only means of changing those lives. Like the supporters of scientific management, they were driven less by aesthetics than by rational thought and an interest in the activities that went on in the home. The means of transforming the status quo advocated by them were above all practically conceived. Transferring communal eating, for example, such as might occur in a hotel, a factory canteen or a hospital, to a site outside the workplace or the institution, would, they believed, put an immediate end to the isolation of the housewife preparing food in her kitchen, whether rationally conceived or otherwise. Similar solutions were offered for childcare and for doing the laundry.

Yet another, this time European, face of the development of the modern interior – which was also heavily ideologically driven and committed to the implementation of ideas developed within the rational, functional, public sphere – emerged as a direct result of the work on social housing programmes initiated by a number of architects in the early twentieth century. From then, and into the inter-war years, a number of Modernist architects drew upon late nineteenth-century ideas and practices related to public arena interiors as stimuli for their democratically conceived dwellings and interior spaces. They intended them to provide 'minimum existences' for people who had hitherto been deprived of that level of comfort in their homes. The 1920s saw a number

The kitchen in the Haus am Horn, designed by Benita Otte and Ernst Gebhardt, exhibited in Weimar, Germany in 1923.

of developments in social housing, many of them on German soil. Although the re-domestication of women that took place in that country in the years after the First World War was linked to the need for population growth, it also inspired a new approach towards the construction of the domestic sphere.[15] That new way of thinking engaged the minds of both female activists and Modernist architects, who realized that collaboration was the only possible way forward. Many of the ideas were rooted in Christine Frederick's concepts, made available to a German audience through the 1922 translation of her book. One of the first manifestations of rational planning in the domestic context on German soil was the realization of the interior of an experimental house called the Haus am Horn (House at the Horn), which was designed by Georg Muche and Adolf Meyer and built as part of a 1923 exhibition mounted by the Bauhaus design school in Weimar. Colour was used to denote the different interior spaces of the house and built-in furniture was extensively utilized. The Haus am Horn kitchen was designed by Benita Otte and Ernst Gebhardt. It contained a work bench and a stool for the housewife in line with Frederick's recommendations. It went further as well, adding eye-level cupboards, with doors to avoid dust accumulating, and standardized, efficiently labelled containers for cooking ingredients, designed by Theodor Bogler. Christine Frederick's German equivalent was the housewife and writer, Erna Meyer, whose book on the same subject, entitled *Der neue Haudsbalt* (*The New Housekeeping*), was published in 1926. Meyer collaborated with the Dutch architect J.J.P. Oud in the creation of a kitchen in a house designed by the architect and exhibited at the *Weissenhof Siedlung* held in Stuttgart in 1927.[16] Meyer and Oud's kitchen realized a number of Frederick's proposals, among them the familiar open shelving, the housewife's stool and workbench and the rational arrangement of its contents.

One of the visitors to the Oud/Meyer kitchen at Stuttgart was Ernst May, an architect involved in a huge redevelopment of Frankfurt. Impressed by what he saw at the *Weissenhof Siedlung*, he initiated a thorough programme of research as part of the Frankfurt project. 'His design team studied psychology, material and product evaluations, and of course scientific management principles as applicable to the home. They scrutinized every aspect of household design to produce efficient and content housewives: color brightened the housewife's world, making housework more tolerable; enamelled surfaces made for easy cleaning; and furniture with smooth lines eliminated dusting in hard-to-reach

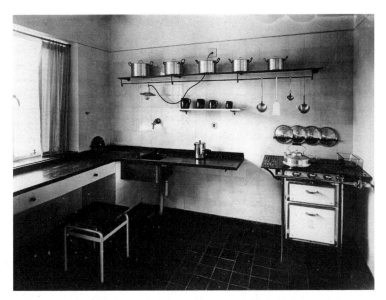

Erna Meyer's kitchen in the house designed by J.J.P. Oud for the *Weissenhof Siedlung* Exhibition, Stuttgart, 1927.

places', one writer has explained.[17] It was beginning to become clear how a rational approach to home design could take on visual and material forms to represent it. One of May's most important decisions was to bring the architect, Margarete Schütte-Lihotzky, from Vienna to work with him on his project. Her lasting contribution to the development of the rational face of the modern domestic interior was the work she undertook on what came to be known as the 'Frankfurt Kitchen'. The design of the small laboratory kitchen that Schütte-Lihotzky developed, along lines already set out by Frederick, was inspired by equivalents in the public sphere – the ship's galley, the kitchen in the railroad dining car and the lunch wagon in particular – which had been designed to facilitate serving food to large numbers of people in as efficient a way as possible.[18] The architect emphasized the importance of step-saving and of efficient, well organized, storage. She also included Frederick's workbench and stool in what has been described as 'a work station where all implements were a simple extension of the operator's hand'.[19] Other notable features included a continuous counter surface attached to the walls of the tiny room, a cutting board fitted into the workbench with a waste bin positioned immediately below it (following Frederick's example), and a

The 'Frankfurt' Kitchen, designed by Margarete Schütte-Lihotzky in 1926–7.

wooden plate holder fixed to the base of the glazed wall cupboards. Schütte-Lihotzky's small 'laboratory' kitchen transformed Frederick's essentially utilitarian spaces into a much more visually elegant solution to the same problem.

While so much of Schütte-Lihotzky's design depended on the ideas and actions of both Beecher and Frederick, it had a more 'modern' look and feel to it than the more overtly functional kitchens the last two women had created. This was achieved through the visual integration of the elements into a whole, a self-conscious use of colour – the cabinet fronts were a deep blue (although even this could be justified functionally as it was a colour which was believed to repel flies), and the employment of strikingly modern materials, linoleum, glass and metal among them. While they could also be justified functionally, they made a significant contribution, nonetheless, to the kitchen's modern look. The impact of the Frankfurt kitchen, which quickly went into mass production, was enormous. It took the idea of rationality into the home on a significant scale and, through the control it gave to her, became a symbol of the professionalization of the housewife. At the same time it removed much drudgery from food preparation. The same principles were soon applied to the bathroom and to the laundry. The emphasis on the kitchen, however, had implications for the conceptualization of the modern house, or apartment, as a whole such that, in the words of Schütte-Lihotzky herself, 'the arrangement of the kitchen and its relationship to the other rooms in the dwelling must be considered first.'[20] That seemingly simple statement had dramatic implications for the evolution of the modern domestic interior, suggesting, as it did, that houses should be designed from the inside out, rather than the reverse. That strategy was soon to become one of the lasting tenets and legacies of architectural Modernism. While on the one hand it had the effect of minimizing the autonomy of the interior by merging it with the architectural shell, on the other, the idea of letting the plan determine the façade imbued the interior with a new level of importance. By giving the elements within the plan utilitarian definitions – the kitchen, the bathroom and the living space for example – they became driving forces behind architectural design as a whole. Indeed the interior became the pivot around which all architectural decisions were made.

The idea of following the processes of efficient production led to a similar level of rationalization in the role of furniture in the 'minimum dwelling'. Bruno Taut addressed the subject in his book *Die Neue Wohnung* (1924), in which he also made references to Christine Frederick, and Ernst May took the idea forward in the Frankfurt project. Indeed May saw a wholesale need to reform the house inside and out. 'Because', he wrote, 'the outside world of today affects us in the most intense and disparate ways, our way of life is changing more rapidly than in previous times. It goes without saying that our surroundings will undergo corresponding changes. This leads us to layouts, spaces and buildings of which every part can be altered, which are flexible, and which can be combined in different fashions.'[21]

Le Corbusier's 'Pavillon de l'Esprit Nouveau', designed for the *Exposition Internationale des Arts Décoratifs Industriels et Modernes*, Paris, 1925.

Germany was not the only European country to take ideas developed in the public arena into the private domestic arena, however. Although he was less systematic and more intuitive than his German counterparts, the French Modernist architect, Le Corbusier, was equally keen to bring ideas generated in the early twentieth-century factory and office into the private residence. His famous statement that 'the house is a machine for dwelling in' indicated his commitment to the influence of the world of industry in the home. His little Citrohan house of 1914 was designed according to the principles of mass production that underpinned automobile manufacture. Interested more in the evocative modernity of factory production, and in the work of the 'heroic' engineer, than in efficiency per se, Le Corbusier envisaged a modern dwelling modelled on the aesthetic implications of rational production. His admiration for open-planning and transparency, and his commitment to the spatial continuity between the outsides and the insides of his buildings, informed much of his domestic architecture,

A chaise longue, designed by Le Corbusier with Pierre Jeanneret and Charlotte Perriand, 1928, photographed in 2007 in the interior of the Villa Savoye.

especially, as has already been noted, his design for the Pavillon de l'Esprit Nouveau, created for the 1925 Paris exhibition. As has also been pointed out, like the constructors of the 1851 Crystal Palace Exhibition, he deliberately left a tree on the site, making a suitable hole in the ceiling for it to pass through, less out of concern for the tree than from a desire not to disturb the space around his building.

Le Corbusier also found other ways of bringing the public sphere into the private arena. They included designing furniture items destined for the former which had their origins in the latter, and using 'off the shelf' items of furniture and pieces of equipment. It has been suggested that the architect took his interest in flat roofs, terraces and balconies from Swiss sanatoria with which he was familiar. Similarly the design for his 1928 Chaise Longue, which he created with Pierre Jeanneret and Charlotte Perriand and used in many of his interiors, could well have been influenced by the reclining chairs used by pulmonary tuberculosis patients during their two-hour daily exposure to fresh air and sunlight.[22] Tuberculosis was a modern disease closely associated with 'the rapid growth of industrialisation and a poorly nourished working class'.[23] By definition, therefore, the reclining chair, part of the cure, was also inherently modern. Furthermore, the removal of dust was a prerequisite of a tuberculosis-free environment, as 'tuberculosis-carrying cough droplets or sputum, although dried, are still infectious and can survive in household dust'.[24] That fact provided the Modernists with yet another rationale for rejecting the dust-collecting surfaces and clutter of the Victorian parlour and for replacing them with open, transparent, clean, white spaces which contained a minimum number of furniture items. Those that were included were defined as items of 'equipment', rather than as providers of comfort. Open-framed reclining chairs, made of wicker or tubular steel, were light enough to be easily moved around, from the terrace back into the living room, and their open forms permitted spatial continuity. The sanatorium provided a recurrent theme within early twentieth-century modern architecture. Josef Hoffmann had designed both the exterior and the interior of the Punkesdorf Sanatorium in 1904, while the Finnish architect, Alvar Aalto, went on to create the Paimio Sanatorium some fifteen years later. He also worked on the building's interior, contributing a number of special features, including non-splash basins and green

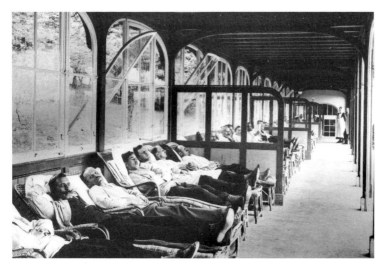

A sanatorium for consumptives, Dannenfels, Germany, 1892.

ceilings to add a level of restfulness when patients were lying down.²⁵ The cupboards in Aalto's sanatorium were all wall-mounted to allow for cleaning to take place beneath them.

Another of the items of furniture equipment introduced by Le Corbusier into several of his interiors was not designed by him but fell, rather, into the category of the 'ready-made'. The leather 'club' armchair, which first made an appearance in his 1925 pavilion, had its origins in the elite male club and provided a very particular alternative to feminine domesticity. From the early eighteenth century onwards the male inhabitants of London, from a range of social groups, had socialized in coffee houses to discuss politics and other affairs of public life and to conduct business. Although they were open access spaces, the coffee houses had served as a means of privatizing public space. They supported a wide range of activities, from business negotiations to literary discussions. Newspapers and magazines could be read and some houses lent books out. They also served as post offices. Gradually certain houses took on a particular political flavour. Whigs visited St James's House, for example, while The Cocoa Tree was frequented by Tories.²⁶ The interiors of the coffee houses were dark and they were fairly sparsely decorated and furnished. Very commonly, 'two or three trestle tables ran the length of a large room, with bench seating and lit by candles. Several pots of coffee warmed on the hob of a large hearth while the hostess dispensed refreshments from the front booth.'²⁷ Those essentially functional interiors had few of the refinements of the domestic arena. However they neither negated domesticity nor embraced it. They merely sought to supplement it.

The private gentlemen's clubs that emerged from the ruins of the earlier coffee houses were much more refined environments, however, and catered for a more exclusive clientele. They emerged in response to the need for enhanced privacy in which to hold discussions of a business or political nature, and to gamble without fear of engaging with suspect characters from the lower classes. They were essentially anti-modern spaces which reinforced social elitism and cultural traditions. From another perspective, however, they were also responding to the effects of modernity, to the increasing accessibility of the city to sections of the population from which 'gentlemen' wished to retain a distance. The clubs were havens both from lower-class men and from the domestic arena that was increasingly being seen as 'belonging' to middle- and upper-class women. They were, therefore, both extensions of, and alternative sites to, domesticity in which political and business matters could be discussed in confidence and like-

The smoking room in the Carlton Club, London, 1890s.

minded people could meet to spend their leisure time together. As interior spaces they were frequently designed in the classical style and contained a number of rooms created for the distinct activities of dining, smoking, playing billiards and cards. Bedrooms were added to many clubs in the second half of the nineteenth century and nearly all had impressive libraries. The style of decoration was usually dark, plush and overtly 'masculine' in nature, and the familiar clutter of the typical middle-class domestic interiors of the period was notable by its absence. The comfortable leather armchair fitted the bill perfectly. The smoking room of London's Carlton Club, for example, was populated with a range of comfortable, upholstered leather chairs and sofas which gave it a masculine appearance. In 'borrowing' the club's leather chair for his residential interiors Le Corbusier was able to introduce an element of semi-private masculine comfort into them, thereby avoiding the 'trap' of bourgeois domesticity.

By the inter-war years, in the US, Christine Frederick had abandoned her attempts to impose a rational model on to the household and had gone into the employ of General Electric to earn her living demonstrating their household technologies in department stores. Her commitment to the efficiency of factory production was overtaken by a realization of the importance of the 'irrational' force of women's consumption to the economy. In 1929 she published a book entitled *Selling Mrs Consumer* in which she outlined the ways in which 'human instincts', she believed at that time, governed consumption decisions. In spite of that volte-face on the part of one of the most important pioneers of the rational household, by the 1920s its impact on the formulation of the modern interior was complete and for many years it remained, in aesthetic if not in ideological terms, one of its key characteristics. As we have seen it found its stylistic expression in the 'machine aesthetic'. Indeed by the inter-war years the modern interior was defined by the modern-looking furniture items, furnishings and decor that appeared in it, made possible by new manufacturing techniques and the use of new materials – aluminium, plastics and bent plywood among them. In spite of the idealism of its protagonists – whether social reformers, feminists or Modernist architects – such was the power of the marketplace and the dominance of the 'irrational' values linked to consumption that, by the 1930s, the modern interior had come to be recognized more by the visual language that represented it than by the efficiency of the work undertaken within it.

The strong desire to embed the rationality underpinning the activities that went on in the production- and work-related interiors of the public sphere in the private dwelling represented a real commitment to its radical transformation. For women it had offered the possibility of their liberation from the drudgery and amateur status of the private sphere, while for the Modernist architects and designers it provided a means of ridding the home of bourgeois domesticity (and thereby de-feminizing it), of making it a healthy environment and of realigning it with the 'masculine' values of work and rationality. In Le Corbusier's case it allowed him to bring the middle-class male camaraderie and companionship of the male club into the home. Ultimately, however, those diverse agendas were all overtaken by the logic – or rather the lack of logic – of the marketplace that transformed that set of abstract idealisms into yet another stylistic option available to consumers.

8   The Mass-produced Interior

The lack of standards in the design of apartments is also a hindrance for the rationalizing of the building trade . . . For rationalization must be based on standardization – as in other spheres of production, the motor-car industry for example.

Stig Lindegren[1]

Together the processes of industrialization, rationalization and standardization, all of which had their origins in the world of work and production, defined modernization.[2] As we have seen their impact was felt not only in the spaces within factories and offices but also in those in the modern home. While industrialization increased the availability of fashionable goods destined for the domestic arena, rationalization radically changed the nature of spaces in the home, firstly in those areas dedicated to work but quickly afterwards in others as well. Standardization also found its way into the domestic arena, both through the mass-produced objects that filled its interiors and through the idea of the standardized, minimal interior.

For Modernist architects, whose thoughts and actions were driven by a desire to democratize design, standardization was hugely important. The idea that objects could, and should, be cheaply mass produced as exact replicas of each other, with interchangeable components, had its origins in American arms manufacturing where the development of standardized parts had ensured that guns could be repaired easily. The principle was subsequently transferred by Henry Ford into automobile manufacture. The 1925 image overleaf of the production line in Ford's Louisville factory depicts the end of the assembly process when the body and chassis come together. The factory workers are checking the last details of the fully assembled, standardized automobiles. Standardization required the existence of a 'model' or 'prototype' that was subsequently replicated. For ease of assembly, distribution and repair all the constituent elements of mass-produced objects had to be exact replicas of each other. The same principles also influenced the development of the modern interior. The effect was a further erosion of the separation between the spheres and a confirmation of the Modernists' desire to minimize the presence of

Workers assembling Model 'T' cars at the new Ford Motors's Plant on South Western Parkway, Louisville, Kentucky, 1925.

nineteenth-century domesticity, and of feminine domestic consumption, within the interior of the modern home. Early ideas relating to the application of standardization to the home were visible in early twentieth-century Germany. In his furniture and interior designs for the new garden city of Hellerau Richard Riemerschmid developed a number of machine-made furniture programmes – his *Maschinenmöbelprogrämme* sets of series, that is, of simple, wooden furniture pieces that could be used, in combination, to create basic interior settings. All his pieces were given numbers – a 1905 kitchen chair was described as 'number 825', for example. They were made simply and their means of manufacture was not concealed. Screw-heads were often left visible, for instance. A model combination living and dining room of 1906, created by Riemerschmid for Hellerau, contained a small table and chairs, a sofa and a storage cupboard. Simple textiles – an embroidered runner for the table and some patterned cushions for the sofa – were included to soften the space as were some reproduced images on the wall, one depicting

Leonardo da Vinci's *Mona Lisa* and another a mountain scene. Bruno Paul worked in a similar way at that time, developing what he called his *Typenmöbelprogrämme* and, like Riemerschmid, numbering his series of replicated furniture pieces. One of his model interiors from 1908/9 was illustrated in *Die Kunst* magazine (see below). The utilitarian appearance of the items of mass-produced furniture it contained was offset, as in Riemerschmid's earlier interior, by a patterned wallpaper, cushions, flowers and paintings hung on the wall.

As we have already seen 1914 saw the eruption of a heated debate about the merits or otherwise of standardization in design between the Belgian architect designer, Henry Van de Velde, and the German champion of modern industrial design, Hermann Muthesius. While the former defended the nineteenth-century ideal of individualism in designed environments, the latter supported an approach towards the manufacture of objects that aligned itself with factory production systems. Within the Modernist architectural model, which dominated progressive ideas

A living room with 'standardized furniture' designed by Bruno Paul, 1908–9, illustrated in *Die Kunst*, 1909.

about the interior through the inter-war years and beyond, Muthesius's view proved to be the more influential. The issue of standardization in, and of, the modern interior was not a straightforward matter, however, and it was interpreted in a variety of ways. While the European Modernists of the middle years of the twentieth century used it to underpin their democratic, egalitarian ideals, and to emphasize the social, the spatial and the functional roles of objects, the American commercial industrial designers of the 1930s utilized standardized machine manufacture to align the interior with the market-led values of industrial modernity.

The architectural Modernists set out to standardize both individual furniture items and the interior as a whole, as far as that was feasible. The latter was most easily achieved in new, large-scale, utilitarian spaces – open plan offices, hotel kitchens, work canteens and student halls among them. Spaces like these were frequently dominated by the presence of mass-produced artefacts, from office chairs to kitchen equipment, to knives and forks. In the canteen of the Bijenkorf Department Store in The Hague (p. 151) the architect P. L. Kramer arranged long trestle tables in straight rows, and included plain white items of standardized crockery to encourage a sense of communal dining. The use of standardized components was also possible inside objects of mass transportation (themselves mass produced), particularly in the more utilitarian spaces destined for lower-class travellers. The interior of one third class railway carriage, or of a third class cabin in an ocean liner, for example, looked very much like the ones either side of them. Both contained minimal levels of comfort. Even in the home – the site, more usually, of individualism and social aspiration – the same issue was enthusiastically addressed by the Modernists. 'Of course a home is a much more complex organism than a car, and is conditioned by many more human functions', the Swedish architect Stig Lindegren admitted in 1949. 'But', he added, 'that only increases the demand for a technical solution of the problem.'[3] Two decades later the French cultural critic Jean Baudrillard devoted a section of his book *The System of Objects* (1968) – a study of the neo-Platonic relationship between the ideas of the 'model' and the 'series' in mass production – to the concept of the 'model interior' in which he emphasized its class implications. He made a distinction between the unattainable, aristocratic interiors depicted in contemporary French magazines such as *Maison Française* and *Mobilier et Decoration*, those 'old eighteenth-century mansions, miraculously well-equipped villas, Italian gardens heated by infra-red rays and populated by Etruscan statuettes, in short the world of

The staff canteen at the Bijenkorf department store, The Hague, designed by P. L. Kramer, 1924, illustrated in *Wendingen* in 1925.

the unique', and what he called 'models in the proper sense of the word', interiors, that is, which contained items that were, through mass production, accessible to a large sector of society.[4]

Although Christine Frederick's rational kitchens, discussed in the previous chapter, were based on the principles of efficiency and productivity, and similar objects appeared in all of them, she had stopped short of advocating the principle of industrialized standardization. Instead she had remained committed to the craft process. By the 1920s, in Germany, the question of 'standards' had emerged as an important issue however, manifested, for example, in the formulation of the DIN (Deutsches Institut für Normung) standards. It was within that climate that Grete Schütte-Lihotzky developed her famous kitchen design, the standardized components of which were manufactured in huge numbers. 'The Frankfurt Kitchen was a factory-assembled module delivered to a building site and lifted into place by crane. Ten thousand were installed in the Frankfurt settlements alone', one writer has explained. As we have seen Lihotsky took her inspiration from ship's galleys and railroad dining-car kitchens so the principle of standardization, inherent in those spaces, moved naturally into the domestic context.[5] Indeed, the role of standardized interior components in determining the appearance of interior spaces became increasingly apparent within the implementation of architectural Modernism in Europe, and in the US through the middle years of the twentieth century. The concept of the idealized 'model interior', which could be replicated through the mass availability of standardized goods, had by that time captured the popular imagination through the media of exhibitions, magazines and other forms of mass dissemination. At the *Weissenhof Siedlung* of 1927, for example, the house designed by J.J.P. Oud, which contained Erna Meyer's rational kitchen, also featured standardized furniture pieces in its combination living and dining room, designed by Ferdinand Kramer.

The need to put any objects into interiors went against the grain of the architectural Modernists and was often undertaken extremely reluctantly. Indeed the Modernist interior was often conceived, at least in ideal terms, as a near empty, uncluttered, dematerialized space. Many architects, as we have already seen, found a solution in the idea of built-in furniture, extensions of the architectural frame, which helped to diminish the impact of the materiality of interior furnishings and to emphasize the dominance of architectural space. 'We would prefer', wrote Le Corbusier, 'that our fittings and our furniture be built into walls, stay there, invisible and practical, leaving the home spacious and aerated'.[6] Given the practical demands of occupying space, however, the total exclusion of material objects was never a realistic option and, inevitably, the modern interior became a container for a variety of material artefacts, both mass-produced and otherwise. Indeed, a tension between abstraction and materiality characterized the Modernist interior. Recognizing the inevitability of the need for material objects in their otherwise abstract, spatial settings, a number of Modernist architects, Le Corbusier among them, chose to complement their built-in furniture with 'free-standing' furnishings, sometimes, as we have seen, mass-produced items bought 'off the shelf' and sometimes objects made to their own designs over which they could maintain a higher level of control. The contemporary materials utilized in many of their designs – tubular steel, glass and plywood among them – determined a particular furniture aesthetic which quickly came to characterize the Modernist interior. They offered a level

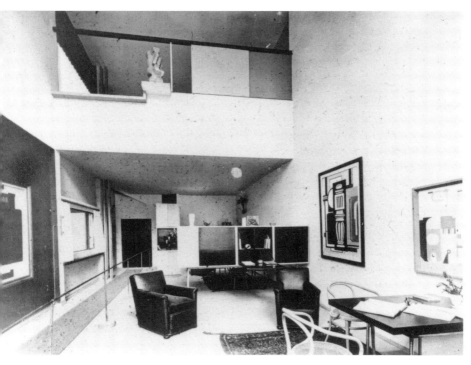

The interior of Le Corbusier's 'Pavillon de l'Esprit Nouveau' for the *Exposition Internationale des Arts Décoratifs et Industriels Modernes*, Paris, 1925.

of materiality to otherwise abstract Modernist settings but the skeletal forms of the furniture items that were included prevented them from disturbing spatial continuity. A subtle balancing act was needed in the design of the material and the spatial aspects of those interiors. Importantly, also, the materials in question were industrially manufactured rather than crafted. Like Adam Smith's identical pins, produced in early pin factories, one industrially produced tubular steel chair looked, therefore, exactly like another.

Le Corbusier's *Pavillon de l'Esprit Nouveau*, designed for the 1925 Paris *Exposition Internationale des Arts Décoratifs et Industriels Modernes*, combined fitted furniture with a number of anonymous 'object-types'. The pavilion itself was a rare instance of a prototype interior designed as a 'model' unit that theoretically, at least, could be replicated many times over in a large apartment block. Le Corbusier chose each item to show his commitment to new materials, industrial production, and standardization.[7] He saw the furniture items he included as aesthetically neutral tools, passive pieces of 'equipment' rather than as elements within a decorative scheme. He selected metal doors, produced by the Roneo company, a manufacturer of steel office equipment; prefabricated metal windows; a tubular metal staircase (inspired by ones used on ships); bentwood armchairs (recalling the communal café rather than the private living room); a metal table made by L. Schmittheisler, a producer of hospital equipment; and some standardized modular storage units, described as 'class-less furniture'.[8] The leather 'club' armchair he included, discussed in the previous chapter, was suggestive of a masculinity that had been created within a semi-public sphere. The overall aim was to eliminate any traces of individualized domesticity and to provide the occupant with the basic utilitarian requirements for everyday life. The architect immodestly described his little pavilion as 'a turning point in the design of modern interiors'.[9] Ironically, though, as was often the case with Modernist proposals, in reality many of its supposedly standardized items had to be custom-made. Special small versions of Maples' leather armchairs, for example, usually produced to standardized measurements, had to be produced to fit Le Corbusier's space.[10]

Although Le Corbusier included a tubular steel stair handrail in his pavilion, he did not at that time realize the potential of that material for the design of furniture pieces that would bring the world of industry into the home.[11] In fact it wasn't until 1927 that, with Pierre Jeanneret and Charlotte Perriand, Le Corbusier began to design chairs in tubular steel. From as early as 1925, however, the Bauhaus-trained architect and designer Marcel Breuer had understood the potential of that material – encountered through his bicycle – to transform the bulky club armchair, of which Le Corbusier was so fond, into a skeletal version of the same design. With its open tubular steel frame Breuer's Wassily chair of 1925 could provide the same utilitarian function as a traditional armchair but without blocking the spatial continuity of the room that contained it. He was dissatisfied with his first version, writing: 'It is my most extreme work, both in its outward appearance and in the use of materials; it is the least artistic, the most logical, the least "cosy" and the most mechanical.' He went on to develop it through several stages until it was finally resolved to his satisfaction.[12] In contrast to Le Corbusier's idea of using 'off the shelf' items, Breuer's approach was to design his own mass-produced furniture pieces to enhance and reinforce the spatiality of his interiors and their standardized nature. It was a strategy that was subsequently emulated by many other Modernist architects, from Mies van der Rohe to Charles Eames.

Over the next few years Breuer designed many other tubular steel furniture items for the numerous interior spaces he created. His tubular steel club armchair appeared in the living area of Walter Gropius's house in Dessau of 1925–6, for example, while a dressing niche in a guest room in the same house featured a little tubular steel stool and a multi-shelf dressing table. The living room in Moholy-Nagy's house of the same years contained a number of Breuer's tubular steel pieces, as did an interior he created in Berlin in 1926 for Erwin Piscator, and the Harnischmacher house of three years later (both pictured overleaf).

Breuer's interest in tubular steel was soon emulated by many other architects and designers. At the *Weissenhof Siedlung* Mies van der Rohe, Mart Stam, J.J.P. Oud, S. van Ravesteyn, Heinz and Bodo Rasch and Arthur Korn were among the architects who displayed tubular steel furniture pieces in the interiors of the buildings they created for that event. A little later the Italian Rationalist architects, Giuseppe Terragni and Gabrielle Mucchi, among others, created furniture pieces in the same material. In the 1930s the British company PEL devoted itself to the mass manufacture of tubular steel furniture, while at the same time in the US Wolfgang Hoffmann, Josef Hoffmann's son, designed a range of items for the Howell Company that were produced in considerable numbers. Only in the US did tubular steel find a place in the popular modern residential interior in the years before 1939, however. In Europe, with the exception of the handful of patrons of Modernist architecture, it was more usually found in church halls, canteens and school classrooms.

By the mid 1930s, as several publications of the time demonstrated, few Modernist interiors were complete without their items of tubular steel furniture. Paul Frankl's *New Dimensions: The Decorative Arts of Today in Words and Pictures* (1928); Dorothy Todd and Raymond Mortimer's *The New Interior Decoration* (1929); Hans Hoffmann's *Modern Interiors in Europe and America* (1930); and Hans Eckstein's *Die Schöne Wohnung* (1931), among others, all depicted numerous examples of interior spaces containing items made of tubular steel.[13] Retail spaces were especially well represented, as were cafés and bars, all of them purveyors of the modern lifestyle. Examples included a Parisian bar designed by Robert Block of Studio Athelia; bars in Helsingfors and Kyoto by Birger Jarl Carlstadt and Isaburo Ueno respectively; a seaside restaurant in San Sebastian by the Spanish architect, Labayen-Aizpurúa; a music shop in Vienna by Ernst

The dining room in an apartment, designed by Marcel Breuer for Erwin Piscator, Berlin, photographed by Cami Stone, 1926.

Marianne Harnischmacher in the living room of the Harnischmacher House, Wiesbaden, photographed by Wolf and Lotte Schede-Foto, 1932.

Lichtblau; a baker's shop in Stockholm by Eskil Sundahl; and a shoe shop by Jock D. Peters in Los Angeles. In private residences, however, tubular steel was for the most part reserved for private bars, smoking rooms and studies, a reinforcement of the material's inherent masculinity. Only a very small number of living rooms were graced by its presence.

As well as playing a strongly visual, material and spatial role within Modernist interiors the emphasis of mass-produced artefacts in interiors also reflected the ideological face of that movement. The Modernist interior was proposed as a solution to the problem of the 'minimum dwelling', that is to the possibility of low income families being able to live their lives in a basic, utilitarian environment.[14] In that context the inclusion of low-priced, standardized, mass-produced artefacts formed part of many Modernist architects' social agendas. A narrow line separated object standardization in the interior from the standardization of the interior itself. Indeed, in the context of the minimum dwelling, the entire interior could itself be seen as a 'model' or a 'prototype' that could be replicated. The British architect Wells Coates's version of the 'minimal flat' was not directed at the less well-off, however, but rather at people with modern, mobile lifestyles who didn't want to be tied down by an excess of material possessions. The interior of the Isokon Minimum Flat

The Isokon Minimum Flat, designed by Wells Coates and exhibited at London's *Exhibition of British Art in Relation to the Home*, 1933.

created for the apartment building he designed in Lawn Road, London consisted of a bed-sitting room and a small kitchenette, and featured Isokon plywood items and PEL tubular steel chairs.[15] It was shown at the *Exhibition of British Industrial Art in Relation to the Home* held in London's Dorland Hall in 1933.

Unless they were created especially by Modernist architects for their own spaces, or for the handful of private residential clients for whom they worked, standardized mass-produced furniture items, such as PEL's simple tubular steel side chairs, could only be produced if there was mass demand for them. From the late nineteenth century onwards the serial production of wooden and metal furniture pieces had developed in the US, focused for the most part in Grand Rapids, near Lake Michigan, in response to the demand from new offices, hospitals, restaurants and other large-scale public sphere buildings which were being constructed at that time. In addition to the growing presence of machine-made furniture and furnishings in inside spaces, inter-war interiors in both the public and the private spheres were also becoming more and more heavily populated by mass-produced, standardized machines. Offices saw the arrival of typewriters and duplicating machines; shops that of cash registers and adding machines; while homes witnessed the influx of a wide range of domestic machines, from irons to kettles, toasters and electric fires. As the spaces designed for work and commerce were gradually modernized and, with domestic spaces absorbing the products of the new technologies, the need for the new machines to reflect that change aesthetically became a priority. Also as the economic depression hit harder in the US, putting increased pressure on manufacturers to differentiate their products, those objects needed to be given modern visual identities that would enhance their suitability for the spaces they were destined to facilitate the introduction of modernity into.

In the late 1920s the members of the newly established American industrial design profession focused on the creation of unified, modern-looking identities for the new machines destined for the newly modernized interiors of both the public and the private spheres. Like their European Modernist architectural contemporaries, they looked to the public sphere for an appropriate aesthetic. Like Le Corbusier, for example, they were inspired by the new, modern machine par excellence, the automobile. While the French architect was more interested in the manufacturing principles underpinning it than the automobile itself (although he did design a 'Minimum Car' with Pierre Jeanneret) his American counterparts went one step further by designing cars and subsequently emulating the streamlined aesthetic they developed for them in the interior. Their objects of transportation were styled to eliminate 'drag' and maximize speed. The symbolic implications of that new, dynamic aesthetic were immediate and compelling and were quickly transferred to inanimate objects such as pencil sharpeners and refrigerators. Inevitably those objects found their way into interiors, both public and private, enabling the interior itself to be 'streamlined'.

The American industrial designers who took upon themselves the ambitious task of streamlining the entire environment, both interior and exterior, came from a variety of commercial backgrounds.[16] Very few were architects by training, the majority having worked in advertising and, in some cases, in theatre and retail design.[17] They were extremely adept, therefore, at creating high levels of visual rhetoric and spectacle in interior spaces. Their work crossed a spectrum from experimental to live projects. While they dreamed of redesigning the city and imagined extraordinary futuristic objects of transport for the 'world of tomorrow', for the most part their everyday work consisted of product redesigns and the commercial interior projects that were associated with them. The link between product and interior design initiated by the American industrial designers offered an alternative approach to the creation of the modern interior to that which had been formulated by the European Modernist architects. While the forms and materials both groups used were often superficially similar – tubular steel and simple geometry featured widely, for example – the contexts in which they worked and their working methods were utterly different. Mass-produced artefacts provided the starting point for the industrial designers and they worked outwards from them into the spaces that contained them. Given that they worked predominantly in the commercial arena their primary aim was to ensure that the objects they designed looked modern, attractive and desirable. The work that Norman Bel Geddes undertook for the Simmons Company, for instance, had that end in sight. In his deliberations about the design of a bed, which in his view had to 'consist of the simplest possible horizontal and perpendicular sections, perhaps molded out of one sheet of metal', he demonstrated the industrial designer's characteristic concern for economical manufacture. He was also interested in ensuring that the bed could be dusted and dismantled easily and, above all, that it 'possess[ed] sheer, graceful lines'.[18] When he moved his focus on to the showroom in which the bed was to be displayed his main preoccupation remained the enhancement of the bed's desirability. Drawing on his earlier experiences in theatre design and shop window dressing he created a complete and enclosed bedroom 'set' featuring streamlined, curved panelled walls, subtle concealed lighting and sufficient simple props to give a sense of realism to the ensemble, but not to outshine the bed, which had to remain the focus of attention.

The interior that Bel Geddes created for the Simmons Company was both an extension and a dramatization of the bed, as well as a form of brand reinforcement. Interestingly, for the design of his private residence Zalmon G. Simmons and his wife Frances adopted a quite different approach, asking the interior decorator Elsie de Wolfe to provide them with a reproduction eighteenth-century French 'Chinoiserie' setting. While the redecoration of their home was probably led by Frances Simmons, her husband's commercial interior was targeted at a mass audience that sought to embrace signs of modernity in their homes. The Simmons's home interior, which subtly combined modernity with tradition, was an appropriate expression of the couple's significant financial and social achievements and their (acquired) position in society. Bel Geddes also worked for the advertising agency J. Walter Thompson, which commissioned him to create a combined conference room and auditorium. He approached that project in two ways, firstly as the creation of an efficient machine, ensuring the inclusion of a screen for projection and an advanced ventilation system, and secondly as a space in which ambiance was all important. To that latter end he included concealed lighting operated by twenty-two dimmer switches.[19] The room was described as being made up of 'impressive plain surfaces, restfully colored, supremely comfortable and completely modern'.[20]

The American industrial designers created a wide range of interiors for offices, showrooms, shops and exhibitions, as well as for objects of transportation. They understood offices, first and foremost, as appropriate spaces for their modern machines. In his book *Horizons* (1934) Bel Geddes described the office as the sum of the artefacts and machines it contained – from the telephone, to the fountain pen, to the calendar pad, to the lamps, to the clock, to the receptacles for cigarettes, to the adding machine, to the calculating machine, to the dictating machine, to the filing cabinet. His was a strongly 'object-centric' view of interiors which were defined by their material contents. In the mock-up corner of *An Industrial Designer's Office* (already described in chapter Five), created by Raymond Loewy and Lee Simonson for the 1934 exhibition at New York's

The interior of the Eastman Kodak Shop designed by Walter Dorwin Teague, New York, 1931.

Metropolitan Museum of Art, the aesthetic of streamlining was applied both to the contents of the interior and to its frame. The walls were covered with curved, horizontal metal bands. The same metal was also used as edging on the curved cantilevered desks, for the frame of an upholstered chair, and for the support for a display stand. Repetition was used to accentuate the unity of that streamlined environment as it had been by the *Gesamtkunstwerk* architect-decorators, Henry Van de Velde and Peter Behrens, earlier in the century. The space was dominated by the objects within it, however, from Loewy's model for his Hupmobile automobile, which was positioned on a plinth centre stage, to his drawing for the Princess Anne ferryboat, to his dramatically modern-looking glass and metal furnishings.

The same designers also worked on numerous shop interiors. Loewy created the W. T. Grant store in Buffalo, among others, while Walter Dorwin Teague designed Eastman Kodak's New York store in 1931. The scheme for the latter shop interior exhibited the same horizontal metal strips, albeit on a different scale, that the designer had used in his redesign of one of the company's cameras. The design for the camera shop was a low-key affair, however, in which the visibility of the goods on sale was paramount. Lighting was concealed behind wall cases fitted flush with the walls. Commenting on that interior, a contemporary critic explained that, 'The entire design was conceived as providing a neutral setting for the display of the photographic enlargements and the various colourful objects of Eastman Kodak manufacture. It was executed, therefore, in varying tones of silver, gray and black. The finish of the various materials was chosen with the same object in view. The display space draws the eye because it is of a light, dull finish in contrast to the dark, polished enframement', adding that: 'The display counters have been kept low, better to attract attention, and the objects are displayed on plain standards of a similar finish to that of the walls.'[21]

Some of the American industrial designers' most overtly modern ideas were reserved for their designs for the interiors of objects of transportation. Transport was their first love and they developed exciting visions of, and wrote extensively and rhetorically about, their streamlined planes, trains, boats, automobiles and even their space rockets, of the future. Only a few of their designs were realized, however. Bel Geddes was responsible for the interior of the Chrysler Airflow of 1933, while the automobile's exterior was the creation of the engineer, Carl Breer. Loewy's powerful locomotive designs for the Pennsylvania Railroad Company and

The main lounge and observation end of the 20th Century Limited train, designed by
Henry Dreyfuss, 1938.

Dreyfuss's 20th Century Limited model for New York Central both went
into production also. The designers in question were equally at home
working inside trains, planes and ships. The specific constraints presented by those projects, including the need to appeal to paying passengers and to build on the important symbolic relationship of transport
objects with modern life, made those interiors especially challenging.
Passenger plane interiors were perhaps the most demanding of all. Bel
Geddes's office designed a mock-up for Pan American's China Clippers
which began flying in 1935. He made a number of innovative proposals
including the provision of sleeping facilities, a galley with a refrigerator
and sound insulation. Ship interiors also received the attention of the
industrial designers. In 1936 Raymond Loewy created a number of rooms, 163

including the main hall and the state room, for the Panama Railways Steamship Company's liner, the ss *Panama*. His spaces exuded an air of modern luxury and recalled the interiors shown in contemporary Hollywood films and glamorous hotels more closely than they did the usual standardized spaces of mass travel. A range of modern materials was employed including stainless steel, aluminium and glass, and Loewy rounded off the corners of the objects in the interior both for safety reasons and as a strategy for making those compact spaces look as large as possible.

Many of the same requirements underpinned the industrial designers' work for train interiors. Henry Dreyfuss's settings for the 20th Century Limited were strikingly controlled, modern-looking, and deceptively spacious. His use of concealed lighting enhanced the luxurious ambiance that he had set out to create. Muted colours – blue, grey and brown – were combined with new materials, including cork and Formica. 'Fully enclosed by glass and rounded surfaces, protected from weather and engine-soot by air-conditioning, and lulled by radio music, they [the passengers] could forget they were travelling as they experienced a rubber-cushioned ride.'[22] In the train's main lounge and observation car, the designer's use of top lighting and the addition of metal strips to the columns combined with a number of other features to create an extremely elegant travelling environment. Loewy's interior designs for the Broadway Limited provided a similarly comfortable experience for its passengers. The train's luxurious interior was enhanced by the presence of a circular bar as glamorous as anything that could have been found in a New York or a Parisian nightclub.

In spite of their significant impact on interior spaces in the commercial sphere the industrial designers made very little difference to the design of the modern home. Exceptionally Bel Geddes was involved in a project to visualize 'The House of Tomorrow'. The result was spatially unadventurous however, most of its rooms being conventional rectangles, and its design details echoed those of the European Modernists for the most part. The design was published in the *Ladies' Home Journal*, thereby reaching a much wider audience than its European equivalents, however. Another group of American designers, several of who had European roots and architectural backgrounds, focused exclusively upon furniture and interior design. They were more successful than the industrial designers in modernizing the American home at that time. Gilbert Rhode, Paul Frankl, Kem Weber, Russel Wright and a few others worked with some of the progressive American furniture mass manufacturers of the day – the Kroehler Company, Herman Miller, and Conant Ball, among them – to create mass-produced sets of simple, light, wooden furniture items, inspired by Swedish models, that were ideally suited to the spatial constraints of modern, urban apartment living. A 1928 living room designed by Kem Weber was illustrated in *Innen-Dekoration*. It brought together modern and traditional items in a single setting. In Mary McCarthy's 1936 novel, *The Group*, a story about the lives of a group

A room designed by Kem Weber, Los Angeles, 1928, illustrated in *Innen-Dekoration*, 1928.

of Vassar graduates living in inter-war New York, Kay, one of the main characters, was among those for whom the new, compact furnishing style was enormously appealing. Her apartment consisted of

> Two rooms, plus dinette and kitchen, plus a foyer, plus, Kay's pride and joy, a darling little dressing room. Every stick of furniture was the latest thing; blond Swedish chairs and folding table . . . in the dinette . . . in the living room a bright-red modern couch and armchairs to match, a love-seat covered in striped grey-and-white mattress ticking, steel standing lamps, and a coffee table that was just a sheet of glass that Harald had had cut at the glazier's and mounted on steel legs, built-in bookcases that Harald had painted canary yellow. There were no rugs yet and, instead of curtains, only white Venetian blinds at the windows. Instead of flowers, they had ivy growing in white pots.[23]

Those designers positioned themselves somewhere between European Modernism on the one hand and American commercial product design on the other. Above all they sought to exploit the possibility of modularity and standardization in furniture manufacture. Their contribution was defined by their 'willingness to make use of the language of the marketplace to reach potential users'.[24]

With the exception of their emphasis on the curved forms of streamlining, the interior designs developed by the American designers of the inter-war years were not especially visually innovative as they tended to combine the strategies of the European Modernists with those of the exponents of the Art Deco style in a fairly straightforward way. The impact of their strongly commercial approach to interior design was more significant, however, especially in the years after the Second World War when their influence provided a counterbalance to that of the Modernists. The approach to the modern interior adopted by the American industrial designers was much more pragmatic and less idealistic than that of their European counterparts and they anticipated a world in which, increasingly, objects were to take centre stage and define the interiors that contained them.

9 The Abstract Interior

We are in need of a new interior.
Theo van Doesburg[1]

As well as allying itself with the twin forces of rationality and efficiency rooted in the world of modern technology and industry, the early twentieth-century modern interior also developed a close relationship with the highly irrational world of contemporary art. Early twentieth-century avant-garde fine art, particularly as it was manifested in Cubism, the Dutch De Stijl movement and Constructivism, sought to distance itself from the domesticated, pictorial aesthetic of the nineteenth century and, by embracing abstraction, to align itself with the spirit of modernity. In the years after 1914 it also sought an alliance with Modernist architecture in the spirit of the *Gesamtkunstwerk*. Together, their protagonists believed, art and architecture could bring about a transformation of the environment that would unite the separate spheres. That new alliance reinforced the approach towards architecture and the interior that defined them, first and foremost, as the results of the manipulation of space. In turn space was seen as being continuous and unbroken, existing both within and beyond the picture plane, the piece of sculpture, and the architectural construction. In that sense, at least conceptually, the abstract interior had no fixed boundaries and existed both inside and outside at the same time. By extension, architectural constructions were not restricted to exclusively private or public functions. Space was simply space and the artists and architects associated with those avant-garde movements set out to reclaim it as a neutral concept, cleansed of all the ideological baggage it had acquired in the nineteenth century through its relationship with domesticity.

By the 1920s an increasing number of progressive architects sought to erode the boundaries between the inside and outside and to enhance the porosity of their architectural structures. As we have seen they linked the house, metaphorically, with the machine, and they defined the artefacts within it as items of equipment, rather than as providers of comfort and pleasure. Above all, as we have also seen, Le Corbusier and others aimed to minimize the role of domesticity in the private dwelling. The influence of ideas emanating from fine art on the interior had the effect, at the progressive, avant-garde end of the spectrum, of reinforcing that mission and of eliminating domesticity and the psychological associations that went with it once and for all. Although in search of classless, gender neutral (although they were, in effect, heavily masculinized) spaces which were neither public nor private, a number of architects completely redefined the modern interior at that time. In the 1920s in its pure form the models they created were restricted to the exhibition and the world of the intellectual elite, by the 1930s the popular 'machine aesthetic' interior had been absorbed into what by that time had become a generic 'modern' style, widely available in the marketplace.

Prior to the nineteenth century, adding art to the domestic interiors of the wealthy, or to significant public spaces, had been a relatively straightforward process related to the power and status of ruling families and of the church. By the second half of the nineteenth century the inclusion of art in the interior was still one of the means of marking one's level in society, although by then that opportunity had been extended to the middle classes. In his seminal 1979 study *Distinction: A Social Critique of the Judgement of Taste* the French social theorist Pierre Bourdieu elaborated the role of 'art' in the context of modern consumer society demonstrating how the ownership and display of 'cultural capital', that is the acquisition of knowledge about art and other forms of high culture, and the demonstration of that acquisition in the context of daily life, whether through interior decor or the presentation of food on a plate, was one of the key means by which the middle class distinguished itself from the class immediately below it.[2] The avant-garde artists of the early twentieth century sought to make artistic practice more self-referential and less part of everyday life. As a result artistic 'knowledge' became more difficult to acquire and increasingly powerful as a mechanism for achieving 'distinction'. By the inter-war years that principle had been extended to architecture, and, by implication, to the interior as well.

A merging of the worlds of fine art and the interior could already be observed, on a number of different levels, in the last decades of the nineteenth century. Several artists had involved themselves with the spaces in which their work was displayed at that time. In 1883, for example, fifty-one of James McNeill Whistler's etchings were installed at an exhibition at London's Fine Art Society, displayed in a setting that contained 'yellow velvet curtains – pale yellow matting – yellow sofas and little chairs – lovely little table – own design – with yellow pot and Tiger Lily'. The exhibit demonstrated the significance that Whistler bestowed on both the domesticity and the theatricality of the space in which his art was shown.[3] In 1912 a group of avant-garde French artists exhibited a similar preoccupation when they created the *Maison Cubiste* at the Paris Salon d'Automne of that year. Although its facade and three interior spaces were masterminded by the decorator André Mare, in reality they were the result of a collaboration of a group of twelve artists associated in various ways with Cubism.[4] Works by Fernand Léger, Roger de La Fresnaye, Jacques Villon, Raymond Duchamp-Villon, Marcel Duchamp, Albert Gleizes, Jean Metzinger and Paul Vera were displayed within the house. The interiors were also filled with eclectic collections of brightly coloured furniture and furnishings from different moments in French history. *Un salon bourgeois* was also included. The intention may have been to subvert the Art Nouveau *Gesamtkunstwerk* and to present, in its place, a more fragmented, cacophonous and discordant interior that paralleled the strategies of the Cubist painters.[5] It could also have been a result of the lack of equivalence between what was considered progressive in the world of fine art and what counted as the 'state of the art' in the area of interior decoration at that time. In 1912 the two areas still inhabited parallel universes. Within a couple of years, however, that was to change and they were to move much more closely together.

After 1914 a number of closer alignments between art and architecture, and by extension the interior, were evident. Indeed the interior was drawn into the heart of the artistic avant-garde's search for new forms and concepts. At that time artistic 'knowledge' became, increasingly, the exclusive terrain of avant-garde artists who sought to distance themselves from the everyday world of taste and status, and to inhabit a more rarefied, conceptual domain. Their interest was in abstraction rather than in narrative, representation, ornamentation or social display. They felt that art should depend upon its own internalized conceptual world and relinquish any dependency on lived-in spaces. In their determination to include architecture within their remit, however, they were forced to embrace the idea of the interior, both idealized and realized.

The transformation of the modern interior in that context began as an intellectual and ideological exercise. Early projects were rarely realized as spaces for occupancy. Ironically, however, given the avant-garde's desire to sever art's links with lived reality, and to lift it to a level above that of fashionable taste and the commercial system of exchange (an unfulfilled aspiration, of course), the long-term effect was a new direction for the lived-in modern interior through the twentieth century. The absorption of the interior into a sequence of modern art movements served to transform it, both theoretically and actually, from a visual, material and spatial reality into an abstract concept. That new direction of travel had two distinct manifestations. Firstly, in the work of the Dutch De Stijl artists, the interior became part of a highly abstracted redefinition of space that took place, in the first instance, in two dimensions on the painted canvas, but which was subsequently reintroduced into three dimensions in the form of architectural models and constructions. Secondly a number of Modernist architects, inspired by the work of the Cubists and the Constructivists, began to see the creation of architecture, and of the interior, as being synonymous with the abstract manipulation of space.

A set of collaborations between artists and architects characterized the developments that took place in The Netherlands in the years immediately after the First World War. The result was the emergence of a new definition of the interior and of the furniture items within it. Those artists and architects established their collaborations, in broad terms, upon the premise that painting and architecture were two very distinct and different disciplines that could, nonetheless, complement each other through the relationship of colour's potential for spatial construction.[6] The Dutch architect, Bart van der Leck, was a key protagonist in those collaborations. He had begun his career as an applied artist in the 1890s and he acted as an important bridge between the ideas of the English Arts and Crafts architects and designers and the work of the De Stijl group of which he was a member. He subsequently worked on a range of architectural projects with the Amsterdam-based architect H. P. Berlage. The artist Theo van Doesburg worked with the architects Jan Wils and J.J.P. Oud, who were also both heavily influenced by Berlage. Another applied artist and painter, Vilmos Huszár, collaborated with the architect Piet Klaarhamer in the development of a number of sophisticated ideas about the difference between the decorative and the plastic arts. He also ventured into furniture design. Piet Zwart, another De Stijl artist with an Arts and Crafts background, also took an interest in interiors and made a significant contribution to exhibition design. His designs were temporary, highly branded structures, intended as frames for the commodities

on display within them. Projects he worked on included a stand for a celluloid manufacturer at the Utrecht Annual Industrial Fair of 1921 and a 1928 design for a display stand for the Nederlandse Kabelfabriek which was illustrated in the Dutch magazine, *Wendingen*. They were both highly innovative designs combining graphics and three-dimensional display design in striking abstract compositions. Although Piet Mondrian, the most prominent of all the De Stijl artists, did not have a background in the applied arts, he developed a special relationship with the interior nonetheless, understanding it as a series of flat planes on to which art could be placed.[7] He applied his ideas to his own studios, creating a series of spaces at one with the work he produced within them.

The programme to which the De Stijl artists and architects signed up was not only aesthetically driven, however. It also had a strong social

Theo van Doesburg, tiled corridor in the De Vonk holiday house in Noodwijkerhout, 1917, illustrated in *Innen-Dekoration*, 1925.

agenda. Although they began from completely different starting points, with very different agendas, like the American material feminists, the members of the De Stijl group were firmly committed to the idea that the new environments would bring about new behaviours. In 1918 van Doesburg and Oud created a holiday residence at Noordwijkehout for *De Vonk*, a social centre for workers, especially women. The former was responsible for the tiled floors and the colours of the doors. He explained to his fellow architect, in characteristically De Stijl rhetoric, that 'we can bring our emotion, realised in space and atmosphere, to its full independence precisely through our coloristic and formal projects.'[8] The projects in which the De Stijl artists and architects engaged crossed, or rather ignored, the public–private divide. They created a number of private residences – among them van Doesburg and Jan Wils's town house for the de Lange family in Alkmaar – but they also worked on numerous projects linked to commerce and leisure – cafés, theatres and exhibition halls among them. The abstract, geometric forms and colours of the typical De Stijl interior environment were eminently suitable for both private and public spaces, and helped to erode the differences between them. Van Doesburg's 1923 design for a hall for Amsterdam University provided a

Theo van Doesburg and Cornelis van Eesteren, a draft in pencil, gouache and collage for Amsterdam University Hall, 1923.

strong and appropriately modern frame for the students living within it, for example. The ten rooms, created by van Doesburg together with Hans Arp and Sophie Taeuber-Arp for the Café Aubette in Strasbourg, built between 1926 and 1928, were among the most striking of all the De Stijl public interiors. The aim was to create 'a harmonious whole that conveyed the dynamic quality of modern urban life'.[9] The cinema-dance hall represented the realization of all the interior strategies that the 'coloristes' and the architects had developed together over the previous decade. It was a highly complex, dramatic space dominated by diagonal lines used to mobilize it spatially and to demarcate blocks of colour. The hall was one of the most abstract of all the De Stijl interiors and, not surprisingly, in advance of the taste of the public for which it had been created.[10]

    With its spatially-inspired form and human scale the cabinet-maker/architect, Gerrit Rietveld's 'Red/Blue' chair looked deceptively like a 'sitting-object', albeit an uncomfortable one. In reality, however, it was an abstract, sculptural exercise composed of intersecting and overlapping planes cutting through space. The first version was made of plain wood but in a later version Rietveld added basic colours as a means of reinforcing the chair's planar intersections. He abandoned the idea of working with mass in favour of articulating space, a strategy he was able to apply as equally to a house as to a chair. His design for the inside of the home of the widowed Mrs Truus-Schroeder and her three children was a prime example of an interior design that embodied the De Stijl group's ideas

A facade of the house designed by Gerrit Rietveld for Mrs Truus-Schroeder, Utrecht,
1924.

about colour and space at their most sophisticated. In that house Rietveld developed a number of innovative interior strategies that were to influence designers through the rest of the century. It also represented an ideal model of the way in which a relationship between an avant-garde architect and his client could work. The Schroeder house, designed in 1924, has usually been discussed in the context of the history of modern architecture, rather than in that of the development of the modern interior. Rietveld was first and foremost a cabinet-maker so, from one perspective, the house can be seen also as a large-scale piece of furniture, a container with multiple folding and moveable parts within it. Conceptualizing the house in that way makes sense of the fact that its facades were not formal, architectural statements dictating the nature of its interior spaces but rather reflections of the house's inner functions and spaces. It also makes sense of Rietveld's determination to minimize the idea of the inward-looking, middle-class home by blurring the distinctions between the inside and the outside, and creating a single spatial continuum. That determination was visible in several areas of the house, especially in one of the upstairs corners where Mrs Schroeder's desk was positioned. Two windows met at that corner, opening outwards at ninety degree angles away from each other, such that the corner could be completely eliminated and, when she was at her desk, Mrs Schroeder could almost feel that she was sitting outside. The whole space could be left open, as depicted overleaf, or screens could be added to create a number of discrete spaces. An impression of outside/inside ambiguity was also achieved by Rietveld's detailing of the window in the ground floor guest bedroom. He divided it horizontally positioning half of it in front of a vertical structural pillar and half behind it. The pillar was, therefore, simultaneously both inside and outside the room. The sense of the permeability of the house's walls was reinforced by the presence of balconies in every room which served to bring the outside in and take the inside out.

The house was designed by Rietveld as a dramatic alternative to the large, sixteen-roomed villa in which Mrs Schroeder had lived when her husband had been alive. Situated at the end of a terrace of conventional houses, her new home was conceived as a setting for a modern lifestyle that involved living an active and engaged intellectual life with a minimal number of material possessions. Denying themselves the usual trimmings of middle-class comfort, Mrs Schroeder's family lived in a small, eminently flexible space that was as efficient as it possibly could be. (The presence of a housekeeper in the household undoubtedly made the

The first floor of the house designed by Gerrit Rietveld for Mrs Truus-Schroeder, Utrecht, 1924.

rather arduous work required to transform the house at different times of the day manageable.) Inasmuch as it was made up of distinct spaces – a hallway, a kitchen, a housekeeper's room, Rietveld's own workspace (a space initially left for a garage but never used as such) and a guest room – the ground floor was laid out fairly conventionally. It was a deliberate ploy on Rietveld's behalf to gain building approval. In order to be able to undertake the innovative design he had planned for it he also described the upper space to the local authorities as an 'attic'. In complete contrast to the ground floor the upper area was left as a single open space, although, as we have seen, rooms for sleeping and for privacy could be created through the movement of sliding and folding screens.

In his design for the interior of the Schroeder house Rietveld fulfilled a number of ambitions. The first was to merge painting and architecture. He achieved that aim in a number of ways which included placing coloured squares and rectangles on various parts of the ceilings and walls to achieve different spatial and light effects. In the entrance hall the presence of a white rectangle served to reflect light from the window situated above the door. Colour was used in a much more practical way in the kitchen. Dark-coloured rectangles were painted around the handles of the white cupboard doors to prevent dirty finger-marks being visible. In the same room, the edges of the dark-coloured wooden shutters, stored by day on the top of the wall-mounted cupboards but placed on the windows at night, were painted white so that they wouldn't stand out when stored. The good-sized window sills in all the rooms were painted different colours and, upstairs, a red area on the linoleum floor demarcated the boundaries of the boys' bedroom when the screens closed it off at night. Rietveld's second aim was the efficiency and flexibility of the house's limited interior space. To that end he borrowed a number of strategies from the traditional Japanese interior, including the use of movable, sliding screens (shojis) and the storage of items when not in use (like futons in the Japanese interior). In the guest room, used by the children as a private space, bedding could be stored in a cupboard hidden above the window beneath the upstairs balcony. Two small tables, one yellow and the other blue, folded out from the wall when needed. Indeed folding wooden items could be found all over the house. In several of the rooms folding flaps of wood covered slits in the window frames included for ventilation purposes, while in the girls' bedroom the folding flaps at the ends of the beds transformed them into sofas for daytime use. In the entrance to Mrs Schroeder's own bedroom a small, blue, fold-down desk could be created, topped by a small red shelf. A small washbasin was concealed inside the room.[11]

In line with the ambitions of the De Stijl movement, Rietveld's ultimate aim, however, was the creation of an immaterial environment determined by a sophisticated handling of colour, light and space, and the inter-relationships between them. The children's sparse toys were kept in grey boxes, while a yellow wooden cover concealed the gramophone. The interior of the house was a completely controlled environment with a high level of aesthetic harmony. Given the client's high level of commitment to the project, it was one that worked. The radicalism of the Schroeder house marked it out as a beacon in the history of the abstract interior and it proved hugely influential on the Modernists' subsequent formulation of the interior. It embodied De Stijl's ideas about art and architecture but went beyond them as well, suggesting that an interior space could facilitate a completely new way of living. Idealism continued to underpin the development of the Modernist interior through the 1920s, combining ideas about function and rationality with that of spatial abstraction.

A view of the interior looking out on to the ramp of the Villa Savoye, designed by Le Corbusier, Poissy, 1928–31.

The highly rarefied and individualistic climate of De Stijl was further developed through work undertaken at the Bauhaus in Germany, and by the Purists in France. Not all of those later experiments proved as inhabitable as the Schroeder house, however.[12] Le Corbusier's Villa Savoye, for example, built between 1928 and 1931, was never really a 'home'. It remained an exercise in space, light, texture and colour and was among the most coherent and uncompromising of interior spatial compositions of the Modern Movement. Its most striking characteristic was its sense of internal dynamism, created by what Le Corbusier called the 'architectural promenade' that dominated the occupant's experience of the interior. The architect's total control, both of the pace of movement through the house, either on the ramp or the spiral staircase, and of the vistas experienced en route, all of which took in aspects of both the inside and the outside in a single glance, was evident throughout the house. The view from the interior out on to the exterior ramp through the large expanses of plate glass that were used in the house indicated the high level of inside/outside ambiguity in the house. The absence of distracting colour, the importance given to built-in furniture – from tables canti-levered out from walls and pillars, to cupboards with sliding doors posi-tioned under the windows – the open-endedness of many of the spaces, made possible by new construction techniques and the extensive use of glass, combined to force the occupant to focus exclusively upon the artic-ulation of space and its interplay with light within the building.

The Modernists' desire for transparency was double-edged, how-ever.[13] While it symbolized the death knell for the heavily interiorized middle-class home it could also create unwanted exposure for the occu-pant. Edith Farnsworth's experience of living in a house designed by the German Modernist architect Ludwig Mies van der Rohe and built between 1945 and 1951 brought that point home forcefully. When she lived there Edith Farnsworth furnished the interior of her glass house with a combination of traditional and modern items (see overleaf). Emphasizing the strongly ideological base-line of its Modernist interior Mies's grandson commented that, 'So unconventional was the house that every move and every activity in it assumed an aesthetic quality which challenges behaviour patterns formed in different surroundings.'[14] The difficulty of living up to that level of idealism in the course of everyday life, of being an 'art object', proved to be excessively demanding in that instance.

Mies van der Rohe had been one of the pioneers of the abstract interior. From as early as 1923, in a design for a brick country house which was never built, he had been searching for a way of creating open, fluid spaces within his architectural constructions, of defining areas according to their functions by clustering appropriate items of furniture together, as Frank Lloyd Wright had done before him, and partially separating them with free-standing wall elements.[15] In 1927 his ambition was realized in two projects, a Glass House created with Lilly Reich for the Werkbund's exhibition in Stuttgart and a Velvet and Silk Café, also designed with Reich, for a Berlin trade fair. In both cases he used materials – glass, velvet and silk – to create spaces within his constructions. The apartments he designed for the *Weissenhof Siedling* had movable walls within them. Mies's full realization of fluid space in a residential setting came, however, with the open layout of the interior of a model house he designed, with Reich, for the Berlin Building Exhibition of 1931.[16] The architect supplemented his use of open floor plans and free-standing, movable wall elements, with his furniture items. The effects of the abstract lines, surfaces and masses that they provided added to the spatial sophistication of his interiors. Often with Reich, he designed many of his own pieces of furniture for use within his own interior spaces. Like Le Corbusier, and undoubtedly for the same reasons, he introduced club armchairs into a number of his spaces, complementing them with his own designs, many of them made from tubular steel. His use of daybeds in living spaces suggested the mobile, modern lifestyles of their inhabitants. In 1929 Mies created a little pavilion intended solely as a reception space through which the King of Spain would make his entrance to the International Barcelona Exhibition of which the pavilion was a part. The sophisticated, open-plan building he created rested on slim steel columns and consisted of free-standing walls made of different kinds of marble and glass, forming a circulation space for the king and his entourage. The

An interior of the Farnsworth House, Plano, Illinois, designed by Mies van der Rohe, 1945–51, showing Edith Farnsworth's own furnishings.

interior space was extended outwards into an open area containing a pool, along one side of which Mies constructed a marble wall with a long, low bench at its base. The emphatically horizontal roof of the building appeared to float over the interior space of the pavilion which, itself, was defined by its strong sense of horizontality in combination with the architect's skilful articulation of space, light and texture. Inside the pavilion Mies positioned a chair he had designed especially for it. His modern 'throne', made up of a padded leather seat and back supported by an elegant steel substructure, brought together the qualities of solemnity, dignity and lightness in a single sitting object. Later Mies's Barcelona chair would become an iconic object used in numerous corporate reception areas and architects' homes.

It was not only European artists and architects who set out to explore the idea of the abstract interior defined by its commitment to space, light, colour and texture. The emergence of the abstract interior in the us in the inter-war years was the result, for the most part, of European immigrants taking it there. A striking example of a building that embraced those ideas was the house that the Austrian architect Rudolph M. Schindler created in 1922 for himself and his wife Pauline, along with another couple, Marian and Clyde Chase, in Los Angeles' Kings Road. It contained shared areas – a bathroom and kitchen among them – as well as dedicated studio spaces. The interior's dominant features were the link the architect created between the inside and the outside and his desire to make the building's internal walls thin and movable such that they would not inhibit the interior's open plan. Sliding canvas doors opened from the studios on to patios to create an inside/outside spatial continuum, reinforced by the presence of roof canopies over the patios. As it had been in British Arts and Crafts houses, such as Baillie Scott's 'Blackwell' created two decades earlier, and the work of Charles Rennie Mackintosh in the early century, the light entering into the building from outside was carefully controlled. Most innovative was Schindler's choice of materials. The floor consisted of a flat concrete slab and a few solid concrete walls were also included. A three-inch gap was left between the floor and the walls which the architect filled either with concrete or with clear, or frosted, glass to create a variety of degrees of transparency within the interior space. The other, movable walls were light wooden frames filled with a variety of transparencies provided by frosted glass, clear glass, and a solid insulation board called 'Insulite'.[17] In a corner of the living area the architect placed a fireplace adjacent to a vertical glazed area. The Schindler House took the abstract interior's

The interior in Rudolf M. Schindler's Kings Road House, Los Angeles, 1921–2.

obsession with transparency to an extreme level of sophistication, combining it with a strong awareness of the effects of texture. Schindler had worked in the office of Frank Lloyd Wright at the time when that architect was designing Tokyo's Imperial Hotel. Like Wright himself, and many other Modernist architects, Schindler was indebted to the minimal, functional, and spiritually-unified spaces of the traditional Japanese home

The living room of a San Francisco apartment designed for J. Templeton Crocker by Jean-Michel Frank, 1927, illustrated in Katherine Kahle's *Modern French Decoration*, 1930.

with its 'fusuma' – sliding doors covered with opaque paper; its 'shoji' – wooden lattice sliding doors covered with paper; its 'tokonama' – a small alcove; and its tatami mats.

Texture, used in combination with transparency, became increasingly important to the abstract interior as it developed through the 1930s. It eventually entered the world of the interior decorator, in particular through the work of the French designer Jean-Michel Frank, who introduced a wide variety of textures and materials – vellum, varnished straw marquetry, terracotta and leather among others – into the highly minimal, sensuous interiors he created for wealthy clients in the 1920s and 1930s.[18] The interior spaces he created for Templeton Crocker in San Francisco were among the most dramatic of his creations. By that time the abstract interior had lost its earlier social idealism and its reliance on architecture, however, and had moved into the realm of stylish, modern luxury. The striking Modernist private residences of the inter-war years, with their sophisticated inside spaces, offered a high cultural model of the modern domestic interior which remained in place in the years after 1945. They provided a level of artistic aspiration that was rarely fulfilled in occupied spaces. In artistic terms the Barcelona Pavilion was, perhaps, the ultimate modern interior but, significantly, it was only ever meant to be inhabited for a matter of minutes. Although the Modernist interior was rarely successful in the context of the home, where commercial interiors were concerned, however – spaces that were not meant to be lived in but that needed to make an instant impact on their occupants – the stark Modernist interior, complete with Mies van der Rohe chairs, was soon to come into its own.

10 The Designed Interior

Whether a home is hand- or machine-built, it is no good unless it is properly designed.
George Nelson and Henry Wright[1]

By 1945 all the components of the modern interior were in place. Its formation had been driven by the shifting identities of the inhabitants of the modern world and by the complex, and ever-changing, relationship between the private and the public spheres that inevitably accompanied that level of identity instability. While, on the one hand, the domestic model had broken through the physical boundaries of the 'home' to inhabit a wide variety of semi-public and public inside spaces, on the other, through the intervention of reforming architects and designers, aspects of the public sphere had also entered the private arena. As a result a stylistic spectrum of modern interiors, developed by architects, designers and decorators of all kinds, had emerged, communicating a wide range of cultural, psychological, social, economic and technical values.

In the years between 1945 and the late 1960s the Modernist interior reinvented itself yet again. It did so through the continuing movement of its visual, material and spatial languages between the spheres. Above all its defining characteristics – formed both within modern domestic spaces and in interior sites dedicated to modern public sphere activities – came closer together, both in the home and outside it. In essence a hybrid aesthetic, defined both psychologically and technically, and referred to in writings of the time as 'humanised Modernism', emerged, first in the domestic context but almost immediately afterwards outside it as well. It was 'engineered' by a new generation of reforming architects and designers who extended the ambitions of the inter-war Modernists, in particular their desire to create a *Gesamtkunstwerk*, to prioritize the role of the architect, to create overtly modern spaces that reflected their own era and to cross the private and the public divide. Although that new approach was driven by idealistic architects and designers working at the highest social and cultural levels, in that era of accelerated mass mediation it quickly became a popular ideal as well. The mass media also brought architects and designers themselves into the public arena and the modern 'designed interior', understood both as a mechanism for social elevation and as a means by which large numbers of people could participate in the exciting new world of progressive modernity, became a mass phenomenon, as the modern idioms of Art Deco and Streamlining had been in the inter-war years.

The message of inter-war European architectural and design Modernism was especially strong in the US in the years after 1945. Following the migration of Josef Urban, Gilbert Rhode, Rudolph Schindler and others across the Atlantic, the additional presence of German Modernists such as Walter Gropius, Mies van der Rohe and Marcel Breuer on American soil – as well as that of a number of other Europeans, including the Finnish Jugendstil architect Eliel Saarinen, who took the directorship of Michigan's Cranbrook Academy – helped to further disseminate that message. The ideas adopted by those Modernist giants relating to the interior – the open plan, the continuity between inside and outside, the use of built-in furniture and items of 'equipment', and the emphasis upon spatial articulation, among many others – inevitably fed into American post-war developments. The 'organic' interiors of the American Modernist, Frank Lloyd Wright, were also frequently referenced in both contemporary architectural and interior magazines as well as in more popular publications. Attention focused on his commitment to the idea of the *Gesamtkunstwerk*, on his use of texture – exposed stone on chimney breasts, for example – and on the hearth as a focal point for open-plan living spaces. The interiors of his own home, Taliesin, were widely reproduced in those years offering a seductive model for others to follow. An image of Wright's living area in that house appeared in a 1955 Italian publication titled *L'Arredamento Moderno*.[2] George Nelson and Henry Wright, in their influential book *Tomorrow's House* (1945), which appealed for a new architecture that would break free from the bonds of stylistic revivalism, described Taliesin as 'one of the most wonderful houses ever built'.[3]

Nelson and Wright's commitment to move beyond the shadow of stylistic revivalism, nostalgia and the obsession with antiques that had dominated both elite and popular American domestic interiors through the twentieth century was echoed by others. In *Goodbye, Mr. Chippendale*, published in 1944, the American interior designer T. H. Robsjohn-Gibbings, for example, blamed the decorators. 'The words "interior

The living area of Taliesin, Wisconsin, the home of Frank Lloyd Wright, designed by
Wright, illustrated in Roberto Aloi's *L'Arredamento Moderno*, 1955.

decorating" today', he wrote, 'bring a mental picture of busy people
running around with a pick-me-up for wilting upholstery, and scouring
Third Avenue for "something amusing and chic" all for ten per cent
profit'.[4] Significantly Robsjohn-Gibbings described himself as an 'interior
designer', a member, that is, of a new community of aesthetic practitioners
who saw themselves as highly professionalized and closely aligned with,

and above all equal to, architects. A few years later an English writer defined the interior design profession's preoccupations as being with planning, scale, heating, lighting, surfaces, furniture, pattern and colour, thereby complementing those of the architect.[5] Importantly, also, the interior designer was seen to play a more significant role in public interiors as well as in domestic spaces. The same English writer explained that, 'This distinction between public and private is not always understood . . . There is no point in dressing up the hall of an Insurance building to look like the entrance to a stately home. No-one will be deceived. The great bowl of florist's flowers will smell of money rather than of earth. Such nostalgic gestures, indeed any attempt to introduce a bogus personal touch into a public place, are mistaken.'[6]

Interior designers largely displaced interior decorators and took on the mantle of architectural Modernism. Their remit was to integrate interiors with their architectural frames and to create interior spaces that were conceived as integrated wholes.[7] As the post-war years progressed, and the concept of the interior decorator became increasingly linked with antiquated upper-class interiors and feminine amateurism in the domestic sphere and the designer with masculine professionalism in the public arena, the difference between decorators and designers came to be seen as a gendered one. In spite of the fact that they continued to work with wealthy, upper-class clients for the most part, and mostly, but not exclusively, in the domestic arena, professional interior decorators were significantly marginalized. Latter-day Modernists saw the work of the decorators as feminized, trivial and superficial and believed that it overemphasized the role of textiles and ignored that of architectural structure. Furthermore they associated interior decoration with social aspiration and an excessive proximity to the media. Interior designers increasingly distanced themselves from what was, by the turn of the twentieth and twenty-first centuries, being relabelled, in both higher educational and professional circles, as 'interior architecture' or 'spatial design'. The gendered and sexual implications of that hierarchy have remained largely unchanged since then and, although the interior's capacity for self-expression and identity formation have become widely acknowledged, the concept of 'interior decoration' has still to be recuperated.

Much attention was directed at the domestic sphere in the years after 1945 but the post-war US also devoted most of its energies to the reworking of Modernism in the context of corporate interiors. That the same approach could be adopted in both spaces lay in the fact that a generation of American architect-designers – among them Charles and Ray Eames, Eero Saarinen (the son of Eliel), George Nelson, Harry Bertoia, Alexander Girard and Hans and Florence Knoll – became preoccupied with extending Modernism's commitment to creating mass-produced furniture items that could be used equally well at home and in the office. Though the preoccupations of those designers were primarily aesthetic and technical, and significantly less political and social than those of their European predecessors, ironically the furniture items and interiors they created fed into a new form of popular domesticity, as well as into the public spaces of post-war corporate capitalism, on an unprecedented scale.

Charles Eames was not an interior designer but a *Gesamtkunstwerk* architect in the Modernist tradition. He turned towards furniture design as a means of translating his ideas about materials and manufacturing technologies into modern forms. Like Le Corbusier before him Eames looked to factory mass production and other areas outside the home as starting points for a renewed language of design for the interior. While Le Corbusier had looked to the sanatorium and the gentleman's club Eames found his inspiration in technological developments, in particular plywood moulding, used by the military in the creation of leg splints, and cycle-welding, developed by the Chrysler Corporation in 1941 but which was also adopted by the military.[8] Created with Eero Saarinen, the furniture designs that Eames exhibited at the New York Museum of Modern Art's *Organic Design in Home Furnishings* exhibition of 1941 were shown in a range of settings. One installation included a dining table and chairs, positioned on a patterned rug and accompanied by two credenzas and a collection of chairs located around a triangular coffee table. The scene evoked an open plan, multi-functional domestic space. Another installation at the same exhibition, consisting of two chairs combined with a low storage cabinet topped by plants and containing books, was more ambiguous and could have been read either as a domestic scene or as an office space. That domestic/workspace ambiguity rapidly became a hallmark of Eames's designs. Focusing on their technical innovations he created furniture pieces which offered a level of modern comfort both in the home and in the workplace. A simple change of upholstery fabric could transform one of his chairs from a domestic object into a non-domestic one in an instant. Depending on whether it was upholstered in a textured cloth or vinyl, a 1954 steel-framed sofa, modelled on a built-in sofa in the seating alcove of Eames's own house in Santa Monica, could be read

Charles Eames's Tandem Sling Seating in Washington (later Dulles) International Airport, Virginia, 1962.

either as a domestic artefact or as one destined for an office or a reception area in an office building.[9] All the furniture pieces that Eames created through the 1940s and '50s displayed the same schizophrenia. His aluminium group furniture pieces of 1958, for example, originally created for Alexander Girard, who had wanted some lightweight pieces to use both within and outside a house he was building in Ohio, were quickly developed for use in a wide range of public spaces.[10]

While Eames worked in the context of mass production and defined his furniture designs as technical achievements first and foremost, he was also fully aware of the significance of the interior settings for which they were destined. Like Henry Van de Velde and others before him, Eames created a home and studio for himself and his family. The house was built from pre-fabricated parts and resembled, from the outside, a glass 'shed' or, alternatively, a simple Japanese house. He filled the interior with his own furniture designs and numerous personal mementos which have been linked to Eames's commitment to the notion of 'functioning decoration', an important characteristic of the new, humanized face of Modernism.[11] The high levels of decoration in the interior of Eames's Santa Monica house have been attributed to the intervention of Charles's wife Ray.[12] A continuum undoubtedly existed in the couple's minds between their domestic spaces and their work environments.[13] They ate breakfast in their home and their other meals at their office, for example.[14] Eames's furniture functioned equally effectively within his pre-fabricated home and in his work area. By extension he offered his clients – both individual and corporate – the possibility of moving seamlessly between their domestic and their non-domestic spaces. Although his chairs were frequently depicted as isolated objects they also acted as powerful representations of a newly defined model of the modern interior that recognized little difference between the private and public spheres. While the mass-produced multiple seating Eames created for airport waiting spaces – Washington's Dulles airport and Chicago's O'Hare airport among them – established a blueprint for stylish public leisure and travel spaces internationally from the late 1950s onward, no self-respecting contemporary house would be complete without an Eames chair, most probably his 1956 lounge chair and ottoman created originally for film director Billy Wilder. A stylish interior by Vittoriano Viganò illustrated in an Italian book on interiors, *Forme et colore dell'arredamento modern*, of 1967 (overleaf), demonstrates the ease with which Eames's 1956 lounge chair, complete with ottoman, could be integrated into modern domestic spaces at that time.[15] Eames's designs reflected the ubiquity and iconicity that Marcel Breuer's earlier tubular steel chairs had set out to achieve in a previous era, but with the advances in manufacturing technologies, the expansion of office spaces and other public sphere interiors, and the democratization of the modern style, Eames's achievements were arguably more significant in the early post-war years.

Charles Eames's refusal to acknowledge the separation of the spheres also underpinned the work of the designer Florence Knoll and her involvement with the Knoll Planning Unit. Her distinctive achievement was not only to create modern furniture designs both for the home and the

A 1960s interior, designed by Vittorio Vigano, containing a lounge chair and ottoman made of leather and rosewood, designed by Charles Eames in 1956, illustrated in *Forma e Colore dell'Arredamento Moderno,* 1967.

office but also to bring the iconic work of others, both older Modernists such as Mies van de Rohe, as well as her contemporaries, Harry Bertoia and Eero Saarinen among them, into that new context. The model of 'corporate Modernism' that she helped to create was an extremely powerful one, mirroring the developments in office block building in the US of the immediate post-war years. An architect by training who had worked with Gropius and Breuer, Florence Knoll created a new language for the modern office and the home that was both modern and inhabitable.[16] Her approach was exemplified in a number of the interiors she created, among them an office for Connecticut General in 1957 and another for the National Bank of Miami in 1957–8.[17] Her 1950s design for Knoll Associates'

The entrance area of the Knoll Showroom in San Francisco, 1954, designed by Florence Knoll.

An interior containing a range of furniture items designed by Alvar Aalto, late 1930s, illustrated in Mary Davis Gillies's *All About Modern Decorating*, 1942.

San Francisco showroom, which contained a number of Mies van der Rohe's Barcelona chairs positioned on a textured carpet around a glass-topped coffee table, provided a model for countless Modernist domestic interiors and commercial reception areas in 'architect-designed' interior spaces for years to come. An illustration in the 1967 book *Forme et colore dell'arredamento moderno* depicted a highly stylish combination living/dining room which combined Barcelona chairs with a pedestal table and chairs designed by Eero Saarinen, also manufactured by Knoll.

Caricaturing the language of the modern interior style some years earlier in *Interiors* magazine George Nelson had described it as compris-

An interior in Philip Goodwin's New York apartment containing chairs designed by Bruno Mathsson, late 1930s, illustrated in Dan Cooper's *Inside Your Home*, 1946.

ing 'a large rubber plant . . . , a couple of Aalto stools and armchairs, a modern coffee table, and a few pieces of prehistoric-looking pottery'.[18] The inter-war work of the Finnish architect, Alvar Aalto, which, like that of Frank Lloyd Wright, had embraced an 'organic' aesthetic, was also widely reproduced and admired in the US in the years after 1945. His bent ply birchwood furniture featured in a living room illustrated by Nelson and Wright in their 1945 book.[19] A more popular book, *All About Modern Decorating*, written by the editor of *Interior Decorating* magazine, Mary

Davis Gillies, also included an interior containing Aalto furniture. The caption explained that 'its comfortable but svelte lines point a finger to the future'.[20] The interior contained bent plywood armchairs, a drinks trolley, a number of three-legged stackable stools, and a round coffee table, all designed by Aalto and arranged to create an overtly modern, yet comfortable, setting (p. 194). Gillies emphasized the importance to her readers of acquiring a modern interior as a means of raising their social profile through the creation of a fictional consumer. 'Mrs. Smart Set', she explained, 'didn't need a separate dining-room'.[21] She also referred to a number of contemporary American architects and interior designers who were fast becoming household names, among them Gilbert Rhode, Ed Wormley, William Pahlmann, George Kosmak and Russel Wright. Frequent references in popular interior-related publications were also made to other Scandinavian achievements, especially those of Sweden. The author of *Inside Your Home* (1946), exhorting his readers to appreciate the changes that could be made to the small home, remarked that 'Sweden, a country wise in the humanities, understands these simple things better than we do'.[22] Many iconic Swedish designs were introduced into American interiors at that time, among them Bruno Mathsson's iconic bentwood armchair with a webbed seat, which was introduced into the living space in Philip Goodwin's New York apartment, illustrated in *Inside Your Home*. The austerity of that small space with its plain walls and carpets was humanized by the inclusion of striped curtain fabric, pictures on the wall, and vase of flowers, as well as by the organic forms of Mathsson's chairs.

Through the 1940s and '50s developments in Sweden focused on the continuation of the democratic, rational programme of inter-war Modernism that had played such an important role in that country, and on the importance of treating the environments of the home, leisure, work and commerce in similar ways. An article published in the Swedish magazine *Kontur* in 1958 titled 'Meet a Swedish Family', demonstrated that although family members might be involved in a variety of different activities – resting at home, filling the car with petrol, working in the office, being educated at school, having a manicure and swimming at the local pool – they could all be undertaken in equally modern-looking spaces. The message was clear. There was no longer, as there had been in the Victorian era, one interior aesthetic for the home and another for public interiors. Through the transfer, in the hands of the inter-war Modernists, of the language of the public sphere into the home, and the post-war movement of that language, humanized through its encounter with domesticity, back into the interior spaces of the public arena, the two spheres had come to resemble each other much more closely. The distinction in people's lives between the private world of domesticity and the public world of work, commerce and leisure did not collapse completely, of course, but the languages and values of those different spaces came to have more and more in common with one another and to facilitate movement between them. While a negative interpretation might suggest that privacy became more elusive and that enhanced levels of engagement with work and consumption were encouraged, a more positive reading could highlight the emergence of a less enclosed and repressive domesticity and of more humanized public interior spaces.

Whatever the interpretation of the desire on the part of architects and interior designers to create a closer relationship between the interiors of the private and the public spheres, the presence of that rapprochement was acutely felt in the us, and in many European countries as well, in the years after 1945. Several of the latter also used the arrival of the 'designed interior' as a vehicle through which to express the distinctiveness of their modernized, post-war national identities. Italy was particularly quick to build on its pre-war relationship with international Modernism, the existence of a post-war generation of trained architects willing and able to work on interior, furniture and product design projects, and its wide availability of small-scale manufacturing firms specializing in furniture production. These came together to exchange the development of a neo-Modernist interior and furniture movement predicated upon the named designer as a 'guarantor' of enhanced social status and added value. The names of Gio Ponti, Achille Castiglioni, Marco Zanuso, Ettore Sottsass, Jr, Vico Magistretti, Joe Colombo and others filled the pages of Italy's glossy interior magazines – *Interni*, *Abitare* and *Domus* among them. A living/dining room created by Osvaldo Borsani for the Tecno company in Milan and containing a flexible sofa/day-bed also created by that designer, provided just one example of the way in which many Italian designers, educated as architects for the most part, worked on both individual furniture pieces and their interior settings (see overleaf). While, in the 1940s, the Italian neo-Modern Movement set out with the aim of building new, furnished homes for the homeless and the working classes, it was rapidly transformed in the 1950s and '60s into a more elitist phenomenon embracing new materials and forms and aligning itself with the idea of the 'good life'. An aesthetic of modern luxury marked out the culturally aware

A combined living and dining area containing mass-produced furniture, designed by Osvaldo Borsani, Milan, 1955, illustrated in Roberto Alois's *L'Arredamento Moderno*, 1955.

middle classes from the rest of society at that time. As in the US the new Italian interior could be found both in private homes and in the inside spaces of public buildings. While also designing interiors for private clients Achille Castiglioni created interiors for the Splügen Bräu Brasserie in Milan in 1960 and the Gavina shop in the same city two years later.[23] Joe Colombo also created a number of commercial interiors including, between 1962 and 1964, an entrance hall for Sardinia's Pontinental hotel, and interiors for the Lella Sport store and the Mario Valentino shoe shop, both in Milan, in 1966 and 1967 respectively.[24]

The Italian neo-Modernist interior was more strongly rooted in domesticity than its American equivalent, however. In Italy itself it represented the domestic modernization of a population that had not long ago been working on the land and that had had to engage with modernity very quickly. In the international marketplace, however, it stood for middle-class domestic sophistication. In 1972 an exhibition titled *Italy: The New Domestic Landscape: Achievements and Problems of Italian Design* was held at New York's Museum of Modern Art, which positioned the domestic interior at the heart of Italian post-war design, questioned the continuing relevance of the optimistic Modernist project in an era that was characterized by the impact of popular culture, and emphasized the emergence of a

An interior containing Pop objects designed by Paul Clark, mid-1960s.

new set of design values that were more at home in the art gallery than the home.

A similar crisis occurred on British soil in the 1960s. The transient values of popular culture confronted those of Modernism at that time resulting in a flurry of designs for materially and stylistically expendable lifestyle accompaniments – from clothing, to posters, to drinking mugs –

which were characterized by their 'massive initial impact and small sustaining power'.[25] Seen as a highly transient area of visual, material and spatial culture that could be changed at will to suit to the shifting identities of its inhabitants, the interior was heavily implicated in that crisis of values. From the poster-festooned bedrooms of young people, to the spaces in the clubs in which they danced, to the brightly coloured patterned surfaces of the retail stores where they shopped for clothes and other lifestyle accessories, the 'Pop' interior quickly became a reality. Retailers, from Terence Conran to Dodo Designs, supplied young British consumers with many of the objects they needed to embellish their interior spaces.

By the 1970s however, the progressiveness that had characterized Pop design had been replaced by a new mood of retrospection that encouraged a reworking of the modern interior. Beginning its journey by reviving the Arts and Crafts Movement before quickly moving on to Art Nouveau and thence to Art Deco and on to 1950s' 'Mid-century Modern', the style-based 'retro' movement embraced, in only a few years, the entire historical period of the modern interior. In so doing it was re-enacting the Victorian interior's embrace of the past as a means of addressing the present. By the 1970s however, the past being revisited was a modern, rather than a pre-modern, one. That spirit of retrospection also stimulated a popular interest in the history of modern architecture, and by implication in the modern interior. The 'period room' concept – hitherto restricted to pre-modern spaces – was extended over the next few decades to include interiors created within the era of industrial modernity. International organizations, such as DOCOMOMO, dedicated themselves to restoring modern buildings and their interiors. In Germany the Bauhaus building in Weimar was restored, in Poissy in France the Villa Savoye was made accessible to visitors, and in Utrecht Rietveld's Schroeder House was also opened, marking the growing interest in those iconic Modern buildings and their interior spaces. In England, the National Trust opened a number of late nineteenth- and early twentieth-century houses to the public, including Edwin Lutyens's Castle Drogo in Devon and Erno Goldfinger's family house in Willow Road in London.[26] Driven by developments in social, rather than architectural history, homes that had been inhabited by people located at the margins of society, such as those located in New York's tenement buildings, were also restored and opened to visitors. Tinged with nostalgia, they proved to be highly popular.

Adding the revival of early modern spaces to its more contemporary stylistic alternatives, the modern interior continued to develop through the last years of the twentieth century, and into the early years of the twenty-first century, in response to many of the same forces that had determined it passage through earlier years. The determination of many architects to influence and control the interior spaces of their buildings continued to play an important role. The English architects John Pawson and Norman Foster, for example, took full responsibility for their interiors, the former supervising every last detail of his strikingly minimal creations, the latter controlling the design of many of the items destined for the inside spaces of his buildings. Many other contemporary architects, including Arata Isozaki in Japan, Jean Nouvel in France and Frank Gehry in the US, also sought to control the interiors of their buildings. In recent years the role of architects as the creators of interiors has been joined by that of product designers, including the French Philippe Starck, as well as by fashion designers, the American Ralph Lauren, the Italian Giorgio Armani and the English Jasper Conran among them. The enhanced role of 'designer-culture' in recent decades has meant that all designers, whatever their specializations, have come to be seen first and foremost as creators of 'lifestyles' and capable, therefore, of designing the interior environments in which those lifestyles are lived out.

The 'minimal interior', based on Modernism's machine aesthetic, emerged in the 1980s but has sustained its popularity into the early twenty-first century. It was especially visible in the abstract forms of late twentieth-century and early twenty-first century commercial spaces, including Tokyo's fashion boutiques and international luxury hotels. A 2005 design by the Japanese group Superpotato, led by Takashi Sugimoto, for the Park Hyatt Seoul Hotel, exemplifies minimalism in action. With its white walls, minimally furnished spaces and sparse, cantilevered shelves, Shiro Kuramata's 1987 store, created for Issey Miyake, provided a highly theatrical backcloth for the 'art objects' displayed within it, while the interior of Giorgio Armani's flagship fashion store in Hong Kong, designed by Claudio Silvestrin in 2002, took the idea of the minimal interior to new levels. Its exaggerated simplicity and use of concealed lighting produced a dramatic backcloth for the stylish clothing displayed within it. So ubiquitous was the minimal interior at the beginning of the twenty-first century that it even entered the realm of popular television. In a 2004 episode of the popular BBC comedy series, *Absolutely Fabulous*, for example, lead character Edina was so desperate for her kitchen to be in the latest, 'ultra-minimal' style, she had her angst-ridden, heavily bespectacled female interior designer remove the stairs.[27] On entering the room, Edina nearly

A bathroom in the Park Hyatt Seoul Hotel designed by Superpotato, 2005.

plummeted to her death to the sound of canned laughter. 'It's not enough now to have the latest clothes', explained the tortured victim of fashion, frantically flipping the pages of *The World of Interiors* and calling in a medium to help her discover her past lives so that she could see where she had come from, 'you have to have the latest interior as well'. 'Other people have art, I have my bar', proclaimed an interviewee in yet another BBC television programme, *Home*, aired in 2006, as he proudly pointed to the minimal bar counter and stools, made mostly of metal and glass, located in his living room.[28] The mere possession of minimally styled domestic

The interior of Giorgio Armani's flagship store in Hong Kong, designed by Claudio Silvestrin, 2002.

furniture items fabricated in modern materials was sufficient to denote the presence of 'art' or 'value' in that interior.

However accelerated the changes to the contexts in which it has manifested itself, most of the defining characteristics of the modern interior are still in place. Its simultaneous commitment to two, often opposing, sets of values denoting modern private domesticity and public life; its inherent dynamism created by the need to continually address the divide between the spheres; its familiarity with the ever increasing demands of the mass media; and its integration into the fashion system, have combined to give it an inbuilt facility for constant adaptation and self renewal. In the early twenty-first century it continues to mutate and to address the continually renewed context in which it finds itself.

Conclusion

Wouldn't you rather be inside?
Southside Shopping Arcade, Wandsworth, London, 2005

While the forces of industrial modernity that surfaced in the mid-nineteenth century remained substantially in place through the twentieth century, the speed at which they effected change inevitably accelerated. Through the work of architects, designers, decorators and others, and the dissemination of their ideas and practices through the mass media, the appearance of the modern interior *did* change continually over that time period. Those style changes did not disturb the basic role of the modern interior, however, as the location for the key experiences of modernity. In that capacity it was influenced by the ever-changing relationship between privacy and publicity, and linked to mass production and mass consumption, identity formation, the enhanced role of 'art' in everyday life and the continually strengthening role of the mass media.

In the early twenty-first century the models of private domesticity and public anti-domesticity that were established in the nineteenth century are still visible, even though they continue to transform themselves and to become almost indistinguishable from each other. The divide between the separate spheres continues to exist. On the one hand, the comfort, refuge and privacy, opportunities for self-reflection, and links to tradition offered by 'home' remain in place, while the public spaces within the giant 'sheds' housing shopping malls, cinemas, leisure centres and exhibition spaces, continue to provide their paradoxical mix of anonymity and surveillance. An anonymous crowd of people, for example, go about their daily activities – some shopping, some resting – in the public spaces of shopping malls, unaware that they are under continual observation. On the other hand domestic 'living rooms', complete with sofas and coffee tables, populate not only the home but also bookshops, coffee shops, dentists' waiting rooms and shopping malls. In addition, with the advent of multiple television channels and the internet, the

A shopping mall in Calgary, Alberta, 2005.

intrusion of the media into our private spaces has reached new and unprecedented levels.

As we have seen, Modernism's legacy continues into the early twenty-first century. However, the power of commerce has stripped it of its ideological underpinnings and transformed it into just one more fashionable interior style. Unable to resist the pull of consumerism it has been transformed into the 'minimal interior', a result of the encounter of modern art with architecture and a marker of modern luxury connoting high levels of 'cultural capital' through what is absent rather than what is present. In contrast to the nineteenth-century home interior, which displayed its occupants' social status through an accretion of objects, the minimal interior has declared itself an artwork and a sign of the enhanced social status that now flows from merging art with everyday life. The approach towards the modern interior which, in the hands of Gerrit Rietveld, Mies van der Rohe and other Modernists focused on the immateriality of space and the idea of a new, anti-materialistic lifestyle had, by the late twentieth century, succumbed to the power of the marketplace and the imperatives of the fashion system. Another of Modernism's legacies – the adoption of the rational processes developed in the workplace into the home – is less stylistically determined. That approach is still visible today in women's magazines and consumer advice publications. The author of an article published in *Good Housekeeping* magazine in January 2003, for instance, offered '50 expert ideas for organising your home', which included the implementation of a clothes storage system involving 'grouping tops and bottoms separately in co-ordinating colours', 'filing appliance instructions in document files' and 'allocating an area [of the house] for household administration'.[1] With the advent of the 'home office', Frederick's 1913 dream has, on one level, finally became a reality.

By far the strongest force to influence the development of the modern interior in recent years, however, has been its relationship with the mass media. In the 1940s in the US, and later elsewhere, television began to take on a parallel role to magazines in the home. As they had been in nineteenth-century theatre productions and inter-war films, interiors were presented to consumers through the medium of television in a variety of ways. They were the subjects of advertisements, the backcloths for other products in advertisements, and the settings for dramas and comedies. This brought into play yet another version of the 'interior within the interior', this time one located, like Loos's 'theatre', within the domestic sphere. The American comedy programme *I Love Lucy* is just one example among many of a 1950s American comedy set within a strikingly modern-looking domestic environment. While room sets in department stores encouraged a level of identification with their audience with the sole purpose of stimulating consumption, the main role of televised interiors was, rather, to offer their audiences a level of familiarity that would persuade them to 'consume' the programmes on offer. Consuming the interior in that sense was, therefore, more about television viewing figures than buying a set of chairs. The increasingly popular activity of DIY (Do-It-Yourself) reached the television screen in the 1950s. At that time the emphasis was firmly upon the role of the 'handyman' in the house – the constructor of shelves and the installer of kitchen units.

By the early years of the twenty-first century however, in order to retain and expand its audiences television has had to use subtler strategies. The domestic interior, in which people are most 'themselves', and which, for many people, represents one of their largest financial investments, inevitably plays several important roles in that context. Firstly it is the most frequently used setting for many different kinds of programmes. Cooking programmes are often filmed in domestic kitchen sets. More recently a range of 'public' interiors has begun to feature in television programmes, sometimes taking on the central dramatic role. *The Office*, a British comedy set in the workplace which has also been very successful in the US, focuses on that space as one which, stereotypally, facilitates certain kinds of social behaviour. Another British television drama series of the early twenty-first century, *Hotel Babylon*, is based in a glamorous, ultra-modern hotel, closely resembling those in the Schrager chain. The role of social realism in television programmes has also meant that many popular drama series are set in hospitals, prisons or police stations, among other places, in an attempt to mirror 'everyday life' and make the viewer feel part of the action. Other television programmes focus on the interior as its main subject matter. They include 'make-over' programmes – most famously the British *Changing Rooms*, which has already been discussed in the introduction to this book. That programme is still enormously successful internationally, playing as it does on its audience's voyeuristic desire to enter other people's lives and living rooms.[2] It embraces a theatrical 'anything goes stylistically' approach to the interior, which is defined, first and foremost, as an agent in identity formation. It also grants a significant level of power to designers, one of the key agents of change, as we have seen, in the development of the modern interior. They are portrayed as having unlimited imaginations and the capacity to change the appearance of the interior with the wave of a wand. Other programmes approach the domestic interior from slightly different perspectives. One, for example, builds on the long-standing fascination of the public with celebrities' homes, while others set out to provide information and advice to people who see their homes as a form of investment which would benefit from the addition of an enhanced interior.

By the early years of the twenty-first century the idea of 'lifestyle' has come to dominate private consumption and, along with fashionable dress, holidays, leisure activities and private transportation ownership, the home has become increasingly important in that context. Especially in its idealized and desired form, home is the place where personal identities are still formed, for the most part, and the destination for most consumed goods, from new technology products to furniture and furnishings. It is not only the goods within interiors that are consumed, however. Interiors themselves, particularly those in hotels, shopping malls, supermarkets, restaurants, banks, theme parks, airport lounges, ocean liners, and other commercially oriented spaces, have themselves become objects of consumption. As the idea of 'lifestyle' became the end in sight within consumer culture, the role of branding also increased in significance and interiors were integrated into marketing and branding strategies.

Increasingly global companies seek to brand themselves through the language of their interiors as well as through their graphic design. The experience of a McDonald's restaurant, of a Hard Rock Café, or of a Planet Hollywood, is, in any city in the world, a more or less standardized one. The same principle applies to shops – from Max Mara fashion stores, to the Body Shop, to Gap, the interiors of which utilize the same colour schemes and display techniques across the world, to chains of hotels, such as the Madonna Inn in the US, theme parks and shopping malls where the same franchised shops appear together in different venues. In those contexts the interior has become less an extension of architecture than of graphic design, advertising and branding. The more standardized mass-produced interiors become however, the greater is the desire to create 'difference' at a higher level of the market through an open alliance with designer-culture. The luxurious stylishness of the interiors of French designer Philippe Starck's New York hotels, for exam-

ple – which have a family resemblance but are highly individualized

The interior of the Royalton Hotel in New York, designed by Philippe Starck, 1988.

nonetheless – fulfil the same market need as couture clothing and hand-crafted objects.

Alongside the erosion of 'place', a result of the corporate standard-ization of the interior, the well-documented lack of differentiation between shopping malls and theme parks is another consequence of the branded interior. As the appeal of lifestyle dominates everything else within consumer culture it becomes increasingly hard to differentiate between the experiences of pleasure and leisure and the act of consump-tion. Themed interiors can be found in both leisure spaces and shopping malls. SeaWorld in San Diego for example, has been described as a 'mall with fish'. Much has been written about Canada's West Edmonton Mall in Alberta which, until fairly recently, was the largest mall in the world. At its centre is an enormous artificial seaside complete with beach and waves. The spectacular nature of that surprising element within a shop-ping mall parallels the use of spectacle in early department stores. Its presence evokes an endless debate about the nature of authenticity and pushes to an extreme the idea that fantasy is an inherent feature of the modern interior. Given its long-standing role as a 'stage set', this is, perhaps, not surprising.

Another notable feature of contemporary urban and suburban life is the merging of spaces and the interiorization that have gone on within commercial buildings. As a result ever larger conglomerations of spaces, and of spaces within spaces, have emerged. In Shibuya, one of Tokyo's busiest shopping areas, for example, the spaces that house the railway and subway stations also contain a department store and a large food court boasting a wide variety of restaurants. The travellers/shoppers/eaters passing through Shibuya can move from one area to another with-out ever needing to go 'outside'. That phenomenon is familiar to many of us living in the early twenty-first century, experienced in both the shop-ping mall and the leisure complex, among other places. Tropical Islands, a huge covered resort in eastern Germany, contains a rainforest and a Balinese lagoon inside what was previously a zeppelin hangar, a favourite structure of the Modernists. The mall in Caesar's Forum in Las Vegas takes the idea of being 'outside inside' to an extreme, providing shoppers and tourists with an overhead 'inside' sky and clouds. That phenomenon, an example of the 'hyper-reality' observed by Jean Baudrillard, has an obvious relationship with the need to control the weather.[3] In Las Vegas it provides protection from the scorching summer heat. In the interior of the Venetian hotel, for example, the narrow streets, bridges, canals and

'Venice' in the interior of the Venetian Hotel, Las Vegas, Nevada, 2006.

gondolas of Italy's Venice have been recreated in an inside space with a blue sky/ceiling overhead. It provides an opportunity for tourists to fantasize about being in that exotic European city, or even believe that they really are there, and above all to consume the goods in the shops constructed in that space. Peter Weir's 1998 film *The Truman Show* provided a filmic parallel to the inside/outside ambiguity of Las Vegas's shopping malls. Seemingly set in a small American town on an island, it is revealed that the entire film has taken place within a huge dome containing a television set, and that the audience has been watching a television programme being made within a film, and a television set within a film set. What Truman believed to be an open horizon was in fact a backcloth with a blue sky painted on to it. The film represents media intrusion into the private sphere, hidden surveillance and the ambiguous relationship between the 'inside' and the 'outside' at their most extreme.

The increasing levels of complexity that characterize realized, represented and idealized interiors in early twenty-first-century private and public spaces suddenly seem unproblematic, however, when they are considered alongside the implications for the interior of the concept of 'virtual space'. Perhaps in that context, in which new inside and outside spaces can be accessed through a computer screen – which can be viewed at home, at work, in the gym, in the garden, in an aeroplane or on the top of a mountain – the idea of modernity, of the separate spheres, and above all of the modern interior, cease to have any meaning.

References

Introduction

1 In his book *The Emergence of the Interior: Architecture, Modernity, Domesticity* (London and New York, 2007), p. 2, Charles Rice discusses the idea of the 'double interior', borrowed from Walter Benjamin. He describes it as being 'both as a physical, three-dimensional space, as well as an image'.

2 Marshall Berman's account of modernity, expressed in his book *All That is Solid Melts into Air: The Experience of Modernity* (London, 1983), is described by Bernhard Rieger as 'a maelstrom of perpetual disintegration and renewal that left no stone unturned', in 'Envisioning the Future: British and German Reactions to the Paris World Fair in 1900', in *Meanings of Modernity: Britain from the Late-Victorian Era to World War II*, ed. M. Daunton and B. Rieger (Oxford and New York, 2001), p. 145. David Frisby explains that for Max Weber modernity was a result of 'modern western rationalism', in 'Analysing Modernity', *Tracing Modernity: Manifestations of the Modern in Architecture and the City*, ed. Mari Hvattum and Christian Hermansen (London and New York, 2004), p. 11. Yet another approach to the concept of modernity is provided by Don Slater: 'consumer culture is bound up with the *idea* of modernity, of modern experience, and of modern social subjects', in *Consumer Culture and Modernity* (Cambridge, 1997), p. 9.

3 M. Nava, 'Modernity's Disavowal: Women, the City and the Department Store', in *The Shopping Experience*, ed. P. Falk and C. Campbell (London, 1997), p. 57.

4 Walter Benjamin, *The Arcades Project*, trans. H. Eiland and K. McLaughlin (Cambridge, MA and London, 2004), p. 8.

5 See J. Wolff, 'The Invisible Flâneuse: Women and the Literature of Modernity', in *The Problems of Modernity: Adorno and Benjamin*, ed. A. Benjamin (London and New York, 1989), pp. 141–56, and E. Wilson, *The Sphinx in the City* (London, 1991).

6 Mari Hvattum and Christian Hermansen explain in their introduction to *Tracing Modernity: Manifestations of the Modern in Architecture and the City* (London and New York, 2004), that 'modernity is embedded in the very fabric of society', p. xi.

7 David Frisby, for example, pointed out that Georges-Eugène Haussmann's reconfiguration of Paris in the mid-nineteenth century could be seen as a redefinition of the city as an 'interior' space, dedicated to the bourgeoisie, which sought to exclude the working classes from its centre. 'The *flâneur* in Social Theory', in K. Tester, *The flâneur* (London and New York, 1994), pp. 81–110.

8 See L. Davidoff and C. Hall, *Family Fortunes: Men and Women of the English Middle Class, 1780–1850* (London, 1987) for an account of the separate spheres.

9 Although the reality of middle-class men and women inhabiting separate spheres has been

questioned (see A. Vickery, 'Golden Age to Separate Spheres? A Review of the Categories and Chronology of English Women's History', in *The Historical Review*, XXXVI/2 (1993), pp. 383–414), it was a dominant ideology at the time, and the existence of two sets of interiors – domestic and non-domestic – helped to make it a physical reality as well.

10 The architectural historian Beatriz Colomina has suggested that 'modern architecture becomes "modern" not simply by using glass, steel, or reinforced concrete . . . but precisely by engaging with the new mechanical equipment of the mass media: photography, film, advertising, publicity, publications and so on.' *Privacy and Publicity: Modern Architecture as Mass Media* (Cambridge, MA and London, 1994), p. 73.

Chapter One: The Private Interior

1 Walter Benjamin, *The Arcades Project*, trans. H. Eiland and K. McLaughlin (Cambridge, MA and London, 2004), p. 220.

2 Quoted in Penny Sparke, *As Long as It's Pink: The Sexual Politics of Taste* (London, 1995), p. 57.

3 Ibid., p. 63.

4 Ibid., p. 104.

5 See R. G. Saisselin, *Bricabracomania: The Bourgeois and the Bibelot* (London, 1985).

6 More recently the architectural historian, Hilde Heynen, has reminded us of the Modernist's belief that domesticity and modernity were fundamentally opposed to each other. See introduction to H. Heynen and G. Baydar, *Negotiating Domestictity: Spatial Productions of Gender in Modern Architecture* (London and New York, 2005). 'A metaphorical "homelessness"', she has written, 'is often considered the hallmark of modernity'. Christopher Reed's 1996 collection of writings, *Not at Home: The Suppression of Domesticity in Modern Art and Architecture* (London, 1996), has also suggested that Modernism was deeply antagonistic to domesticity.

7 See Anthony Giddens, *Modernity and Self-Identity: Self and Society in the Late Modern Age* (Cambridge, 1991), for an extended discussion of the relationship between individualism and modernity.

8 Benjamin, *The Arcades Project*, p. 9.

9 Quotation from a pamphlet accompanying the exhibition *At Home in Renaissance Italy* at the Victoria and Albert Museum in London (5 October 2006–7 January 2007), p. 4.

10 In his book *Home: The Short History of an Idea* (Harmondsworth, 1987), Witold Rybczynski explained that the idea that 'a room conveys the character of its owner' first emerged in the sixteenth century in Northern Europe, while intimacy and privacy became features of seventeenth-century Dutch homes. Both, he explains, were responses to forces within early modernity – the expansion of city life and of commercial activity; the development of new forms of manufacturing; and the emergence of the middle classes. According to Rybczynski, it was in seventeenth-century Holland that the modern concept of domesticity – a phenomenon that, in his words, 'has to do with family, intimacy, and a devotion to the home, as well as with a sense of the house as embodying . . . these sentiments' – was formed. Significantly it was created for the most part by women who, with the growing exodus of men into the public workplace, had been largely left on their own to form it, an early manifestation of the 'separate spheres' which spread to many other places over the next two centuries.

11 See C. Rice, *The Emergence of the Interior: Architecture, Modernity, Domesticity* (London and New York, 2007) for further discussion of this topic.

12 Walter Benjamin, 'Paris, Capital of the Nineteenth Century', in *Reflections*, trans. Edmund Jephcott (New York, 1986), pp. 155–6.

13 R. Dutton, *The Victorian Home: Some Aspects of Nineteenth-century Taste and Manners* (London, 1954), p. 84.

14 See Juliet Kinchin, 'Interiors: Nineteenth-century Essays on the "Masculine" and the "Feminine" Room', in *The Gendered Object*, ed. P. Kirkham (Manchester, 1996), p. 20. Kinchin has written that 'a level of civilising "refinement" was expressed in the proliferation and complexity of objects'.

15 T. Logan, *The Victorian Parlour: A Cultural Study* (Cambridge, 2001), p. 97.

16 Kinchin, 'Interiors', p. 13.

17 Saisselin, *Bricobracomania: The Bourgeois and the Bibelot*, p. 30.

18 Edith Wharton and Ogden Codman, Jr, *The Decoration of Houses* (London, 1897).

19 Edith Wharton, *The House of Mirth* (Basingstoke and Oxford, 2000), pp. 38–9.

20 H. Maguire, 'The Victorian Theatre as a Home from Home', in *Journal of Design History*, XIII (Oxford, 2 November 2000), p. 107.

21 Ibid.

22 M. Guyatt, 'A Semblance of Home: Mental Asylum Interiors, 1880–1914' in *Interior Design and Identity*, ed. S. McKellar and Penny Sparke (Manchester, 2004), pp. 48–71.

23 In her book *Shopping for Pleasure: Women in the Making of London's West End* (Princeton, NJ, 2000) Erika Diane Rappaport notes the advent of 'a new notion of bourgeois femininity, public space and conceptions of modernity' and the emergence of a number of women's clubs – Berner's Club, the Woman's University Club, formed in 1891; the Writers' Club, established in 1878; the Somerville; the Pioneer Club; the Empress Club and the Lyceum Club, opened in 1904, among many others.

24 Rappaport, *Shopping for Pleasure*, p. 254

25 Elsie de Wolfe, 'The Story of the Colony Club', in *The Delineator* (November 1911), p. 370.

26 See www.british-history.ac.uk/report.aspx?compid=40571 (accessed 8 February 2008).

27 With his wife Marie-Louise, César Ritz was known for creating striking neo-rococo interiors. See Elaine Denby, *Grand Hotels: Reality and Illusion* (London, 1998).

28 Denby, *Grand Hotels*, p. 8.

29 Many of the women attached to the English Arts and Crafts movement, among them Janie Morris, Kate Faulkner, Phoebe Traquair and Edith Dawson, helped to encourage women's domestic production, see I. Anscombe, *A Woman's Touch: Women in Design from 1860 to the Present Day* (London, 1984).

30 K. Halttunen, 'From Parlor to Living Room: Domestic Space, Interior Decoration, and the Culture of Personality', in *Consuming Visions: Accumulation and Display in America, 1880–1920*, ed. S. J. Bronner (Wintherthur, DE, 1989), p. 164.

31 See Halttunen, 'From Parlor to Living Room', 1989, p. 8, and B. Gordon, 'Woman's Domestic Body: The Conceptual Conflation of Women and Interiors in the Industrial Age', in *Wintherthur Portfolio: A Journal of American Material Culture*, XXXI/4 (Winter, 1996), p. 283. Gordon wrote: 'In a world of urban strangers, appearance became ever-more important as the outward sign of such achievement. This in itself was not new; wealthy individuals since the Renaissance had been very concerned with the impression created by what they wore. However, this preoccupation was now extended to whole new categories of people, comprising the majority of the population. Individuals on nearly every step of the social ladder had to be vigilantly concerned with and conscious of their presentation of self. Dress – the decoration of the body – and interior furnishings – the decoration of the home – together formed what in more contemporary terms has been called the *front* that projected the desired image to the world at large.'

32 Halttunen, 'From Parlor to Living Room', p. 158.

33 Ibid., p. 187.

34 Ibid.

35 Ibid., p. 188.

36 Kinchin, 'Interiors', p. 25.

Chapter Two: The New Interior

1 Walter Benjamin, *The Arcades Project*, trans. H. Eiland and K. McLaughlin (Cambridge, MA and London, 2004), p. 6.

2 For a detailed account of Art Nouveau and Jugendstil, see P. Greenhalgh, ed., *Art Nouveau 1890–1914* (London, 2000).

3 See Benjamin, *The Arcades Project*, p. 6.

4 L. Tiersten, *Marianne in the Market: Envisioning Consumer Society in Fin-de-Siecle France* (Berkeley and Los Angeles, CA and London, 2001), p. 157.

5 Quoted in J. Heskett, *Design in Germany 1870–1918* (London, 1986), p. 52.

6 A. Crawford, *Charles Rennie Mackintosh* (London, 1995), p. 66.

7 See A. Ellis, *The Hill House* (2004).

8 G. Fahr-Becker, *Wiener Werkstatte 1903–1932* (Cologne, 1995), p. 18.

9 See *Glasgow's Hidden Treasure: Charles Rennie Mackintosh's Ingram Street Tearooms* (Glasgow, 2004).

10 Noted in the text to the display at Glasgow's Kelvingrove Museum and Art Gallery.

11 Ellis, *The Hill House*.

12 Elaine Denby, *Grand Hotels: Reality and Illusion* (London, 1998), p. 148.

13 Ibid.

14 See A. Wealleans, *Designing Liners: A History of Interior Design Afloat* (New York and London, 2006).

15 J. Stewart, *Fashioning Vienna: Adolf Loos's Cultural Criticism* (London and New York, 2000), p. 132. In the words of Janet Stewart, 'the rich man preferred to spend as little time at home as possible and began to hanker after his old belongings which had been sacrificed in the name of art.'

16 Benjamin, *The Arcades Project*, p. 6.

Chapter Three: The Mass-consumed Interior

1 Mrs C. Frederick, *Selling Mrs Consumer* (New York, 1929), p. 220.

2 D. Slater, *Consumer Culture and Modernity* (Cambridge, 1987), p. 8.

3 B. Colomina, *Privacy and Publicity: Modern Architecture as Mass Media* (Cambridge, MA and London, 1998), p. 244

4 J. Moran, *Reading the Everyday* (London and New York, 2005), p. 131.

5 Ibid.

6 For an account of 'supermodernity' which links to the idea of 'lifestyle' see M. Auge, *Non-Places: Introduction to an Anthropology of Supermodernity* (London, 1995).

7 *La Revue de Femme*, May 1927, no. 6, p. 42.

8 M. Beetham, *A Magazine of Her Own? Domesticity and Desire in the Woman's Magazine, 1800–1914* (London and New York, 1996), p. 8.

9 Ibid., p. 21

10 D. Ryan, *The Ideal Home Through the Twentieth Century: "Daily Mail" Ideal Home Exhibition* (London, 1997), p. 45.

11 See G. Crossick and S. Jaumain, eds, *Cathedrals of Consumption: The European Department Store, 1850–1939* (Aldershot, 1999).

12 Ibid.

13 W. R. Leach, 'Transformations in a Culture of Consumption: Women and Department Stores, 1890–1925', in *The Journal of American History*, LXXI/2, (September 1984), p. 323.

14 Ibid., p. 328–9.

15 R. Laermans, 'Learning to Consume: Early Department Stores and the Shaping of Modern Consumer Culture (1860–1914)', in *Theory, Culture and Society*, X/4 (November 1993), pp. 79–102.

16 Crossick and Jaumain, *Cathedrals of Consumption*, p. 321.

17 See M. F. Friedman, *Selling Good Design: Promoting the Early Modern Interior* (New York, 2003).

18 Ibid., pp. 6–7.

19 Quoted by Donald Albrecht on www.russelwrightcenter.org/russelwright.html (accessed 15 September 2007).

20 E. O. Burdg, *The Manual of Show Window Backgrounds for Mercantile Display* (Chicago, IL, 1925), p. 175.

21 Ibid., p. 171.

22 See history.sandiego.edu/gen/soc/shoppingcenter.html. (accessed 8 February 2008)

23 Ryan, *The Ideal Home Through the Twentieth Century*.

24 Walter Benjamin, *The Arcades Project*, trans. H. Eiland and K. McLaughlin (Cambridge, MA and London, 2004), p. 7.

25 See R. C. Post, ed., *1876: A Centennial Exhibition* (Washington, DC, 1976).

26 J. Aynsley, 'Displaying Designs for the Interior in Europe and America, 1850–1950' in *Imagined Interiors: Representing the Domestic Interior since the Renaissance*, ed. J. Aynsley and C. Grant (London, 2006), p. 192.

27 Private e-mail from Eric Anderson to the author, 13 December 2006.

28 See www.morrissociety.org/writings.html (accessed 8 February 2008)

29 R. Houze, 'National Internationalism: Reactions to Austrian and Hungarian Decorative at the 1900 Paris Exposition Universell' in *Studies in the Decorative Arts*, XII/1 (Fall/Winter 2004/5), p. 75.

30 T. Gronberg, *Designs on Modernity: Exhibiting the City in 1920s Paris* (Manchester, 1998, p. 13.

31 Ryan, *The Ideal Home Through the Twentieth Century*.

32 P. Greenhalgh, 'The Style and the Age' in *Art Nouveau 1890–1914*, ed. P. Greenhalgh (London, 2000).

33 *The Architect and Building News*, 27 September 1946, pp. 193–4.

34 Aynsley, 'Displaying Designs for the Interior in Europe and America, 1850–1950', p. 197.

35 N. Harris, 'The Drama of Consumer Desire', in O. Mayr and R. C. Post, *Yankee Enterprise* (Washington, DC, 1981), p. 186. As Neil Harris has written, 'Film's influence on consumer products, however subtle and complex, was probably as important as its provision of a new set of celebrities . . . the objects redeemed by the camera ran the gamut from expensive playthings, traditional objects of luxury, to the ordinary appliances of everyday life. The presence of a certain style of clothing, a set of furniture, an interior décor, in a major film, could touch off considerable public demand.'

36 L. Ray, 'Achieving Eighteenth-Century Luxury with Modern Comfort', in *Arts and Decoration* (January 1938), p. 35.

37 A. Massey, *Hollywood Beyond the Screen: Design and Material Culture* (Oxford and New York, 2000), p. 67.

38 Ibid., p. 67.

39 K. Wilson, 'Style and Lifestyle in the Machine Age – the Modernist Period Rooms of "The Architect and the Industrial Arts"' in *Visual Resources*, vol. XXI, pt 3 (September 2005), pp. 245–8.

40 Massey, *Hollywood Beyond the Screen*, p. 70.

Chapter Four: The Fashionable Interior

1 Elsie de Wolfe, *The House in Good Taste* (New York, 1913), p. 55.

2 Charles Baudelaire is quoted from 'The Painter of Modern Life', in *The Painter of Modern Life and Other Essays*, trans. J. Mayne (London, 1964), p. 12. For further information about ideas relating fashion and modernity see U. Lehmann, *Tigersprung: Fashion in Modernity* (Cambridge, MA, 2000); E. Wilson, *Adorned in Dreams: Fashion and Modernity* (London, 1985); C. Breward and C. Evans, eds, *Fashion and Modernity* (London and New York, 2005) and D. L. Purdy ed., *The Rise of Fashion: A Reader* (Minnesota, 2004).

3 Lisa Tiersten, *Marianne in the Market: Envisioning Consumer Society in Fin-de-Siècle France* (Los Angeles, CA, and London, 2001), p. 125. As Tiersten explained, 'late nineteenth-century taste media proclaimed fashion and home decorating to be not simply art forms, but art forms inscribed in modernity'.

4 B. Gordon, 'Woman's Domestic Body: The Conceptual Conflation of Women and Interiors in the Industrial Age', in *Wintherthur Portfolio: A Journal of American Material Culture*, XXXI/4 (Winter 1996), p. 281. Gordon explained that: 'Women are still primarily identified in our culture with the arrangement and outfitting of both the interior and the body.'

5 Ibid., p. 286.

6 Ibid., p. 289.

7 See D. Fuss, *The Sense of an Interior: Four Writers and the Rooms that Shaped Them* (New York and London, 2004) and V. Rosner, *Modernism and the Architecture of Private Life* (New York, 2005).

8 Walter Benjamin, *The Arcades Project*, trans. H. Eiland and K. McLaughlin (Cambridge, MA and London, 1999), p. 6.

9 See C. Breward, *The Culture of Fashion: A New History of Fashionable Dress* (Manchester, 1995).

10 See E. Saunders, *The Age of Worth: Couturier to the Empress Eugenie* (Bloomington, IN, 1955).

11 Ibid., p. 110

12 Ibid.

13 For more details see N. J. Troy, *Couture Culture: A Study in Modern Art and Fashion* (Cambridge, MA and London, 2003).

14 Ibid., p. 46.

15 Rooms by Paul Poiret for the Herrmann Gerson exhibition in Berlin, in *Deutsche Kunst und Dekoration*, vol. XXXI (October 1913–March 1914), pp. 147 and 148.

16 See Penny Sparke, *Elsie de Wolfe: The Birth of Modern Interior Decoration* (New York, 2005).

17 In *Couture Culture: A Study in Modern Art and Fashion*, Nancy Troy highlighted the paradox involved in the couturiers' practice of producing unique, custom-made gowns for wealthy clients while simultaneously creating 'models', intended to be copied by department stores and other clothing outlets and sold in significant numbers.

18 Tiersten, *Marianne in the Market: Envisioning Consumer Society in Fin-de-Siècle France*, p. 166. Tiersten has described how in France, in this period, the fashion for eclecticism that had begun in dress moved, at a later date, into the interior. While, as she explained, the columnist Lucie Crete wrote in *La Mode francaise* of 1876 that 'Mélange has become . . .

obligatory', she also pointed out that Henri de Noussane had echoed the same words in *Le Gout dans l'Ameublement* twenty years later, proclaiming that 'the salon of the bourgeois home and apartment is furnished preferably in a modern style. Understand what we mean by modern: here it signifies a mélange of styles'.

19 Ibid., p. 51.

20 Troy, *Couture Culture*. Troy explained that, 'by the late nineteenth century clothing was losing its ability to provide a readily available guide to rank or social standing'.

21 Tiersten, *Marianne in the Market: Envisioning Consumer Society in Fin-de-Siècle France*, p. 150.

22 *Artistic Houses* illustrated a wide range of very wealthy homes in the Aesthetic Movement style. For more details of American home decorating advice books published in these years see K. Halttunen, 'From Parlor to Living Room: Domestic Space, Interior Decoration and the Culture of Personaloity' in S. J. Bronner, ed., *Consuming Visions: Accummulation and Display in America, 1880–1920* (New York and London, 1989).

23 Much of the material in the numerous advice books was first published in magazines. The interior featured in fashion and etiquette-oriented periodicals, in domestic magazines, as well as in more specialist furniture and interior decoration publications. For more details about American advice publications see C. E. Clark, Jr, *The American Family Home* (Chapel Hill, NC, and London, 1986) and J. Scanlon, *Inarticulate Longings: The Ladies Home Journal, Gender and the Promise of Consumer Culture* (New York and London, 1995). *Godey's Lady's Book* was the first popular women's magazine to be edited by a woman, Sarah Josepha Hale.

24 Edith Wharton and Ogden Codman, Jr, *The Decoration of Houses* (London, 1897).

25 Among many others Lucy Abbot Throop's *Furnishing the House of Good Taste* appeared in 1912; George Leland Hunter's *Home Furnishing* in 1913; and Mary J. Quinn's *Planning and Furnishing the Home: Practical and Economical Suggestions for the Homemaker* in the following year. They all covered similar ground to a certain extent but had their own unique characteristics as well.

26 D. De Marly, *Worth: Father of Haute Couture* (New York and London, 1980), pp. 174–5.

27 Troy, *Couture Culture*, p. 85. Troy has suggested that the latter was highly theatrical in nature and that the couturier was deliberately blurring the boundaries between Spinelly as an actress, an interior client and as a mannequin for his clothes.

28 See M. B. Miller, *The Bon Marché: Bourgeois Culture and the Department Store 1869–1920* (New Jersey, 1981).

29 Ibid. As Miller explained, 'the Bon Marché showed people how they should dress, how they should furnish their homes'.

30 See Troy, *Couture Culture*, for more detail.

Chapter Five: The Decorative Interior

1 D. Todd and R. Mortimer, *The New Interior Decoration: An Introduction to its Principles, and International Survey of its Methods* (London, 1929) p. 21.

2 Elsie de Wolfe, *The House in Good Taste* (New York, 1913), p. 5.

3 M. Snodin and M. Howard, *Ornament: A Social History since 1450* (New Haven, CT, 1996), p. 142.

4 Ibid.

5 Ibid.

6 Ibid., p. 143, and C. Rice, *The Emergence of the Interior: Architecture, Modernity, Domesticity* (London and New York, 2007), p. 2.

7 Snodin and Howard, *Ornament: A Social History since 1450*, p. 143.

8 Ibid.

9 Rice, *The Emergence of the Interior*, pp. 37–54.

10 See K. Livingstone and L. Parry, *International Arts and Crafts* (London, 2005).

11 N. J. Troy, *Modernism and the Decorative Arts in France: Art Nouveau to Le Corbusier* (New Haven, CT, and London, 1991), p. 116.

12 See Caroline Constant, *Eileen Gray* (London, 2000).

13 See *Wiener Werkstätte 1903–1932* (Cologne, 1995).

14 Ibid., p. 58.

15 See C. Witt-Dörring, ed., *Josef Hoffmann Interiors 1902–1913* (Munich, 2006).

16 Elsie de Wolfe, *The House in Good Taste* (New York, 1913), pp. 66–7.

17 L. L. Christensen, *A Design for Living: Vienna in the Twenties* (New York, 1987), p. 23.

18 H. H. Adler, *The New Interior: Modern Decoration for the Modern Home* (New York, 1916), p. i.

19 Ibid.

20 Ibid. An interior designed by Paul Zimmerman was captioned, for example, 'a Dining-room fulfilling the decorative principles of beauty, utility and color'. Others were decorated by the Ascherman Studio.

21 L. O. Duncan, 'The Belle of Yesterday', *The Store of Greater New York* (August 1939), referred to in C. F. Peatross, *Winold Reiss: A Pioneer of Modern American Design*, http://www.winold-reiss.org/works/architectural.htm (accessed 10 August 2007).

22 N. Stritzler-Levine, 'Three Visions of the Modern Home: Josef Frank, Le Corbusier and Alvar Aalto' in *Josef Frank: Architect and Designer* (New Haven, CT, and London, 1996), p. 24.

23 Stritzler-Levine, 'Three Visions of the Modern Home', p. 119.

24 Ibid., p. 22.

25 'European Influences in Modern Interior Decoration', in *International Studio*, LVI/224 (1915), p. 83.

26 K. M. Kahle, *Modern French Decoration* (New York and London, 1930), p. 35.

27 See D. Silverman, *Art Nouveau in Fin-de-Siècle France: Politics, Psychology and Style* (Los Angeles, CA, 1989).

28 E. Genauer, *Modern Interiors Today and Tomorrow* (New York, 1939), p. 11, and Todd and Mortimer, *The New Interior Decoration*, p. 22.

29 C. Benton, T. Benton and G. Wood, *Art Deco 1910–1939* (London, 2003).

30 See M. F. Friedman, *Selling Good Design: Promoting the Modern Interior* (New York, 2005).

31 See A. Massey, *Hollywood Beyond the Screen: Design and Material Culture* (Oxford and New York, 2000).

32 *The Home of Today: Its Choice, Planning, Equipment and Organisation* (London, undated), pp. 194, 195.

33 W. Fales, *What's New in Home Decorating?* (New York, 1936), p. 152.

34 Todd and Mortimer, *The New Interior Decoration*.

35 Genauer, *Modern Interiors Today and Tomorrow*, p. 22.

36 Todd and Mortimer, *The New Interior Decoration*, p. 2.

37 J. Sharples, *Merchant Palaces: Liverpool and Wirral Mansions* (Liverpool, 2007), p. 6.

38 C. Wheeler, 'Interior Design as a Profession for Women', in *Outlook* (6 April 1896), pp. 559–60 and (20 April 1895), p. 649.

39 See P. Kirkham and Penny Sparke, 'A Woman's Place…?' in *Women Designers in the USA, 1900–2000* (New Haven, CT, and London, 2000), p. 307.

40 Penny Sparke, *Elsie de Wolfe: The Birth of Modern Decoration* (New York, 2005).

41 Edith Wharton and Ogden Codman, Jr, *The Decoration of Houses* (New York, 1897).

42 See G. Wood, ed., *Surreal Things* (London, 2007).

43 Ibid.

44 Quoted in C. Varney, *In the Pink: Dorothy Draper, America's Most Fabulous Decorator* (New York, 2006), p. 43.

45 Ibid.

46 P. McNeil, 'Designing Women: Gender, Sexuality and the Interior Decorator, *c.* 890–1940' in *Art History*, xvii/4 (December 1994), pp. 631–57.

47 Ibid., p. 634.

Chapter Six: The Public Interior

1 V. Woolf, cited in V. Rosner, *Modernism and the Architecture of Private Life* (New York, 2005), p. 3.

2 Le Corbusier, *Towards a New Architecture* (London, 1974 [1923]), p. 19.

3 S. Giedion, *Mechanisation Takes Command: A contribution to anonymous history* (New York, 1969 [1948]), pp. 364–5.

4 For more information about the relationship between the city and modernity see P. Hall, *Cities of Tomorrow: An Intellectual History of Urban Planning and Design in the Twentieth Century* (Oxford, 1991); J. Rykwert, *The Seduction of Place: The History and Future of the City* (New York, 2002), and R. Sennett, *The Fall of Public Man* (New York, 1992 [1974]).

5 The title of Richard Sennett's book serves to reinforce this gender bias.

6 For more ideas about the concept of the 'flâneur' see K. Tester, ed., *The Flâneur* (London and New York, 1994).

7 G. Lambert, *The Covered Passages of Paris* (Paris, undated), p. 9.

8 Walter Benjamin, *The Arcades Project*, trans. H. Eiland and K. McLaughlin (Cambridge, MA and London, 2004), p. 3.

9 Ibid.

10 Ibid., p. 14.

11 Ibid., p. 20.

12 Ibid., p. 7.

13 C. Hobhouse, *1851 and the Crystal Palace* (London, 1945), p. 57.

14 E. D. Rappoport, *Shopping for Pleasure: Women in the Making of London's West End* (Princeton, NJ, 2000), p. 27.

15 Ibid., p. 28.

16 In feminist writings the *flâneur* has been joined by the parallel concept of the *flâneuse*, the modern female (middle-class for the most part) shopper, who sought pleasure as she moved outside the safety of her home to join the mass of consumers crowding the commercial areas of London, Paris, New York and the other main cities of the second half of the nineteenth and the first decade of the twentieth centuries. See J. Wolff, 'The Invisible *Flâneuse*: Women and the Literature of Modernity', in *Theory, Culture and Society*, ii/3 (1985) pp. 37–48, and Rappaport, *Shopping for Pleasure*, p. 13.

17 Paradoxically public interiors, including those in exhibition halls, shops and shop windows, contained commodities destined for the private arena. As Beatrix Colomina has explained, 'The private had become consumable merchandise.' See Beatrix Colomina, *Privacy and Publicity: Modern Architecture as Mass Media* (Cambridge, MA and London, 1996), p. 8.

18 Rappaport, *Shopping for Pleasure*, p. 154.

19 See M. Miller, *The Bon Marché: Bourgeois Culture and the Department Store 1869–1920* (Princeton, NJ, 1981).

20 Rappaport, *Shopping for Pleasure*, pp. 167–8.

21 Miller, *The Bon Marché*, p. 154.

22 See http:/www.pdxhistory.com/html/marshall_fields.html (accessed 2 June 2007).

23 See F. W. Taylor, *Principles of Scientific Management* (New York, 2005 [1911]).

24 Giedion, *Mechanisation Takes Command*, p. 98.

25 Ibid., p. 99.

26 D. Hounshell, *From the American System to Mass Production 1800–1932: The Development of Manufacturing Technology in the US* (Baltimore, MD and London, 1982), p. 70.

27 A. Forty, *Objects of Desire: Design and Society 1750–1980* (London, 1986), p. 120.

28 See A. Delgado, *The Enormous File: A Social History of the Office* (London, 1979), pp. 24–5.

29 Ibid., p. 41.

30 Quoted in Q. Colville, 'The Role of the Interior in Constructing Notions of Class and Status: A case-study of Britannia Royal Naval College, Dartmouth, 1905–1939', in S. McKellar and Penny Sparke, eds, *Interior Design and Identity* (Manchester, 2004), p. 115.

31 S. Darling, *Chicago Furniture: Art, Craft and Industry, 1833–1983* (New York and London, 1984), p. 132.

32 It should be remembered, of course, that women did not only visit the above interiors. By the late nineteenth century they also worked in them and the entry of women into the workplace was one of the most dramatic ways in which they entered into modernity. Working women entered a whole range of workspaces at this time, among them shops, offices, factories, sweat shops, restaurants, offices, telephone exchange, schools and commercial laundries.

Chapter Seven: The Rational Interior

1 Walter Benjamin, *The Arcades Project*, trans. H. Eiland and K. McLaughlin (Cambridge, MA and London, 2004), p. 9.

2 See P. Collins, *Changing Ideals in Modern Architecture 1750–1950* (London, 1965).

3 G. Matthews, *'Just a Housewife': The Rise and Fall of Domesticity in America* (New York and Oxford, 1987), p. 98.

4 Ibid., p. 145, and D. Hayden, *The Grand Domestic Revolution: A History of Feminist Design for American Homes, Neighborhoods and Cities* (Cambridge, MA and London, 1981), p. 151.

5 S. Strasser, *Never Done: A History of American Housework* (New York, 1982), p. 186.

6 Ibid., p. 189.

7 Hayden, *The Grand Domestic Revolution*, p. 57.

8 Christine Fredrick, 'The New Housekeeping', in *Ladies' Home Journal* (September–December 1912), p. 2.

9 G. Wright, *Building the Dream: A Social History of Housing in America* (Cambridge, MA and London, 1981), p. 129.

10 Strasser, *Never Done*, p. 217.

11 For a full account of Material Feminism see Hayden, *The Grand Domestic Revolution*.

12 See http:/womenshistory.about.com/od/quotes/a/c_p_gilman.htm (accessed 6 April 2007).

13 Strasser, *Never Done*, p. 219.

14 One model put forward was that of the apartment hotel. See Hayden, *The Grand Domestic Revolution*, p. 194 and Wright, *Building the Dream*, p. 144, for more details.

15 See S. R. Henderson, 'A Revolution in the Woman's Sphere: Grete Lihotzky and the Frankfurt Kitchen' in *Architecture and Feminism*, ed. D. Coleman, E. Danze, and C. Henderson (New York, 1996).

16 Coleman, Danze and Henderson, *Architecture and Feminism*.

17 Ibid., p. 232.

18 Ibid., p. 235.

19 Ibid.

20 Quoted in N. Bullock, 'First the Kitchen – Then the Façade', in *Journal of Design History*, 1/3 and 4 (Oxford, 1988), p. 187.

21 H. Heynen, *Architecture and Modernity: A Critique* (Cambridge, MA and London, 1999), p. 47.

22 See M. Campbell, 'What Tuberculosis did for Modernism: The Influence of a Curative Environment on Modernist Architecture and Design', in *Medica History*, XLIX/4; (1 October 2005), pp. 463–88 (online at http:/www.pubmedcentral.nih.gov/articlerender.fcgi?artid =1251640.

23 Ibid., p. 2.

24 Ibid., p. 3.

25 See A. A. Fou, *Paimio Tuberculosis Sanatorium, City of Turku 700th Anniversary Exhibition* (London and New York, 1994).

26 For more information on London's eighteenth-century coffee houses see J. and L. Pelzer, 'The Coffee Houses of Augustan London', in *History Today*, XXXII (9 October 1982), pp. 40–47.

27 www.rakehell.com/article.php?id=206 (accessed 8 February 2008).

Chapter Eight: The Mass-produced Interior

1 Stig Lindegren, 'A Swedish Housing Investigation', in *Ten Lectures on Swedish Architecture* (Stockholm, 1949), p. 81.

2 See J. Giles, 'Introduction' to *The Parlour and the Suburb: Domestic Identities, Class, Femininity and Modernity* (Oxford and New York, 2004).

3 Lindegren, 'A Swedish Housing Investigation', p. 82.

4 Jean Baudrillard, *The System of Objects*, trans. J. Benedict (London and New York, 1996), p. 19.

5 For the feminist writer, Henderson, this incursion of the public sphere into the private space of the home simply replaced one form of patriarchy with another, that of the family with that of industry and government. See S. R. Henderson, 'A Revolution in the Woman's Sphere: Grete Lihotzky and the Frankfurt Kitchen', in *Architecture and Feminism*, ed. D. Coleman, E. Danze and C. Henderson (New York, 1996).

6 N. J. Troy, *Modernism and the Decorative Arts in France: Art Nouveau to Le Corbusier* (New Haven, CT and London, 1991), p. 216.

7 Ibid., p. 220.

8 Ibid., pp. 222–4.

9 Le Corbusier, *Le Corbusier et Pierre Jeanneret, Oeuvres Completes, 1910–1929* (Zurich, 1964), p. 104.

10 Troy, *Modernism and the Decorative Arts in France*, p. 224.

11 J. Stewart Johnson 'Introduction' to C. Wilk, ed., *Marcel Breuer: Furniture and Interiors* (New York, 1981), p. 13.

12 Quoted in C. Wilk, *Marcel Breuer: Furniture and Interiors* (New York, 1981), p. 38.

13 See D. Todd and R. Mortimer, *The New Interior Decoration: An Introduction to its Principles and an International Survey of its Methods* (London, 1929); H. Hoffmann, *Modern Interiors in Europe and America* (London, 1930); H. Eckstein (intro), *Die Schöne Wohnung: Beispeile Neuzeitlicher Deutscher Wohnraumer* (Munich, 1931); and P. T. Frankl, *New Dimensions: the Decorative Arts of Today in Words and Pictures* (New York, 1928).

14 See I. B. Whyte, *Bruno Taut and the Architecture of Activism* (Cambridge, 1982).

15 See *Thirties: British Art and Design before the War* (exh. cat., Arts Council with v&a, 1980), p. 267.

16 See J. L. Meikle, *Design in the usa* (Oxford and New York, 2005).

17 Ibid.

18 'Bel Geddes' in *Fortune* (July 1930), pp. 51–7, p. 53.

19 J. L. Meikle, *Twentieth Century Limited: Industrial Design in America, 1925–1939* (Philadelphia, pa, 1979), p. 53.

20 *Fortune* (July 1930), p. 55.

21 'The Eastman Kodak Shop: New York City', in *The Architectural Forum* (April 1931), p. 449.

22 Todd and Mortimer, *The New Interior Decoration*, p. 179.

23 Mary McCarthy, *The Group* (Harmondsworth, 1969 [1936]), pp. 89–90.

24 K. Wilson, *Livable Modernism: Interior Decorating and Design during the Great Depression* (New Haven, ct and London, 2005), p. 4.

Chapter Nine: The Abstract Interior

1 Quoted in N. Troy, *The De Stijl Environment* (Cambridge, ma and London, 1983), p. 19.

2 Pierre Bourdieu, *Distinction: A Social Critique of the Judgement of Taste* (London, 1984).

3 Whistler's own description of this exhibit is contained in an article on a website edited by the Freer Gallery of Art, http:/www.tfaoi.com/aa/4aa/4aa170.htm. (accessed 11 February 2007)]

4 See N. Troy, *Modernism and the Decorative Arts in France* (New Haven, ct and London, 1990).

5 Troy, *Modernism and the Decorative Arts in France*, pp. 85–90. Troy's argument represented a fundamental revision to her statement made in her earlier book, *The De Stijl Environment*, that the Maison Cubiste was a 'superficial stylization'.

6 Troy, *The De Stijl Environment*, p. 6.

7 Ibid., p. 62.

8 Ibid., p. 19.

9 Ibid., p. 169.

10 Ibid., p. 176.

11 Information gathered on a visit to the Schroeder house on 24 March 2006.

12 The relationship of the modern interior aesthetic and domesticity was addressed by Tim Benton in *The Modernist Home* (London, 2006), written to coincide with the *Modernism: Designing a New World, 1914–1939* exhibition held at London's Victoria and Albert Museum in the same year. Describing Le Corbusier's famous Villa Savoye, built between 1928 and 1931, one of the icons of architectural Modernism, Benton explained, 'Even when it was occupied by the Savoye family, the few items of furniture could not make this luminous space "home."' As in a Palladian villa, you had to appreciate the architectural values of space and light, colour and texture to find satisfaction in a house like this.' He continued: 'Perhaps the key to understanding the Modernist house is that it was not designed for just anyone. This was an art movement, intended for those who could understand and appreciate it.'

13 Tim Benton's view that buildings such as the Villa Savoye were not easy to live in had already been poignantly expressed by Alice T. Friedman in her book *Women and the Making of the Modern House: A Social and Architectural History* (New York, 1998).

14 Friedman, *Women and the Making of the Modern House*, p. 128.

15 See C. Lange, *Ludwig Mies van der Rohe and Lilly Reich: Furniture and Interiors* (Krefeld, 2006), p. 51.

16 Lange, *Ludwig Mies van der Rohe and Lilly Reich*.

17 Information taken from a booklet edited by Peter Noever, entitled *Schindler by mak*

(Munich, 2005) and from a visit to the Schindler House in July 2006.

18 See F. Baudot, *J.M. Frank* (New York, 1998), p. 11.

Chapter Ten: The Designed Interior

1 George Nelson and Henry Wright, *Tomorrow's House: A Complete Guide for the Home-Builder* (New York, 1945), p. 2.

2 R. Aloi, ed., *L'Arredamento Moderno* (Milan, 1955), p. 573.

3 Nelson and Wright, *Tomorrow's House*, p. 43.

4 T. H. Robsjohn-Gibbings, *Goodbye, Mr. Chippendale* (New York, 1944), p. 43.

5 D. Rowntree, *Interior Design* (Harmondsworth, 1964).

6 Ibid., p. 199.

7 Writing in *The Art of Interior Design and Decoration* (London, 1951), John H. Holmes explained that he was conscious of the schism that was developing between these two areas of activity. In his view decoration and design were interchangeable in what he called 'great periods of design', but there was, he believed, a danger, at times when their integration was not understood, that 'the decorator may study expression . . . rather than the purpose which is expressed'.

8 A. Drexler, *Charles Eames: Furniture from the Design Collection* (New York, 1973), p. 12.

9 Ibid., p. 38.

10 G. Koenig, *Eames* (Cologne, 2005), p. 70.

11 See P. Kirkham, *Charles and Ray Eames: Designers of the Twentieth Century* (Cambridge, MA, and London, 1995), pp. 164–99.

12 Ibid.

13 Ibid.

14 See Koenig, *Eames*, p. 47.

15 *Forme e colore dell'arredamento moderno* (Milan, 1967).

16 See B. Tigerman, '"I am not a Decorator": Florence Knoll, the Knoll Planning Unit and the Making of the Modern Office', in *Journal of Design History*, xx/1 (2007), pp. 61–74.

17 Ibid.

18 G. Nelson, 'Problems of Design: Modern Decoration', in *Interiors* (November 1949), p. 69.

19 Nelson and Wright, *Tomorrow's House*, p. 23.

20 Mary Davis Gillies, *All About Modern Decorating* (New York and London, 1942).

21 Ibid.

22 D. Cooper, *Inside Your Home* (New York, Inc.), p. 73.

23 See V. Gregotti, *Achille Castiglioni* (Paris, 1985).

24 See I. Favata, *Joe Colombo and Italian Design of the Sixties* (Milan, 1988).

25 See R. Banham, 'A Throw-away Aesthetic', in Penny Sparke, ed., *Design by Choice* (London, 1981), pp. 90–93.

26 DOCOMOMO International defines itself as an 'international working party for documentation and conservation of buildings, sites and neighbourhoods of the modern movement', see: www.docomomo.com (accessed 8 February 2008).

27 Broadcast on 25 December 2004.

28 Broadcast on 8 August 2006.

Conclusion

1 '50 Expert Ideas for Organising Your Home', in *Good Housekeeping* (January 2003), pp. 101–108.
2 See V. Narotzky, 'Dream Homes and DIY: Television, New Media and the Domestic Makeover', in J. Aynsley and C. Grant, *Imagined Interiors: Representing the Domestic Interior since the Renaissance* (London, 2006), pp. 258–73.
3 See Jean Baudrillard, *America* (London, 1989).

Bibliography

Abbot, J. A., *Jansen* (New York, 2006)

Abercrombie, S., *A Century of Interior Design, 1900–2000: The Design, the Designers, the Products, and the Profession* (New York, 2003)

Adler, H. A., *The New Interior: Modern Decoration for the Modern Home* (New York, 1916)

Albrecht, D. and C. B. Broikos, eds, *On the Job: Design and the American Office* (New York, 2000)

Anscombe. I., *A Woman's Touch: Women in Design from 1860 to the Present Day* (New York, 1984)

Attfield, J., 'Design as a Practice for Modernity: A Case for the Study of the Coffee Table in the Mid Century Domestic Interior' in *Journal of Material Culture*, ii/3 (1997), pp. 267–89

Augé, M., *Non-Places: Introduction to an Anthropology of Supermodernity* (London and New York, 1995)

Aynsley, A. and C. Grant, eds, *Imagined Interiors: Representing the Domestic Interior since the Renaissance* (London, 2006)

Aynsley, J. and K. Forde, *Design and the Modern Magazine* (Manchester, 2007)

Bachelard, G., *The Poetics of Space: The Classic Look at How We Experience Intimate Spaces* (Boston, MA, 1994)

Baldwin, B. and M. Gardine, *Billy Baldwin: An Autobiography* (Boston, MA, 1985)

Banham, J., S. Macdonald and J. Porter, *Victorian Interior Design* (London, 1991)

Bartlett, A. P. and S. B. Crater, *Sister: The Life of Legendary American Interior Decorator, Mrs. Henry Parish ii* (New York, 2000)

Battersby, M., *The Decorative Twenties* (London, 1988)

Baudot, F., *J. M. Frank* (New York, 1999)

Bauhaus Furniture: A Legend Reviewed (Berlin, 2003)

Baxter, P., 'Thirty Years of Growth in the Literature of Interior Design', in *Journal of Design History*, iv/4 (1991), pp. 241–50

Bayer, P., *Art Deco Interiors: Decoration and Design Classics of the 1920s and 1930s* (London, 1990)

Beecher, C. E., and H. Beecher Stowe, *The American Woman's Home; Or, Principles of Domestic Science* (Hartford, CT, 1975 [1869])

Beetham, M., *A Magazine of Her Own? Domesticity and Desire in the Woman's Magazine, 1800–1914* (London and New York, 1996)

Benjamin, W., *The Arcades Project*, trans. H. Eiland and K. McLaughlin (London, 2004)

Benton, C., T. Benton, and G. Wood, *Art Deco 1910–1939* (London, 2003)

Benton, T., *The Modernist Home* (London, 2006)

Berman, M., *All That's Solid Melts into Air: the Experience of Modernity* (London, 1982)

Bevier, I., *The House: Its Plan, Decoration and Care* (Chicago, IL, 1907)

Blumin, S., *The Emergence of the Middle Class* (New York, 1989)

Bourdieu, P., *Distinction: A Social Critique of the Judgement of Taste* (London, 1984)

Breward, C., and C. Evans, *Fashion and Modernity* (Oxford and New York, 2005)

Bronner, S. J., ed., *Consuming Visions: Accumulation and Display of Goods in America, 1880–1920* (New York, 1989)

Brown, E., *Sixty Years of Interior Design: The World of McMillen* (New York, 1982)

Brucker, C., 'In the Public Eye: Women and the American Luxury Hotel', in *Winterthur Portfolio*, xxxi/4 (Winter 1996), pp. 211–25

Bryden, I., and J. Floyd, *Domestic Space: Reading the Interior in Nineteenth-century Britain and America* (Manchester, 1999)

Bryman, A., *Disneyization of Society* (Thousand Oaks, CA, 2004)

Buckley, C., *Designing Modern Britain* (London, 2007)

Burman, B., ed., *Dress, Body, Culture* (Oxford, 1999)

Butler, J., *Gender Trouble: Feminism and the Subversion of Identity* (London, 1999)

Calloway, S., *Twentieth-Century Decoration: The Domestic Interior from 1900 to the Present Day* (London, 1988)

Carter, R. and R. R. Cole, *Joseph Urban: Architecture, Theatre, Opera, Film* (New York, 1992)

Cieraad, I., ed., *At Home: An Anthropology of Domestic Space* (Syracuse, NY, 1999)

Clark, C. E., Jr., *The American Family Home, 1800–1960* (Chapel Hill, NC, 1986)

Cohen, D., *Household Gods: The British and Their Possessions* (London, 2006)

Coleman, D., E. Danze and C. Henderson, eds, *Architecture and Feminism* (Princeton, NJ, 1996)

Colomina, B., *Privacy and Publicity: Modern Architecture as Mass Media* (London, 1996)

——, *Sexuality and Space* (New York, 1992)

Constant, C., *Eileen Gray* (London, 2000)

Cook, C. C., *The House Beautiful: Essays on Beds and Tables, Stools and Candlesticks* (New York, 1878)

Crawford, A., *Charles Rennie Mackintosh* (London, 1995)

Crossick, G., and S. Jaumain, *Cathedrals of Consumption: The European Department Store* (Aldershot, 1999)

Crowley, J., *The Invention of Comfort: Sensibilities and Design in Early Modern Britain and Early America* (Baltimore, MD, 2000)

Daunton, M., *House and Home in the Victorian City: Working Class Housing 1850–1914* (London, 1983)

——, and B. Rieger, eds, *Meanings of Modernity: Britain from the Late Victorian Era to World War II* (Oxford and New York, 2001)

Davidoff, L., and C. Hall, *Family Fortunes: Men and Women of the English Middle-Class, 1780–1950* (London, 1987)

Demetrios, E., *An Eames Primer* (New York, 2001)

De Wolfe, E., *The House in Good Taste* (New York, 1913)

Denby, E., *Grand Hotels: Reality and Illusion* (London, 1998)

Doid, A., *Theo Van Doesburg: Painting into Architecture, Theory into Practice* (New York, 1986)

Drexler, A., *Charles Eames: Furniture from the Design Collection* (New York, 1973)

Duncan, A., *Art Deco Furniture* (London, 1984)

Eastlake, C. L., *Hints on Household Taste in Furniture, Upholstery and Other Details* (London, 1869)

Eckstein, H., introduction to *Die Schöne Wohnung; Beispeile Neuzeitlicher Deutscher Wohnraumer* (Munich, 1931)

Eleb, M., 'Modernity and Modernisation in Postwar France: The Third Type of House', in *Journal of Architecture*, ix/4 (2004), pp. 495–514

Ferry, E., '"Decorators may be compared to Doctors": An Analysis of Rhoda and Agnes Garrett's "Suggestions for House Decoration in Painting, Woodwork and Furniture" (1896)' in *Journal of Design History*, XVI/1 (2003), pp. 15–33

Flinchum, R., *Henry Dreyfuss, Industrial Designer: The Man in the Brown Suit* (New York, 1997)

Fogg, M., *Boutique: A 50s Cultural Phenomenon* (London, 2003)

Ford, J., and K. M. Ford, *Design of Modern Interiors* (New York, 1942)

Foy, J. H., and K. A. Marling, eds, *The Arts and the American Home* (Knoxville, TN, 1994)

Frank, J., L. Botstein and N. Stritzler-Levine, *Josef Frank, Architect and Designer: An Alternative Vision of the Modern Home* (New Haven, CT, 1996)

Frankl, Paul, T., *New Dimensions: The Decorative Arts of Today in Words and Pictures* (New York, 1928)

Friedman, A. T., *Women and the Making of the Modern House: A Social and Architectural History* (New York, 1998)

Fuss, D., *The Sense of and Interior: Four Rooms and the Writers that Shaped Them* (New York and London, 2004)

Geist, J. F., *Arcades: History of a Building Type* (London, 1982)

Genauer, E., *Modern Interiors Today and Tomorrow: A Critical Analysis of Trends in Contemporary Decoration as seen at the Paris Exposition of Arts and Techniques and Reflected at the New York World's Fair* (New York, 1939)

Gere, C., *Nineteenth-century Decoration: The Art of the Interior* (New York, 1989)

——, *The House Beautiful: Oscar Wilde and the Aesthetic Interior* (London, 2000)

Giddens, A., *Modernity and Self-Identity: Self and Society in the Late Modern Age* (Cambridge, 1991)

Giedion, S., *Mechanisation Takes Command: A Contribution to Anonymous History* (New York, 1969)

Giles, J., *The Parlour and the Suburb* (Oxford, 2004)

Gillies, M. D., *Popular Home Decoration* (New York, 1940)

Gilman, C. P., *The Home, Its Work and Influence* (New York, 1903)

Girouard, M., *Life in the English Country House: A Social and Architectural History* (New Haven, CT, 1978)

Glancey, J., *The New Moderns* (London, 1990)

Goodnow, R. R., *The Honest House* (New York, 1914)

Gordon, B., 'Woman's Domestic Body: the Conceptual Conflation of Women and Interiors in the Industrial Age', in *Wintherthur Portfolio*, XIII/4 (1996), pp. 281–301

——, Interiors, 1898–1940', in *Journal of Popular Culture*, XXII/4 (Spring 1989), pp. 35–47

Gordon, J., 'Interior Decorating as Popular Culture. Women's Views Concerning Wall and Window Treatments, 1870–1920', in *Journal of American Culture*, IX/3 (Autumn 1986), pp. 15–23

——, and J. McArthur, 'Popular Culture, Magazines and American Domestic' in C. Grafe and F. Bollerey, eds, *Cafés and Bars: The Architecture of Public Display* (Oxford, 2007)

Gray, S., *Designers on Designers: The Inspiration Behind Great Interiors* (New York, 2004)

Greenhalgh, P., ed., *Art Nouveau 1890–1914* (London, 2000)

——, *Ephemeral Vistas: The Expositions Universelles, Great Exhibitions and World's Fairs, 1851–1939* (Manchester, 1990)

Grier, K., *Culture and Comfort: Parlor Making and Middle Class Identity, 1850–1930* (Washington, DC, 1997)

Gronberg, T., *Designs on Modernity: Exhibiting the City in 1920s Paris* (Manchester, 1998)

Guffey, E. E., *Retro: The Culture of Revival* (London, 2006)

Guillén, M. F., *The Taylorized Beauty of the Mechanical: Scientific Management and the Rise of Modernist Architecture* (Princeton, NJ, 2006)

Hampton, M., *Legendary Decorators of the Twentieth Century* (New York, 1992)

Hanks, D. A., *Donald Deskey: Decorative Designs and Interiors* (New York, 1987)

——, *The Decorative Designs of Frank Lloyd Wright* (Washington, DC, 1978)

Hayden, D., *The Grand Domestic Revolution: A History of Feminist Designs for American Homes, Neighborhoods and Cities* (Cambridge, MA, 1981)

Heal, J., *Interior Decorating: Your Career* (London, 1945)

Hennessey, W. J., *Russel Wright: American Designer* (Cambridge, MA, 1983)

Heskett, J., *Designed in Germany 1870–1918* (London, 1986)

Hetherington, K., *Capitalism's Eye: Cultural Spaces of the Commodity* (London, 2007)

Heynen, H., *Architecture and Modernity: A Critique* (Cambridge, MA and London, 2001)

Heynen, H., and G. Baydar, eds, *Negotiating Domesticity: Spatial Productions of Gender in Modern Architecture* (London and New York, 2005)

Highmore, B., *Everyday Life and Cultural Theory: An Introduction* (London and New York, 2002)

Hine, T., *Populuxe* (New York, 1986)

Hobhouse, C., *1851 and the Crystal Palace* (London, 1937)

Hoffman, H., *Modern Interiors in Europe and America* (London, 1930)

Holmes, J. M., *The Art of Interior Design and Decoration* (London, New York, Toronto, 1951)

Hounshell, D. A., *From the American System to Mass Production, 1800–1932* (London, 1984)

Houze, R., 'From Wiener Kunst im Hause to the Wiener Werkstätte: Marketing Domesticity with Fashionable Interior Design', in *Design Issues*, XVIII/1 (Winter 2002), pp. 3–23

Hvattum, M., and C. Hermansen (eds), *Tracing Modernity: Manifestations of the Modern in Architecture and the City* (London and New York, 2004)

'Interior Design and the Airliner', in *Architectural Review* (December 1966), pp 413–22

Isenstadt, S., 'Picture This: The Rise and Fall of the Picture Window', in *Harvard Design Magazine* (Autumn 1998), pp. 27–33

——, *The Modern American House: Spaciousness and Middle Class Identity* (Cambridge, 2006)

Jackson, L., 'Contemporary': Architecture and Interiors of the 1950s* (London, 1998)

——, *Robin and Lucienne Day: Pioneers of Contemporary Design* (London, 2001)

Jones. C., *Colefax and Fowler: The Best in English Interior Decoration* (Boston, MA, New York, Toronto, London, 1989)

Kahle, K. M., *Modern French Decoration* (New York and London, 1930)

Kaplan, W., ed., *The Arts and Crafts Movement in Europe and America: Design for the Modern World* (London, 2004)

Kaufmann, E., 'What is Modern Interior Design?', in *Introductions to Modern Design* (New York, 1969)

Kiesler, F., *Contemporary Art Applied to the Store and its Display* (New York, 1930)

Knight, A., *The Hollywood Style* (London, 1969)

Kirsch, K., *The Weissenhofsiedlung: Experimental Housing built for the Deutscher Werkbund, Stuttgart 1927* (New York, 1990)

Koenig, G., *Eames* (Cologne, 2005)

Kowinski, W., *The Malling of America: An Inside Look at the Great Consumer Paradise* (New York, 1985)

Lamonaca, M., 'Tradition as Transformation: Gio Ponti's Program for the Modern Italian Home, 1928–1933', in *Studies in the Decorative Arts*, V/(1997), pp. 52–82

Lange, C., *Ludwig Mies van der Rohe and Lilly Reich: Furniture and Interiors* (Krefeld, 2006)

Larabee, E., and M. Vignelli, *Knoll Design* (New York, 1981)

Leach, W., *Land of Desire: Merchants, Power, and the Rise of a New American Culture* (New York, 1993)

Leavitt, S. A., *From Catherine Beecher to Martha Stewart: A Cultural History of Domestic Advice* (Chapel Hill, NC and London, 2002)

Lees-Maffei, G., 'From Service to Self-Service: Advice Literature as Design Discourse, 1920–1970', in *Journal of Design History*, XIV/3 (2001), pp. 187–206

Lefèbvre, H., *The Production of Space* (Oxford, 1991)

Lehmann, U., *Tigersprung: Fashion in Modernity* (Cambridge, MA and London, 2000)

Leslie, F., *Designs for Twentieth-Century Interiors* (London, 2000)

Lewis, A., *Albert Hadley: The Story of America's Pre-eminent Interior Designer* (New York, 2005)

Lind, C., *The Wright Style: The Interiors of Frank Lloyd Wright* (London, 1992)

Livingstone, K., and L. Parry, *International Arts and Crafts* (London, 2005)

Logan, T., *The Victorian Parlour: A Cultural Study* (Cambridge, 2001)

Lukacs, J., 'The Bourgeois Interior', in *The American Scholar*, XXXIX (1970), pp. 616–30

Macdonald, S., and J. Porter, *Putting on the Style: Setting up Home in the 1950s* (London, 1990)

Madigan, R., and M. Munro, 'House Beautiful: Style and Consumption in the Home', in *Sociology*, XXX/1 (1996), pp. 41–57

Maldonado, T., *The Idea of Comfort* (London, 1987)

Marcus, S., *Apartment Stories: City and Home in Nineteenth-Century Paris and London* (Berkeley, CA, 1999)

Massey, A., *Hollywood Beyond the Screen: Design and Material Culture* (Oxford, 2000)

——, *Interior Design of the Twentieth Century* (London, 1990 and 2001)

McCorquodale, C., *History of Interior Decoration* (London, 1983)

McKellar, S., and P. Sparke, eds, *Interior Design and Identity* (Manchester, 2004)

McLeod, M., ed., *Charlotte Perriand: An Art of Living* (New York, 2003)

Matthews, G., *Just a Housewife: The Rise and Fall of Domesticity in America* (Oxford and New York, 1987)

Miller, D., *Home Possessions: Material Culture Behind Closed Doors* (Oxford, 2001)

Miller, M. B., *The Bon Marché: Bourgeois Culture and the Department Store, 1869–1920* (Princeton, NJ, 1981)

'The Modern House Revisited: Twentieth Century Architecture', *The Journal of the Twentieth Century Society*, 2 (1996)

Monro, J., *11 Montpelier Street: Memoirs of an Interior Decorator* (London, 1988)

Nelson, G., and H. Wright, *Tomorrow's House: A Complete Guide for the Home-Builder* (New York, 1945)

Parsons, F. A., *Interior Decoration: Its Principles and Practice* (New York, 1916)

Penner, B., and C. Rice, 'Constructing the Interior', *Journal of Architecture*, [special issue], IX/3 (2004)

Pimlott, M., *Without and Within: Essays on Territory and the Interior* (Rotterdam, 2007)

Post, E., *The Personality of a House: The Blue Book of Charm* (New York, 1948)

Praz, M., *Illustrated History of Interior Decoration from Pompeii to Art Nouveau* (London, 1981)

Quinn, B., *The Fashion of Architecture* (Oxford, 2003)

Rappoport, E. D., *Shopping for Pleasure: Women in the Making of London's West End* (Princeton, NJ, 2000)

Reed, C., *Bloomsbury Rooms* (New Haven, CT and London, 2004)

—— ed., *Not at Home: the Suppression of Domesticity in Modern Art and Architecture* (London, 1996)

Reimer, S., and D. Leslie, 'Identity, Consumption and the Home', in *Home Cultures*, 1/2 (2004), pp. 187–208

Rice, C., *The Emergence of the Interior: Architecture, Modernity, Domesticity* (London and New York, 2007)

Robsjohn-Gibbings. T. H., *Good-bye, Mr Chippendale* (New York, 1944)

Rosner, V., *Modernism and the Architecture of Private Life* (New York, 2005)

Rowntree, D., *Interior Design* (Harmondsworth, 1964)

Ryan, D. S., *The Ideal Home Through the Twentieth Century* (London, 1997)

Rybczynski, W., *Home: A Short History of an Idea* (New York, 1986)

Saisselin, R. G., *Bricabracomania: The Bourgeois and the Bibelot* (London, 1985)

Salny, S. M., *Francis Elkins: Interior Design* (New York and London, 2005)

Sasaki, H., *Modern Japanese Houses, Inside and Out* (Tokyo, 1970)

Scanlon, J., *Inarticulate Longings: The Ladies' Home Journal, Gender, and the Promises of Consumer Culture* (New York and London, 1995)

Segalin, M., 'The Salon des Arts Ménagers, 1923–1983: A French Effort to Instil the Virtues of Home and the Norms of Good Taste', in *Journal of Design History*, VII/4 (1994), pp. 267–76

Silverman, D., *Art Nouveau in Fin-de-Siècle France: Politics, Psychology and Style* (Berkeley and Los Angeles, CA and London, 1989)

Skurkar, N., and O. Gili, *Underground Interiors: Decorating for Alternative Lifestyles* (New York, 1972)

Slater, D., *Consumer Culture and Modernity* (Cambridge, 1997)

Sorkin, M., ed., *Variations on a Theme Park: The New American City and the End of Public Space* (New York, 1992)

Sparke, P., *As Long as It's Pink: The Sexual Politics of Taste* (London, 1995)

——, *Elsie De Wolfe: The Birth of Modern Interior Decoration* (New York, 2005)

——, B. Martin and T. Keeble, *The Modern Period Room: The Construction of the Exhibited Interior 1870–1950* (London and New York, 2006)

Spigel, T., 'Installing the Television Set: Popular Discourses on Television and Domestic Space, 1948–1955', in *Private Screenings: Television and the Female Consumer*, ed. T. Spigel and D. Mann (Minneapolis, MN, 1992), pp. 3–38

Stewart, J., *Fashioning Vienna: Adolf Loos's Cultural Criticism* (London and New York, 2000)

Stewart, S., *On Longing: Narratives of the Miniature, the Gigantic, the Souvenir, the Collection* (Durham and London, 1993)

Tate, A., and C. R. Smith, *Interior Design in the Twentieth Century* (New York, 1986)

Taylor, M., and J. Preston, eds, *Intimus: Interior Design Theory Reader* (Chichester, 2006)

Taut, B., *Modern Architecture* (London, 1929)

Taylor, M., and J. Preston, *Intimus: Interior Design Theory Reader* (West Sussex, 2006)

Tebbel, J., and M. E. Zuckerman, *The Magazine in America, 1741–1990* (New York, 1991)

Tester, K., ed., *The Flâneur* (London and New York, 1994)

Thornton, P., *Authentic Décor: The Domestic Interior, 1620–1920* (New York, 1984)

Tiersten, L., *Marianne in the Market: Envisioning Consumer Society in Fin-de-Siècle France* (Berkeley and Los Angeles, CA and London, 2001)

Tigerman, B., '"I Am Not a Decorator": Florence Knoll, the Knoll Planning Unit and the Making of the Modern Office', in *Journal of Design History*, XX/1 (2007), pp. 61–74

Todd, D., and R. Mortimer, *The New Interior Decoration: An Introduction to its Principles, and International Survey of its Methods* (London, 1929)

Todd, P., *Bloomsbury at Home* (New York, 1999)

Tosh, J., *A Man's Place: Masculinity and the Middle-Class Home in Victorian England* (London, 1999)

Trocme, S., *Influential Interiors: Shaping 20th Century Style: Key Interior Designers* (London, 1999)

Troy, N. J., *Couture Culture: A Study in Modern Art and Fashion* (Cambridge, MA, 2003)

——, *Modernism and the Decorative Arts in France: Art Nouveau to Le Corbusier* (New Haven, CT, 1991)

——, *The De Stijl Environment* (Cambridge, MA, 1983)

Utopia and Reality: Modernity in Sweden, 1900–1960 (New Haven, CT and London, 2002)

Varney, C., *In the Pink: Dorothy Draper, America's Most Fabulous Decorator* (New York, 2005)

Vernet, D., and L. de Wit, eds, *Boutiques and Other Retail Spaces: The Architecture of Seduction* (New York and London, 2007)

Von Falke, J., *Art in the House* (Boston, MA, 1879)

Votolato, G., *Transport Design: A Travel History* (London, 2007)

Wealleans, A., *Designing Liners: a History of Interior Design Afloat* (London and New York, 2006)

McNeil, P., 'Myths of Modernism: Japanese Architecture, Interior Design and the West, *c*. 1920–1940', in *Journal of Design History*, V/4 (1992), pp. 281–94

Wharton, E., and O. Codman, *The Decoration of Houses* (New York, 1897)

Wheeler, C., ed., *Household Art* (New York, 1893)

——, *Principles of Home Decoration* (New York, 1903)

Wigley, M., *White Walls, Designer Dresses: The Fashioning of Modern Architecture* (Cambridge, MA and London, 1995)

Wilk, C., *Marcel Breuer: Furniture and Interiors* (New York, 1981)

—— ed., *Modernism: Designing a New World, 1914–1939* (London, 2006)

Wilson, K., *Livable Modernism: Interior Decorating and Design During the Great Depression* (New Haven, CT and London, 2004)

——, 'Style and Lifestyle in the Machine Age – The Modernist Period Rooms of the Architect and the Visual Arts', in *Visual Resources*, XXI, pt. 3 (September 2005), pp. 245–8

Witt-Dörring, C., *Josef Hoffmann: Interiors, 1902–1913* (Munich, 2006).

Wood, G., *Surreal Things: Surrealism and Design* (London, 2007)

Wood, M., *Nancy Lancaster: English Country House Style* (London, 2005)

Wright, G., *Building the Dream: A Social History of Housing in America* (Cambridge, MA, 1987)

Zukin, S., *Point of Purchase: How Shopping Changed American Culture* (London and New York, 2005)

Acknowledgements

This book is the result of my attempt to address some of the unanswered questions that arose in the late 1990s and early 2000s while researching the work of the pioneer American interior decorator Elsie de Wolfe. The scope of the book I wrote then did not permit me to dwell in any detail on the meaning of the modern interior in the first half of the twentieth century. My overriding question at that time had been whether de Wolfe, working as she did in French eighteenth-century period styles for the most part, was a 'modern' decorator or not. That deceptively simple question took me to the vast literature on the subjects of modernity and identity, especially where they touched on issues relating to gender, class and sexuality. Indeed, I had already begun to interrogate those themes in my 1995 publication, *As Long as It's Pink: The Sexual Politics of Taste*, which had led me to Elsie de Wolfe in the first place. While researching *The Modern Interior* I was reminded again that the scholarship on the subjects of modernity and identity in the fields of history, the social sciences, the humanities and cultural studies operates at a considerable distance from work undertaken in the visually oriented areas of the history and theory of art, architecture and design. This book is a modest attempt to help make that bridge a bit more crossable.

Writing this book has not just been an academic exercise, however, but rather a lived experience. The fact that it exists at all is due to the countless memorable visits I have made to many modern interiors over the years with colleagues, friends and family, and alone. It couldn't have been written, for example, without the experiences of the annual overseas study trips made with the staff and students of the Royal College of Art/Victoria and Albert Museum History of Design MA course, between 1982 and 1999, during which we visited many fascinating modern interior spaces. Hvitträsk knee-deep in snow, and Carl Larsson's house in Dalarna, where we met remaining family members, are among the many memories that come immediately to mind. For those I thank Gillian Naylor, Charles Saumarez Smith, Paul Greenhalgh, Jeremy Aynsley and Christopher Breward, among many others. Among the many debts that I owe to friends and family, one must go to Wendy Caplan who kindly took me to the Eames's Santa Monica House, and another to my daughter Molly, who proved an able research assistant on visits to Gerrit Rietveld's Schroeder House and Le Corbusier's Villa Savoye, among others.

Equally, this book couldn't have been written without the support of my fellow researchers at Kingston University – Trevor Keeble, Anne Wealleans and Brenda Martin in particular – who constitute the core members of the Modern Interiors Research Centre (MIRC). The Centre's annual conferences, held from 1999 onwards, have provided an important international forum in which many of the ideas presented in this study were rehearsed and debated. The US-based visiting professors to the Centre, Alice Friedman and Pat Kirkham, and the numerous speakers and delegates who have travelled from all over the globe – among them Bridget May, Pauline Metcalf, Christopher Reed, Joel Sanders, Rebecca Strum, Nancy J. Troy and John Turpin from the USA; John Potvin from Canada; Hilde Heynen from Belgium; Charles Rice from Australia; and Mark Taylor and Julieanna Preston from New Zealand – have also been, and continue to be, an inspiration to me.

Many of the doctoral students with whom I have worked at the Royal College of Art and at Kingston University – Susie McKellar (my co-editor on *Interior Design and Identity*), Viviana Narotzky, Nic Maffei, Quintin Colville, Maiko Tsutsumi, Fiona Fisher, Patricia Lara and Anthea Winterburn among them – have also opened my eyes to new ways of thinking about the modern interior. Working as my research assistant, Fiona also acquired most of images for this book, for which I owe her an enormous debt, while my PA, Maureen Hourigan, and members of Kingston University's Learning Resource Centre and its Media Department, have been enormously supportive throughout the process. My sincere thanks go to them all.

In making it possible for me to reproduce the images that I have included I would like to thank Lynne Bryant at Arcaid; Paul-Etienne Kisters at the Archives et Musée de la Littérature, c/o Bibliothèque Royale, Brussels; Eike Zimme/Eva Farnberger at the Austrian National Library; Annette Handrich at the BASF Corporate Archives and Projects; Sabine Hartmann at the Bauhaus Archiv; Marcel van de Graaf at Beeldrecht; Laure Lefrancois at the Bibliothèque Nationale in Paris; Ruth Jansen at the Brooklyn Museum; Patricia M. Virgil at the Buffalo and Erie County Historical Society; Edgar van Riessen/Cecile Ogink at the Centraal Museum, Utrecht; Jason Birch at the City of London Libraries and Guildhall Art Gallery; Coi Gehrig at the Denver Public Library; Jessica Casey/Christian Zimmerman at the Design and Artists Copyright Society; Alyson Rogers at English Heritage, National Monuments Record; Whitney French at the Farnsworth House; Isabelle Godineau at the Fondation Le Corbusier; Ben Blake at the Hagley Museum and Library; Franziska Wachter at IMAGNO; Howard Doble at the London Metropolitan Archives; Tracy Hartley/Jane Parr at Manchester City Council; Katja Leiskau at the Marburg Picture Archive; Mark Vivian at the Mary Evans Picture Library; Laura Whitton at the RIBA Library Photographs Collection; Magdaleno Mayo at the Science and Society Picture library; Mrs. K. Miskova at the Netherlands Architecture Institute; Kristina Watson at the Royal Commission on the Ancient and Historical Monuments of Scotland; Monique Comminges at the Roger Viollet Agency; Wendy Hurlock Baker at the Smithsonian Institution, Archives of American Art; Christopher Coutlee at the Toronto Public Library; Elke Handel at the University of Applied Art, Vienna; Bridget Gillies at the University of East Anglia, and Amy Purcell at the University of Louisville, above all. I would also like to thank the British Academy for providing funding to cover the acquisition of, and the rights to reproduce, the images.

Finally I would like to thank Vivian Constantinopoulos at Reaktion Books for her help and imaginative suggestions for improvements to the text, and my husband, John, and three daughters – Molly, Nancy and Celia – for their patience in putting up with my obsession with modern interiors, and for the all too frequent detours that occurred during family holidays to visit many of them.

Photo Acknowledgements

The author and publishers wish to express their thanks to the following sources of illustrative material and/or permission to reproduce it. Every effort has been made to contact the copyright holders for illustrations in this book. If there are any inadvertent omissions these will be corrected in a future reprint.

Photos Arcaid: pp. 203, 209; courtesy Austrian Archives: p. 51; Austrian National Library Vienna (Picture Library): p. 95; photos author: pp. 8, 120, 142, 174, 178, 182, 202, 205, 211; photo courtesy of the author: p. 199; photo courtesy BASF Corporate Archives: p. 143; photo courtesy Bauhaus-Archiv, Museum für Gestaltung: p. 136; photo © Beeldrecht Foundation: p. 138; Bibliothèque Royale de Belgique (Archives et Musée de la Litérature), Brussels: p. 40; photos copyright Bildarchiv Foto Marburg: pp. 41, 94; photo courtesy Brooklyn Museum: p. 69; photo Richard Bryant: p. 203; photo courtesy the Buffalo and Erie County Historical Society: p. 126; from E. O. Burdg, *The Manual of Shop Window Backgrounds for Mercantile Display* (Chicago, 1925): p. 63; Caufield and Shook Collection, Photographic Archives, University of Louisville, KY: p. 148; Centraal Museum, Utrecht (© Beeldrecht Foundation): p. 176; courtesy Christian Brandstätter Verlag: p. 52; photos Denver Public Library (Western History Collection): pp. 10, 24; photo courtesy of the Elsie de Wolfe Foundation: p. 82; reproduced by permission of English Heritage, National Monuments Record (photo Beford Lemere): p. 29; courtesy of the Florence Knoll Bassett Papers, 1932-2000, Archives of American Art, Smithsonian Institution: p. 193; Fondation Le Corbusier, Paris: pp. 93, 141, 153 (© DACS, London, 2008); photo courtesy Guildhall, City of London: p. 116; photos courtesy the Hagley Museum and Library, Wilmington, DE: pp. 122, 123; photos IMAGNO: pp. 51, 52; photo courtesy of Landmarks of Illinois: p. 180; photos Library of Congress, Washington, DC: pp. 14 (Prints and Photographs Division, George Grantham Bain Collection), 190 (collection of the Work of Charles and Ray Eames); reproduced by permission of the London Metropolitan Archives, City of London: pp. 128, 145; photos Manchester Archives and Local Studies, Central Library: pp. 20, 26; courtesy of the Marcel Breuer Papers, 1920-1986, Archives of American Art, Smithsonian Institution: p. 156; photos Mary Evans Picture Library: pp. 61, 127; photo Metropolitan Museum of Art, New York: p. 70; photo MGM/Photofest: p. 71 (foot); Musée Carnavalet, Paris: p. 112; National Railway Museum, York/Science and Society Picture Library: p. 30; photo courtesy Netherlands Architecture Institute, Rotterdam: p. 138; loaned to the Netherlands Architecture Institute by the Van Eesteren-Fluck and Van Lohuizen Foundation, The Hague: p. 173; New York Historical Society (Mattie Edwards Hewitt collection): p. 71 (top); photo The Preservation Society of Newport County (Meservey Collection): p. 27; photo courtesy of the Pritchard Papers, University of East Anglia: p. 157; from *Rapport General: Section Artistique et Technique Vol.4: Mobilier* (Paris, 1925): pp. 66, 67, 102; RIBA Library Photographs Collection: pp. 161, 163; photos Roger Viollet: p. 81 foot (© DACS, London, 2008), 112; Royal Commission on the Ancient and Historic Monuments: p. 31; photo Cami Stone: p. 156 (top); photo copyright Toronto Public Library: p. 33; Collections of the University of Applied Art, Vienna, © Dorothea Stransky: p. 139; photo Wolf and Lotte Schede-Foto: p. 156 (foot).

Index